THE END OF THEOLOGICAL EDUCATION

THEOLOGICAL EDUCATION BETWEEN THE TIMES

Ted A. Smith, series editor

Theological Education between the Times gathers diverse groups of people for critical, theological conversations about the meanings and purposes of theological education in a time of deep change. The project is funded by the Lilly Endowment Inc.

Daniel O. Aleshire
Beyond Profession: The Next Future of Theological Education

Elizabeth Conde-Frazier
Atando Cabos: Latinx Contributions to Theological Education

Keri Day
Notes of a Native Daughter: Testifying in Theological Education

Willie James Jennings
After Whiteness: An Education in Belonging

Mark D. Jordan
Transforming Fire: Imagining Christian Teaching

Ted A. Smith
The End of Theological Education

Chloe T. Sun
Attempt Great Things for God: Theological Education in Diaspora

Amos Yong
Renewing the Church by the Spirit: Theological Education after Pentecost

Mark S. Young
The Hope of the Gospel: Theological Education and the Next Evangelicalism

THE END OF THEOLOGICAL EDUCATION

Ted A. Smith

WILLIAM B. EERDMANS PUBLISHING COMPANY

GRAND RAPIDS, MICHIGAN

Wm. B. Eerdmans Publishing Co.
4035 Park East Court SE, Grand Rapids, Michigan 49546
www.eerdmans.com

29 28 27 26 25 24 23   2 3 4 5 6 7

ISBN 978-0-8028-7887-8

Library of Congress Cataloging-in-Publication Data

A catalog record for this book is available from the Library
of Congress.

Parts of the introduction, chapter 1, chapter 2, and chapter 5 were published in "The Education of Authenticity: Theological Schools in an
Age of Individualization," *Journal of the Society of Christian Ethics* 42.1
(Fall/Winter 2022), https://doi.org/10.5840/jsce2022101469. Used with
permission.

For my father,
and in memory of my mother,
with gratitude, respect, and love

Do not say, "Why were the former days better than these?" For it is not from wisdom that you ask this.

Ecclesiastes 7:10

Contents

Acknowledgments

This book grows out of the joy of working with friends in the Theological Education between the Times project. My fellow authors in the series—Daniel Aleshire, Elizabeth Conde-Frazier, Keri Day, Willie Jennings, Mark Jordan, Colleen Mallon, Hosffman Ospino, Chloe Sun, Maria Liu Wong, Amos Yong, and Mark Young—taught me so deeply that I can only describe it as a kind of healing. I am especially grateful to Willie Jennings and Colleen Mallon, my partners in a small writing group, and to Keri Day and Mark Jordan, who read drafts long after they had rightly moved on to other things. Lucila Crena, Corwin Davis, Julian Reid, Rachelle Green, Tony Alonso, and Ashly Cargle-Thompson—my partners in leading the project—shaped my thinking both through the ideas they voiced around the table and through the practical wisdom they showed in our shared work. Editor and artist Ulrike Guthrie has made every book in this series better, very much including mine. James Ernest, David Bratt, Andrew Knapp, Jenny Hoffman, and Tom Raabe of Eerdmans have been important partners in the work of bringing the series to press. And Chris Coble and colleagues at the Lilly Endowment provided not only the material support that made the whole project possible but also steady guidance over many years. I count participation in this project as one of the great blessings of my life, and I am grateful for all those to whom it has connected me.

In many ways the first life of this book was oral. It arose in speaking with and listening to colleagues in ministry and theological education in many different settings. I learned in all these conversations, and I am thankful for them. Thanks especially to Austin Presbyterian Theological Seminary for the opportunity to share early efforts at this book in the 2017 Currie Lectures. And thanks to Union Presbyterian Seminary for the chance to offer a more developed version in the 2021 Sprunt Lectures. Between and beyond the bookends of these lecture series, I worked through the ideas in this book in lectures, conversations, and podcasts hosted by La Asociación para la Educación Teológica Hispana, the Association of Theological Schools, the Hispanic Theological Initiative, In Trust, Louisville Institute, the Ministry Collective, the Wabash Center for Teaching and Learning in Theology and Religion, a gathering of presidents of seminaries affiliated with the PC(USA), the PC(USA) Committee on Theological Education, Bradley Hills Presbyterian Church (Bethesda), the Episcopal Parish Network, Fourth Presbyterian Church (Chicago), Peachtree Christian Church (Atlanta), Second Presbyterian Church (Indianapolis), Eden Theological Seminary, Garrett Evangelical Theological Seminary, Candler School of Theology, Columbia Theological Seminary, and Vanderbilt Divinity School.

Other crucial conversations were more individual. Thanks to Luke Bretherton, Kathleen Cahalan, Fernando Cascante, Meg Funk, Justo González, De'Amon Harges, Chris Henry, Jennifer Herdt, Susan Hylen, Robby Jones, David Kelsey, Kwok Pui Lan, Kyle Lambelet, Kathryn Lofton, Vincent Lloyd, Gerardo Marti, Mike Mather, Mary Nickel, Joi Orr, Christian Scharen, Chad Wellmon, Barbara Wheeler, and Sara Williams for putting books in my hands or ideas in my head that directly helped me with this book. And thanks to my Candler colleagues Jennifer Ayres, Emmanuel Lartey, Jan Love, Roger Nam, Joanne Solis-Walker, and Jonathan Strom for programmatic collaborations that have both informed and refined many of these ideas. If the first life of this book was oral, the second has been institutional. Publication has come last.

The shortcomings in the book are of course my own. In particular, I have slipped repeatedly into modes of prose the Theological Education between the Times writing group called one another beyond. And this book is much longer than we imagined our books to be. I regret falling away from our better hopes.

My family will not be surprised that I went on too long. And in its deepest center, this is a book from and for my family. Susan Hylen teaches me more than I can say, not least about what it means to be a theological educator. The book simply would not exist without her generosity, partnership, and love. Our sons Bennett and Tobias have been on my mind on every page, as I think about the worlds in which they make their ways. Their capacities to do more wonderful things than I can teach them remain a sign of hope for me. Always with them in my mind as I write are my own parents, Ted and Dede Smith. My mom embodied and my dad continues to embody the highest and best forms of the virtues of the world of voluntary associations. They offered those virtues to my sisters Jackie and Allison and to me, trusting us to cultivate them in our callings. We each do this in our own ways, even as we know we cannot simply pass on what they gave to us. The world has changed too much. But our parents also introduced us to a God whose mercy is wider and deeper even than the virtues they taught us and the institutions they made. With thanks for that gift, I have tried to write by the light of the hope they helped us have. This book is dedicated to them.

Introduction

> We are concerned that liberal Christian theological
> education is headed toward financial, as well as theo-
> logical and educational, bankruptcy. We believe that
> the possibility of its deliverance is rooted in a praxis-
> based transformation of theological and educational
> assumptions that have undergirded the enterprise for
> a hundred years.
>
> The Mud Flower Collective,
> *God's Fierce Whimsy* (1985)

With quarantines closing campuses, uprisings for Black freedom
shaking foundations, denominations splitting, established financial models collapsing, and the role of religion in American
lives changing in deep, epoch-defining ways, the challenges facing theological schools today can make it seem as if the end is
near. And in some sense it is. But these times between the times
are not unprecedented. We've been here before.

A PARABLE

In September of 1814 Lyman Beecher's world was coming to
an end. At thirty-nine years old, Beecher had already emerged

as one of the most influential preachers in New England. He had come of age in a Connecticut that bound church and state closely together. Throughout his life the Congregational church had been established by law and supported by taxes. That established church oversaw the public schools Beecher attended as a boy. When he continued his education at the publicly supported Yale College, church and state were so deeply interwoven that the curriculum scarcely distinguished between preparing students for service in one or the other. Theological education and general education overlapped so significantly that there was no sense in having a separate seminary or divinity school. To prepare for ministry Beecher simply topped up the ordinary curriculum with some studies with a learned divine who happened to be the president of the college. Upon completion of his studies, Beecher was deemed ready to take his place in the tight network that formed the "Standing Order" that held together economic, civil, and ecclesial powers in Connecticut. Those powers held sway over all the most prominent institutions in the state. And they penetrated daily life with laws like the ones that established Sunday as a state-mandated Sabbath. The Standing Order had survived the Revolution and the passage of the First Amendment, which applied only to the federal government. But now, in 1814, it was unraveling. The world into which Beecher had been born, the world he had been formed to lead, was coming undone.

Beecher denounced the crisis in a sermon he preached at the installation of John Keyes as pastor of the Congregational church in Wolcott. Because the Standing Order was weakening, he said, there were towns in which "the church is extinct, and the house of God in ruins."[1] The state was suffering "grievous desolations." These desolations had deep roots, in Beecher's analysis. The revivals that had renewed piety in the middle of the eighteenth century had also produced rival Christian movements. With the proliferation of these nascent denominations, towns that once came together to support a single full-time minister were now divided into smaller societies that could afford only part-time clergy. Worse still, Beecher said, a free market in religion undermined church discipline. Worried that they would lose people to other denominations, preachers started to flatter their listeners, and "infidel philosophy" rose to fill the vacuum created by lax churches. These divisions in religion were mirrored by divisions in the political order, as partisanship threatened any sense of a common good. Now some of those partisans were lobbying for Sunday mail and an end to state subsidies of the established church. "The consequence," Beecher preached, "is the decline, and in some cases, the entire subversion, of that religious order which our fathers established."[2]

Beecher tried to rally the old Standing Order, but he failed. Just four years later, in 1818, the Congregational church was formally disestablished in the Connecticut Constitution. The Standing Order had come to an end.

At the time, Beecher saw this as a calamity with everlasting consequences. In his view, the old order had done more than any other system to provide for the proclamation of the gospel. The loss of that order would leave souls in misery and the land in ruins. "The bondage of corruption, commencing here," he said, "will extend through eternity. The career of iniquity, here begun, will hold on to its unobstructed course and never end."[3]

Yet, less than a decade after disestablishment, Beecher already saw things very differently. Repurposing a discourse he had delivered to the state legislature of Connecticut, Beecher preached a sermon entitled "The Memory of Our Fathers" at Plymouth in 1827. In the sermon he told anew the history of New England. The order founded by the Puritans may have fallen apart, Beecher said, but this is just the way things go. "The history of the world is the history of human nature in ruins." But this was not the end of the story. For "He that sitteth upon the throne saith, 'Behold, I make all things new'" (Rev. 21:15).[4]

For two hundred years, Beecher said, the law had held together a single order of family, church, and state. This was good, but it could not last. The crumbling of the law, though, did not mean that God had abandoned God's people. For "at the very time when the civil law had become impotent for the support of

3

religion and the prevention of immoralities, God began to pour out his Spirit upon the churches; and voluntary associations of Christians were raised up to apply and extend that influence which the law could no longer apply." Now there are "Bible societies, and Tract societies, and associations of individuals, who make it their business to see that every family has a Bible, and every church a pastor, and every child a catechism." Voluntary associations founded schools and colleges and—a new kind of institution for this new dispensation—*seminaries* for the formation of clergy. Everything that the state could no longer do voluntary associations were now doing even better. For this new order depended not on "worldly dominion" but on an inner renewal of free individuals who came together to form associations.[5]

Looking back on the collapse of the Standing Order, Beecher said, "The injury done to the cause of Christ, as we then supposed, was irreparable." It seemed like the end of the world. But the end of the Standing Order turned out to be *"the best thing that ever happened to the State of Connecticut. It cut the churches loose from dependence on state support. It threw them wholly on their own resources and on God."*[6] So many things had changed as the church moved from legal establishment to voluntary association. Congregations took on a new kind of institutional form and were funded in new ways. They related to the state very differently. Ministers were trained in new kinds of schools. They lost some kinds of authority and gained others. In the midst of all these changes, Beecher observed, the work of God was thriving. The new world was still a theater of God's great work of redemption.

* * *

Beecher might have been formed for the old Standing Order, but he quickly adjusted to lead the new world of voluntary associations and, indeed, helped found two of the strongest of these, the American Bible Society and the Domestic Missionary Society. His congregations thrived in the new funding model, gathering more in voluntary contributions than they had received from

4

the state's collection of taxes. He embraced the new print media that arose hand in hand with the voluntary associations, starting a newspaper and publishing a steady stream of articles, pamphlets, and sermons. Beecher's mastery of the new world of voluntary associations catapulted him to national fame. He moved from his congregation in Connecticut to a prominent pulpit in Boston. He also attracted the attention of a new class of wealthy merchants ready to fund an empire of benevolence. Thus, when Beecher moved to Cincinnati in 1832 to become president of the newly formed Lane Theological Seminary, it looked to some like a step down the social ladder he had climbed so skillfully— especially because the city was mired in a cholera epidemic at the time. Beecher's move only made sense if one believed that a Protestant seminary for what then counted as the American West was essential for the salvation of the world.

That is exactly what Lyman Beecher believed. He had gone to Cincinnati because he believed the fate of the nation depended on the lands drained by the Mississippi and its tributaries. Cincinnati was the most established city of that region, "the London of the West," as Beecher called it, and he hoped the new seminary would give him a chance to form ministers who would win the West for Protestant Christianity and evangelical reform. The stakes could not have been higher, Beecher argued. "The moral destiny of our nation, and all our institutions and hopes, and the world's hopes, turns on the West. . . . If we gain the West, all is safe; if we lose it, all is lost."[7] Gaining the West required seeding it with thousands of "well systematized voluntary associations," including schools, congregations, and societies for moral reform. As Beecher saw it, these voluntary associations provided the trellis on which new towns could grow and bloom. Moreover, they formed people for the responsible exercise of freedom that a republic required. This republican freedom not only knit individuals together in a democratic society but also proved the superiority of white Protestant settlers to the "tyrannical" Indigenous and Catholic communities they met as they pushed westward. Such voluntary associations, thought Beecher, didn't merely make the project of white Protestant settlement possible; they made it just.[8]

These all-important voluntary associations required the kind of leaders a world-class seminary would produce. Thus, reasoned Beecher, the seminary was the key to voluntary associations, voluntary associations were the key to the West, the West was the key to the United States, and the United States, as the land where God's millennial reign would begin, was the key to the world.[9] The trustees of Lane shared this vision. They saw themselves as founding a seminary that would train "hundreds and thousands of ministers" whose piety and zeal would bring "the salvation of the country and the world."[10] They planned for Lane to become "the great Andover or Princeton of the West." Like Andover Theological Seminary (founded in 1807) and Princeton Theological Seminary (founded in 1812), Lane was built on the new model for theological schools that had begun to rise with the culture of voluntary associations. Unlike the Yale College of Beecher's own training, seminaries on the Andover model were dedicated entirely to the training of ministers. They received no state support but were funded instead by a mixture of philanthropy and tuition. And they were closely tied to particular religious movements that were rapidly coalescing into a new institutional form: *denominations* that took their place as distinct religious movements under the umbrella of a nation-state that was not directly aligned with any one of them.

Lane offered a Western variation on this form. Like some other schools founded as part of the network of voluntary associations, it sought to form students with manual labor in addition to studies. Because of the lack of strong elementary and secondary schools in the region, it offered preparatory departments designed to get students ready for the seminary, which offered specialized training for ministry. The seminary got its start through a gift of $4,000 from New Orleans businessman Ebenezer Lane. Other donors with interests up and down the Ohio and Mississippi Rivers chipped in. Even when the donors were not involved directly in the slave trade, the rivers linked their profits to economies that depended on slavery. The school maintained a complex denominational identity, initially trying to relate to both Old and New School Presbyterians as well as the Congregationalists who were linked to Presbyterians through the Plan of Union. Denominational, disestablished, and specialized for ministry, Lane was a seminary that fit the times.[11]

After a rocky start with a solo professor who wasn't sure he wanted to be there, Lane's trustees put together a pair of interlocking commitments that they thought would secure the future of the school. Arthur Tappan, one of the wealthiest people in the United States and a major backer of the emerging network of voluntary societies, promised $20,000 if the school could recruit Lyman Beecher to be its president. Beecher agreed to be president if the school could get the kind of funding only someone like Tappan could supply. Beecher and the money arrived together in 1832.

Beecher's celebrity attracted not only funds but also students. His arrival secured the legitimacy of the school and made clear that it would be aligned with the culture of voluntary associations—and so with the revivalism and abolitionist sentiments woven deeply into the fabric of this culture. Tappan certainly expected as much, as did the students. Located just a few miles north of the Ohio River, Lane attracted Southerners who were opposed to slavery, including James Bradley, a Black student who made his way up from Arkansas. Lane also attracted students from the "burned-over" district of western New York, with a large group coming from the Oneida Institute, a hotbed of revival and abolition. Among those students was Theodore Dwight Weld, a charismatic speaker and organizer who had learned the ropes as a member of the "holy bands" that would prepare the ground for the revivals of Charles Grandison Finney. Weld also served as an agent for a Tappan-funded voluntary society dedicated to promoting schools on the manual labor model, like Oneida and Lane. He was not alone in this experience. All in all, a dozen members of the first class of Beecher's tenure had experience as agents for voluntary associations.[12]

With trustees whose business interests were dependent on slavery, students who were committed to immediate abolition, a major donor in New York who expected to see an integrated seminary, and a denomination already coming apart over revivals (and the abolitionism they always seemed to bring with them), Lane was stressed along exactly the lines that defined the new seminary form. It took someone of Beecher's skill and celebrity to hold it all together.

For a while, he could. The cholera epidemic of 1832 and 1833 took a painful toll on the school, killing three students and forcing more than half of the remaining students into quarantine. It also diverted some of the energies that threatened to tear the school apart. But as the epidemic faded in the early months of 1834, those energies surged back to the surface. Led by Weld, the students held extended debates on two questions: "Ought the people of the slaveholding states abolish slavery immediately?" and "Do the doctrines, tendencies, and measures of the American Colonization Society, and the influence of its principal supporters, render it worthy of the patronage of the Christian public?"

Students debated each question for two and a half hours per night for nine nights, for a total of forty-five hours. They gave speeches that juxtaposed the Bible and republican ideals with eyewitness accounts of the horrors of slavery. James Bradley, the lone Black student at the seminary, held the floor one night for two full hours. He made his arguments with sarcastic wit that repeatedly moved the room to supportive laughter. Refuting the claim that free Blacks could not take care of themselves, Bradley argued that enslaved people "have to take care of, and support themselves *now, and their master, and his family into the bargain*; and this being so it would be strange if they could not provide for themselves, *when disencumbered from this load*." His argument was especially powerful because listeners knew that he had purchased his freedom with money he made working beyond the work demanded by the family that enslaved him. He was living proof of all that he said.[13]

Having long speeches night after night made the debates very much like the "protracted meetings" that many of the students had helped lead during revivals. And like the revival meetings, the debates ended with a demand for decision. The students were unanimous in voting for the first proposition and almost unanimous in offering a negative response to the second. They went on the record for immediate abolition and against efforts to deport free Blacks to Africa.[14]

Like converts after a revival meeting, students came out of the debates resolved to take action. Some were rumored to be working with the Underground Railroad. Above ground, students organized a campus Anti-Slavery Society. Beyond the campus, they formed a string of institutions with Black Cincinnatians, including a lyceum, a library, and a reading room. They helped organize Sabbath Schools and Bible classes that Black citizens attended. One white seminary student, Augustus Wattles, took leave from his studies to found a school for Black students. By 1834 there were four schools with five teachers and over two hundred students supported by Cincinnati's Black community, students from Lane, and money from Arthur Tappan and other donors. The schools attracted white women from New England— the "Cincinnati Sisters"—who moved to Ohio to join the movement as teachers.[15]

White Cincinnatians took notice. On campus, theology department professor Thomas J. Biggs fulminated against the students, cloaking his opposition to abolition in procedural objections to students gathering without faculty approval. Biggs's opposition was significant, as he was one of only three professors who taught Lane's seminarians. He also had the ear of trustees. The trustees pressed Beecher to restrain students and make public statements assuring all their constituencies of the school's moderation. Beyond the campus, the *Cincinnati Journal* criticized the seminary as a hub of "amalgamation," especially as reports began to circulate of white students socializing with Black citizens in their homes and churches.[16] Students were cursed, hissed at, and spat upon in the streets of the city. And the threat of greater extralegal violence lurked barely in the background. White mobs had rampaged through Black communities in Cincinnati's First Ward just a few years before, in August of 1829, driving more than a thousand Black citizens from the city. There was now talk that similar mobs would target the seminary.[17]

Beecher faced pressure from every side. Trustees, a prominent professor, and the threat of white terrorism all pressured him to curtail student activism and focus instead on the "proper" task of a theological school: preparing young men to lead congregations and other voluntary associations. At the same time, almost all the students—in a young school that needed students very much—were trying to do some kind of work for Black freedom. And the seminary's biggest donor was bankrolling their efforts. President Beecher scrambled to find a moderate middle way.

In June 1834, after the end of the term that featured the student debates, Beecher gave a speech before the American Colonization Society (ACS) in Cincinnati. His mere presence before the Society whose work the students had condemned was meant to reassure supporters of colonization in and beyond the city. In the speech he stressed the common ground he saw between movements for abolition and colonization. This might have alienated proslavery supporters of colonization, but they were not part of Beecher's core constituency. He sought to hold together Lane's extended community by arguing that both abolitionists and colonizers agreed that "slavery is wrong, and a great national sin and national calamity." The movements now seemed "like opposing clouds . . . rushing into collision." But, Beecher proclaimed, these apparent opponents would surely "pour out their concentrated treasure in one broad stream of benevolence—like rivers, which ripple and chafe in their first conjunction, but soon run down their angry waves, and mingle their party-colored waters, as they roll onward toward the ocean."[18] Like the Miami and Ohio Rivers, which join just a few miles west of Cincinnati, abolition and colonization flowed together to the same benevolent end.

Beecher's speech pleased members of the ACS in Cincinnati and across the country. But it seems not to have changed the minds of abolitionists who opposed colonization. Abolitionist Black clergy like Richard Allen and Absalom Jones expressed sympathy with the desire of some Black people to leave the United States. They knew firsthand the suffering that came with deeply discriminatory laws and the ever-present threat of being kidnapped and sold into slavery. But they worried, with good reason, that colonization could become a vehicle for forced deportation. And they knew that the exodus of free Blacks would remove the people working hardest for abolition. In their view, colonization would only enable the continuation of slavery in the United States. And, Black Presbyterian minister Samuel Cornish argued, the real goal of the colonization movement was an ethnic cleansing that would "rid the country of the free colored population." For a society hellbent on whiteness, a free Black person was a living contradiction, a being whose mere existence threatened the whole social order. The students at Lane were shaped by such Black abolitionist voices. Beecher did not change their minds. In speeches and pamphlets, they called the ACS the American Kidnapping Society.[19]

Beecher tried to find another middle way on a second set of questions about social relations across racial lines. He supported a baseline commitment to welcoming Black and white students— all male—to study together. In an 1833 letter, he reassured Tappan that the seminary would always be integrated. "Our only qualification for admission to the seminary," he wrote, "are *qualifications* intellectual, moral, and religious, without reference to color, which I have no reason to think would have any influence here, certainly never with my consent."[20] The admission of James Bradley made good on this promise. And now, in the heat of controversy, Beecher defended the students' right to serve in Black communities. The seminary would be integrated. And students would be engaged in benevolence that crossed racial lines.

But Beecher distinguished these forms of integration from the deeper relationships that critics denounced as tending toward "amalgamation." He told Theodore Dwight Weld, "If you want to teach colored schools, I can fill your pockets with money, but if you will visit in colored families, and walk with them in the

11

streets, you will be overwhelmed."[21] As historian Vincent Harding has argued, "The primary issue was neither abolition nor academic freedom. Rather, it was the faculty and trustees' fears concerning the results of students and black people developing personal, social relationships."[22] While it was not formally articulated in school policy, that same distinction between institutionalized benevolence and personal, social relationships extended to campus. James Bradley was welcome as a student. But when all the students were invited to an event at Beecher's home, Bradley got the message—unspoken, but clear—that he was not really welcome. Beecher claimed to be puzzled by Bradley's absence. But Bradley was simply reading the contours of Beecher's middle way. The school would be officially integrated but socially segregated. And students might serve Black communities beyond the school, but that service should underscore distinctions based on race, not dissolve them.

Satisfied that his carefully crafted positions could hold the fragile Lane community together—and perhaps just wanting to get out of town—Beecher went back East in the summer of 1834 to raise money and see old friends. He hit the lecture circuit with "A Plea for the West," a speech that shared his vision of a seminary shaping leaders who shaped institutions that shaped the free Protestant Christians who would win the West—and so the nation, and so the world—for Christ. The speech made no mention at all of slavery or campus conflicts around it.[23] Calvin Stowe, professor of biblical literature and Beecher's ally in trying to find a middle way, also left Cincinnati for the summer. This left only one faculty member on campus: Thomas Biggs, who had opposed the students from the start. Biggs worked with sympathetic trustees to get the executive committee to pass a series of resolutions that severely restricted the students' abolitionist activism. While the new policies did not have the force of standards set by the full board of trustees, the intentions were clear.

The students raised the stakes, printing more than three thousand copies of an anticolonization tract on the seminary's press, continuing their organizing in the community, and inviting Black friends from the community to visit them on the Lane campus. The trustees responded by closing the campus on September 13, 1834. Beecher was still back East, raising money and now urgently trying to land desirable jobs for Weld and other student leaders so they could leave freely before he had to expel them. He wrote both students and trustees, asking them to be patient. But on October 6 the full body of trustees ratified the intentions of the executive committee. Existing student societies were dissolved, and new ones could not form without faculty approval. Nor could students meet, speak in public, write for the public, or be absent from campus without permission from the faculty. The executive committee would be empowered to dismiss students for violations of these standards.

Beecher returned to Lane a few days after the trustees met. The campus was in crisis as the fall term began on October 15, 1834. Any mediation was now impossible. Twenty-eight students requested regular dismissal—a kind of honorable discharge—as the term began. Beecher and Stowe fought to keep trustees from expelling Weld before he could submit his own request for regular dismissal. More requests from the students, who came to be known as "the Lane Rebels," came with every passing day. By the end of 1834, only 8 of the 103 students who had started the fall term remained enrolled in the seminary.[24]

The purged seminary received warm acclamation from the *Cincinnati Journal*: "Parents and guardians may now send their sons and wards to Lane Seminary," the paper said, "with perfect confidence, that the proper business of a theological school will occupy their minds; and that the discussion and decision of abstract questions, will not turn them aside from the path of duty."[25] Beecher got the trustees to moderate their strictures and persuaded Tappan to keep paying his salary. And Beecher's celebrity and persuasive powers were such that he soon boosted enrollment back up to forty students.[26]

Lane survived, but it was never the same. The school closed the preparatory departments, and the seminary limped along through the nineteenth century and into the first decades of the twentieth. It produced some notable graduates, including Beecher's son Henry, who became a celebrity preacher himself. But it never regained the vitality it had when Beecher first arrived. Over the course of the nineteenth century, the seminary sold off its endowment of land to keep itself afloat. In 1910 it tried to extend its life by affiliating with the school that is now Columbia Theological Seminary. The partnership did little for Lane, and in 1932—100 years after Beecher became president—it ceased instruction in Ohio and transferred its library and remaining faculty and students to McCormick Theological Seminary in Chicago. Most of what was the campus is now occupied by the Thomson-MacConnell Cadillac dealership. The only bit of Lane that still stands is the house where Lyman Beecher lived, the house where James Bradley knew he was more welcome in the abstract than in the flesh.

Two Leaps

Beecher's world came to an end. He had made one leap, to imagine Christian institutions after their legal disestablishment. He had dreamed and organized his way into a world marked by new kinds of pluralism, mobility, and individual choice. He had mastered new media, cultivated a new kind of persona, and developed new institutional forms that fit the times. But Beecher could not make a second leap. He could imagine a seminary in which Black and white students studied in the same classrooms, and he could imagine sending students out for gospel service to people of all races. But he could not imagine a seminary, or a country, in which Black people and white people shared the fullness of life on terms marked by emancipation, reparations, equality, reciprocity, and love. Beecher could imagine an integrated seminary. But he could not imagine an *abolitionist* seminary.

It's worth remembering that Beecher was regarded as relatively "progressive" among the leaders of his time. He was no radical, as his leadership showed, but even his limited commitments to abolition and integration set him apart from many white seminary presidents. And Lane, with all its tensions, was a beacon that attracted abolitionists like James Bradley and Theodore Dwight Weld. But even the most praiseworthy parts of Lane's mission were assimilated to a larger project of white Protestant settlement, for it was the supposed superior morality of Lane graduates and the institutions they led that legitimated their claims to the Mississippi watershed against those of Catholics and the people of America's First Nations. Beecher could imagine a seminary that formed leaders to work for justice in the world. But he could not imagine the story of God's redemption of the world without the white Protestant settlement of North America at its center. And he could not imagine theological education apart from that project.[27]

Those of us who care about theological education face an analogous double challenge now. We need to make a leap to new institutional forms. We are in the midst of social shifts that run as deep as disestablishment did in the early national period. Historians, sociologists, and social theorists have described these shifts in many different ways over the last half century. Hannah Arendt argued that the collapse of genuine authority left only "atomized" individuals. Christopher Lasch described the rise of a "culture of narcissism." Lionel Trilling warned of the erosion of "sincerity" and the rise of "authenticity." Robert Bellah, Richard Madsen, William Sullivan, Ann Swidler, and Steven Tipton discerned the displacement of "civic republicanism" by "expressive individualism." Robert Putnam traced the collapse of voluntary associations and worried about Americans bowling alone. Ulrich Beck and Elisabeth Beck-Gernsheim offered a more thoroughly materialist account of what they called "individualization." Charles Taylor stretched the historical frame to narrate the shift from an *ancien régime* to an Age of Mobilization to an Age of Authenticity. And in the last decade, countless voices have weighed in on the rise of the "nones" and those who identify as "spiritual but not religious." These accounts differ in important ways, and I have learned from all of them even as I quarrel in one way or another with each of them. But this dense cluster of work points to some significant phenomena. In the present time, people are less likely to join voluntary associations or form new ones. The associations themselves no longer mediate cultural power in the same way. They have lost their aura. The world of voluntary associations that Lyman Beecher discerned and helped create, the social imaginary that had such power to shape an emerging nation for two centuries, is passing away. Even where the shells of its institutions seem to endure, they are transformed by changes in their inner rationale and their loss of power to define norms for others.

Ironically, the unraveling of Beecher's world puts us in a position like Beecher's own. As he saw the end of the Standing Order, so now we are seeing the end of the world of voluntary associations that took its place. Many of the people most advantaged by the old Standing Order could imagine nothing but anarchy and infidelity if it passed away. They mistook the dominant form of social life in their context for the entirety of social life in human community. They missed new and refurbished forms of social connection already coming together in their midst. So, today, those most invested in the world of voluntary associations worry that its passing leaves nothing more than a vacuous individualism that is empty in itself, defined only by the absence of belonging to voluntary associations. Too many of us who are formed by these associations and help lead them have neglected the challenge of cultivating new forms of life together. And we have too often missed new and refurbished forms of social life already emerging within and beyond the centers of power.

Discerning and cultivating new forms of social life and the forms of theological education that make sense with them is so demanding that it can seem to constitute the entirety of the challenge before us. It will be difficult enough to make a leap like the one Beecher made, to forms of theological education that fit with an emerging social world. But it will be even more difficult, especially for those of us who understand ourselves as white, to make the leap Beecher could *not* make: to forms of social life and modes of theological education that break the stranglehold on Christian imaginations of the projects of white supremacy and settlement.

This second leap is demanded by contemporary movements for freedom and dignity for Black, Indigenous, and other people of color. But it is not a new demand. It was already there in Beecher's time, for those with ears to hear prophets like Jarena Lee, David Walker, and Tecumseh. The modalities of white supremacy in North America have changed shape over the centuries, but the demand to undo structures of domination is not new. The demand is as old as the violence that gives it urgency. It is the demand of a slain sibling's blood, crying out from the ground. If we fail to hear it, God does not.

It clarifies the work before us, I think, to distinguish these two demanded leaps from one another. Changes in the modes of social life will not automatically bring racial justice. Those who celebrate new social forms might imagine that because the older forms were shot through with white supremacy, the end of those old forms will bring the end of the racist powers they transmitted. But this misses the shape-shifting power of white supremacy in American history. As it moved from chattel slavery to Jim Crow to mass incarceration, so it migrated from the Standing Order to the world of voluntary associations. There is no reason to assume it cannot slither into whatever is coming next.

DOWNSTREAM FROM LANE

In telling the stories of Lyman Beecher and Lane Theological Seminary, I find myself both blessed and implicated, even *indicted*, as one formed by and for the world they made. It is not just that I identify as white, straight, male, and Presbyterian. These markers are meaningful, of course, but they can mean many things. It is not enough simply to list them as a kind of performative warm-up before a long run that leaves them far behind. As philosopher George Yancy has argued, white people need to "tarry" with whiteness, to "*dwell* with the emotional and cognitive dissonance that will be inevitably experienced as they become more and more attentive to the ways in which they are entangled in the social and psychic web of white racism." This dwelling with dissonance, Yancy writes, "is *not* about seeing how much guilt one can sustain or endure. That sounds like a species of white self-indulgence through a mode of masochism." And it is not about denying the real virtues of people like Beecher and institutions like Lane and worlds shaped by them for the sake of a new Manicheanism. Rather, Yancy writes, "The trick is not to flee, but to have the foundations of one's white being challenged, to lose one's sense of white self-certainty, and to render unstable that familiar white sense of being-in-the-world."[28] For those of us who identify as white, it is to let ourselves be touched, shaken, by Black and Brown and Indigenous thinkers who know us better than we know ourselves. It is to dwell with the end of a world God has already declared to be done, and so to listen for a hope that is more than we can ask or imagine.

I grew up in the Mississippi watershed Lane was founded to redeem, in a church pastored by a graduate of McCormick, the seminary Lane flowed into. More than this, though, I was raised in and for a world dense with voluntary associations. For generations my family has related to our church not just as a place of worship but also as an organization run by its members. Committee service has been handed down as a practice of religious devotion. That ethos has extended out from the church to other voluntary associations, just as Beecher said it should. Across the generations, my parents, grandparents, and great-grandparents joined, led, and sustained everything from direct-service ministries to social clubs, professional associations, advocacy groups, political parties, public schools, and a local college. In this world, service was the cardinal virtue, and serious service was always mediated by a voluntary association. At the center of any meaningful, praiseworthy life were three pillars: professional achievement (especially for men, though, in later generations, for all), a thriving family, and leadership in these voluntary associations. Wealthy people who focused more on consumption and leisure than service were regarded as decadent. Their lives served as warnings about the vices that came with inherited wealth. And people in need deserved help. That help—often real, even life-changing for particular individuals—flowed through voluntary associations that didn't really want the people who received help to join them. The associations were officially integrated by race and committed to serving all people, even as they legitimated and extended the power of a white professional class. They both constituted a local elite and—just as Beecher promised, just as Tocqueville saw—cultivated the republican virtues that let democratic self-governance flourish. For some. In all these complexities, this was the West Lane was founded to create.

I grew up a true believer in this relatively progressive white "mainline" Protestant world. I was active in our Presbyterian congregation in every way a young person could be active. And I followed the ethos beyond the congregation, holding some kind of office in student government every year of my schooling, from the beginning of kindergarten to the end of high school. I threw myself into debate, which promised to cultivate the virtues needed for the world of voluntary associations. (What dueling was to European aristocrats in the nineteenth century, debate was to a Midwestern professional-managerial class in the twentieth: the stylized performance of the signature skill of a world that was already passing away.) I lived out the piety I felt by participating in organized benevolence and serving as a delegate to my denomination's governing body. In high school and college I joined too many organizations and then started new ones. As I tried on different vocations, I thought elected politics involved too many moral compromises. Besides, I'd been raised to believe that voluntary associations were the real heart and soul of the nation. And while I hadn't even heard of Lyman Beecher, I shared his sense that seminary was where one learned how to lead in that world. And so I went to seminary, became a minister, and served congregations that established new voluntary associations that did real good even as they also reproduced and legitimated local elites. And now I have followed Beecher from the congregation to the seminary, teaching in a historically white, now more diverse, relatively progressive Protestant school that trains leaders for a world of voluntary associations. Candler draws on different denominational roots and is in a different watershed. But the muddy ambivalences of Lane still flow through the school.

In dwelling with these details of identity, I don't mean to authorize the speech that follows. The particular race, class, and gender identities that I inhabit usually exert their greatest authorizing power when they fade into the background and try to pass as the natural order of things. Instead, I mean to dwell with the ways the old contradictions continue, not only in institutions but also in my own body. I mean to grapple with what it would mean to take responsibility for those contradictions. And I mean to pray for a hope that runs beyond them.

ESCHATOLOGICAL MEMORIES

The work demanded in this time between the times cannot be done from what Willie James Jennings has called the "commanding heights" of political, cultural, ecclesial, and academic authority.[29] If I were to offer a New Blueprint for Theological Education, the genre itself would amount to a claim to speak from those heights. Failing to recognize my entanglement in present orders, the genre would project those old orders into proposals that presented themselves as newer than they really were. Instead, I'm trying to write from down in the ruts of the world I'm trying to describe. And so I write historically—not from the end of history, as one who can define the meaning of different epochs, but from a more muddled and implicated middle.

From this implicated spot, I try to tell the story of the consolidation of a model of theological education that fits the world of voluntary societies (chap. 1) and the forces of individualization (chap. 2) that are unraveling this model and the world in which it makes sense (chap. 3). A sermon then interrupts the story to announce the end of theological education, even in the middle of things, with a vision of judgment and grace that are two faces of the same divine love. And then, from the blessed, groaning rubble of the present, I try to name practices of renunciation (chap. 4) that open us to God's faithfulness and some affordances we might grasp as we try to respond (chap. 5).

I intend the history that launches this exercise to be a genealogy of established forms. As a genealogy, the story I tell here makes no claim to be comprehensive. Excellent wide-ranging histories already exist, and I am in their debt.[30] I am also in the debt of friends and fellow authors in the Theological Education between the Times series. Each of our books tells stories of particular parts of theological education from particular points of view. Even together, they don't pretend to tell every story. That framing of the series, coupled with the profound work of colleagues, delivers me from illusions of universality that too often envelop histories of dominant forms. I mean to tell something more local, personal, and particular: the family history of one mode of theological education that gained a kind of established status that is now unraveling.

The established quality of this mode has never been primarily about numbers. Indeed, a majority of Christian ministers in the last 250 years have been trained in other ways. And a more expansive understanding of theological education would reveal my sliver of a story to be an even narrower part of the whole. But a truthful story of any kind of establishment is a story not just of numbers, but of power. Essential to that power has been the way that established forms of theological education have come to seem natural, almost ontological, not just the way things are but the way things should be, even the only way things *could* be. In telling a genealogy of how these forms came into being, I want to stress the contingency of the story. Things have been otherwise in the past, could have developed into an otherwise present, and might yet be otherwise in the future. I hope that stressing this contingency will provoke critical, theological reflexivity, both among those who understand this genealogy as the story of a family that has blessed them and among those who have lived with the weight of this history on their backs.[31]

To give shape to this story, I mold the history into three clumps that keep spilling into one another: a *standing order*[32] that runs from the first European settlements through the early national period; an age of *voluntary associations* that runs from pre-Revolutionary times through the middle decades of the twentieth century; and an age of *authentic individuals* that gains power in the Long Sixties and shapes our shared world today.[33] The substantive nouns in these names define what these social imaginaries take as the fundamental building blocks of society: a singular *order*, then plural *associations*, and now even-more-plural *individuals*. And the modifiers in these phrases suggest a core value in each imaginary: the *standing*, or given, quality of the social order; the free and *voluntary* nature of associations; and the *authentic* ideal to which so many individuals aspire today. Of course these clumps fail to capture the whole of anything like an era, epoch, age, or even a single year. Historical realities are wider and weirder than broad categories like these can capture. But organizing disparate data into clumps, eras, and ages can help create narratives that spark reflexivity, even when reality runs beyond them. Indeed, they might be most illuminating when they fail.

A narrative that moves from standing orders to voluntary associations to authentic individuals has a kind of direction. It can be tempting to read this narrative as one of world-historical progress or decline. Such narratives abound now, and with the arrow of history pointing in both directions. Some see a great story of progress, featuring perhaps the steady emancipation of individual selves. Individuals have greater freedom than ever to make and remake themselves, the story goes. Others see a story of decline. Critics identify many different dates as the high point from which we are declining. Perhaps it came when the world was more of a standing order (it's been downhill since Plymouth!), or when voluntary associations defined civic and ecclesial life (downhill since the '50s!). Progressives and conservatives might point to different markers as they sketch the downward line. But a sense that things are getting worse unites a large and disparate group. Narratives of decline fill books and op-ed columns. They haunt institutions' official communications that are meant to show that they are exceptions to the general rule. And they infuse daily conversations. I cannot count the number of retiring pastors or professors who have privately expressed relief to me at getting out before the whole thing collapsed.

There are indeed gains to celebrate and losses to grieve. But it would be a mistake to see the larger story as one of world-historical progress or decline. Narratives of progress imagine a glorious future that we are moving toward, while narratives of decline pin that perfect moment to some golden age in the past from which we are falling away. Both make the mistake of imagining the reign of God as a moment in history that is continuous with but not identical to our own. But the reign of God cannot be reduced to a point on a timeline. It is the power that creates the time line, the grace that redeems it, and the love that breaks into it to give each moment—even now!—whatever life it has. This love makes claims on us. It demands that we renounce the powers of sin and death and respond instead with love. Individuals and whole societies can do better and worse in our responses. We can and must tell stories that evaluate those responses. But the stories of our responses cannot be gathered into grand narratives of progress or decline, as if the reign of God was at some point in the future or the past. Instead, we must risk eschatological memories, stories of judgment and hope, stories in which the reign of God has drawn near.[34]

AFTER THE END

In saying yes to Jesus's proclamation that the time is fulfilled, that the reign of God has drawn near, Christians confess that the end of the world is always at hand. It is by the light of this confession that we read the passing of all the orders of this age. Seeing by this light does not minimize those passings. We live in the midst of them, and real goods are at stake in the ways we navigate them. But this angle of vision does deliver the orders of this age from any appearance of ultimacy. And it helps us see that the end of what we mistake for the whole world is not the end of God's world.

This is the source of our hope: not that we can stop the orders of this world from passing away, nor that we can make an ethical leap into perfect forms, but that the histories in which we find ourselves are caught up in the much larger history of God's redemption of the cosmos.

The end of Lane Theological Seminary was not the end of God's work in the Mississippi watershed. Some of this work happened through the ambivalent achievements of the seminary's mission. If the network of voluntary associations Beecher envisioned projected power, it also formed people for democracy and self-rule. If the associations legitimated white settlement of the land Beecher called the West, they also played an important role in the abolition of slavery.

And some of what I will risk naming as the redeeming work of God came not through the seminary's limited success, but exactly through its collapse. After the trustees cracked down in the fall of 1835, Lane students scattered. About a dozen of them joined Black citizens in grassroots abolitionist study sessions in Cumminsville, a few miles away, piecing together a curriculum from their various areas of expertise. They preached, taught Sunday school, and held lectures in racially mixed gatherings. White and Black people walked together in the streets and visited in one another's homes. They ate, drank, prayed, and enjoyed communion across the lines racialized respectability tried to draw. These practices surely did not completely transcend systemic racism, and they never attained the power to establish enduring institutions, but they were disruptive enough to call forth the threat of violence from white Ohioans. In Ohio, as in the country of the Gerasenes, sometimes it is in the alarm of demons that we can recognize redemption.

A larger group of former Lane students, including both Theodore Dwight Weld and James Bradley, went to Oberlin, where they pushed a fledgling school to open a theological department, hire revivalist Charles Grandison Finney, and become the aboli-

24

tionist institution they thought Lane should have been. Oberlin had moral contradictions of its own, bonding abolitionist politics to the ideology of a redeemer nation first in sending settlers to Kansas and then in sending missionaries to China. But Oberlin was probably the most deeply integrated school of the time, and the school and town became a hub for Black freedom movements. The Lane Rebels would settle for nothing less.

Another fugitive from Lane also came into her own after she left the school. Harriett Beecher had never enrolled in Lane, which was restricted to men at the time. She went instead to a school for women back in Connecticut that was run by her sister Catharine. But she lived with her father, Lyman, on the Lane campus in those crucial early years, and she heard many of the debates of 1834. In 1836 she married her father's faculty ally Calvin Stowe and followed his career to a more stable situation at Bowdoin College in Maine. There they turned their home into a stop on the Underground Railroad. And there she wrote the vivid descriptions of slavery that became *Uncle Tom's Cabin*, the best-selling novel of the nineteenth century. Harriet Beecher Stowe mastered the new media even better than her father had, serializing the writing in multiple publications, gathering it as a novel, turning it into a play, and using it as a springboard to transatlantic lecture tours. *Uncle Tom's Cabin* trades in stereotypes and scenes of subjection that offer white readers both titillation at the sight of degraded Black bodies and the sinuous pleasures of moral superiority.[35] It is no more innocent than Lane itself. But exactly in this compromised state it played a vital role in helping white Northerners see slavery as the abomination it was. There is both grace and judgment in this history, as there is in the fact that the most influential person Lane Theological Seminary helped form was never able to enroll as a student.

As the seminary struggled financially in its later years, trustees sold off parcels of the campus and other lands that made up much of its endowment. At least some of the land was sold to Black buyers eager to establish homes and businesses. The seminary, unlike many other landowners, was willing to sell to them. The sale of its lands helped nurture and sustain a community of Black property owners in and around its Walnut Hills neighborhood, contributing to a base for Black wealth. Precisely in its unraveling, the seminary did more than issue another of the hedged statements for justice that it offered when it was trying to survive. It did material work for justice. The Walnut Hills neighborhood is gentrifying now. But God is not through with it.

1

Consolidation

If many theological schools today seem uncertain about the context in which they are working and about the purposes they serve this may be due in no small part to the confusions present in that contemporary Christianity itself in which they participate. These internal conflicts are doubtless rooted in the perennial human condition; there is no way to eliminate by any single movement of reformation the temptations and the failures from which the last rebirth alone can set us free. But unless the forms in which idolatries appear at any particular time are illuminated and criticized there is no prospect for ultimate health. The critique of education requires the critique of theology and the critique of theology involves the critique of the Church. Such self-criticism in seminary and Church is always part of that total repentance which is the counterpart of faith.

H. Richard Niebuhr et al.,
The Purpose of the Church and Its Ministry
(1956)

An interconnected network of institutions came together in the early national period to create a normative framework for religious and political life in the United States. It involved a whole range of voluntary associations, including special-purpose benevolence societies, congregations, denominations within a shared national polity, ministry as something like a profession, and theological education as preparation for leadership of more-or-less religious organizations. In subsequent decades the institutions in this network grew more fully into their forms even as they absorbed old and new religious movements.

This constellation has become so established, so taken for granted, that it can seem identical with Christian ministry and practice, and even with religion more broadly. If that were the case, then the erosion of this network would mean the end of Christian faith and practice in the United States. But this constellation does not exhaust the possibilities for religious life, nor even for Christian life. Faithful lives might be lived otherwise. Indeed, they already have been.

STANDING ORDERS

European settlers brought imaginations shaped by their experiences with an "established" church that was not fully differentiated from the state. The treaties signed in Westphalia in 1648 stopped the worst of the carnage of the Thirty Years' War and laid the groundwork for a new social order in Europe. Now each sovereign would determine the religion of his or her territory—and be obliged to respect the designations of other sovereigns. That broad framework could accommodate many differences. The established religion might still be contested, as it was in England. Degrees and modes of tolerance for dissenting groups varied from state to state. And the power to make ecclesial and political appointments, along with the flows of wealth between church and crown, took many different (and endlessly disputed) forms. But even with these differences, a shared Westphalian imagination featured some favored religious tradition in a tight circuit of mutual legitimation with a nation-state that asserted sovereignty over a defined territory.

English Puritans brought that imagination to New England, establishing Puritan congregationalism in many different jurisdictions, including what came to be called the Standing Order in

Connecticut. Dissenters in their home country, Puritans came to North America for the chance to be the established political and ecclesial power. Dutch Calvinists brought a similar worldview to their settlements up the Hudson River, and Anglicans carried it with them to Virginia. Even religious traditions not used to established status shared in the social imaginary of a standing order, offering implicit and explicit assent as they took up the role carved out by dissenting groups in European nations. Sometimes they accepted the legitimacy of the establishment of some other tradition in exchange for a measure of tolerance. And sometimes, in colonies where no church was established, they occupied the dissenting role in relation to an establishment left empty. The imaginary was elastic enough to hold many variations.[1]

"Establishment" describes aspirations and imaginations more than the complex realities on the ground. It meant different things in different places. Establishments were stronger and weaker, and took different forms, even within the same colony. But the arrangements of the Standing Order in Connecticut indicate the contours of a widely shared imaginary. In Connecticut, the Standing Order named a tight network of ecclesial, political, and economic powers. The Congregational church enjoyed an established status that assured funding and limited meaningful competition from other bodies of believers. Its values and practices—like a Sunday Sabbath—were written into law. It exercised influence beyond a narrowly defined religious sphere, helping set standards for business practices and overseeing education from primary schools to colleges. The term "standing order" was particular to Connecticut. I use it more generally here because it well describes this loose, plural, and contested social imaginary that exerted so much formative power in the first centuries of European settlement of North America.

The social imaginary of a standing order shaped key institutions in the colonies, including congregations and ministry. It also shaped the form of theological education that prevailed, at least among established churches. Here I consider each in turn.

Whatever they were called, congregations in standing orders were often imagined as something like *parishes*. At least in the imagined ideal, one established congregation served each town or region. Even if a village church was not literally a parish, it enjoyed many of the privileges and performed many of the duties of a parish of the established church in a European country. In E. Brooks Holifield's typology, these early American churches were "comprehensive congregations." They were supported in various ways by at least some public funds. And they had significant public duties. Episcopal congregations in Virginia, for instance, kept records of births and deaths in their parishes. Their church wardens were charged with caring for orphans, protecting children from abusive parents, and providing relief for people experiencing poverty or homelessness. Towns played a larger role in caring for vulnerable people in New England and the middle colonies, but congregations still provided funds and bore responsibility for public welfare. And their buildings often doubled as both worship space for the congregation and meeting space for the town. Looking back from the nineteenth century, Justice Lemuel Shaw described church and town in early New England as a "dual corporation." The two were distinct but deeply joined.[2] If congregations were in the wider social world, that world seeped into congregations as well, as seating arrangements formally reflected local hierarchies. The comprehensive congregation did not operate only in a distinctly religious sphere. It was part of a standing order that featured interlocking religious, economic, familial, and political institutions rather than differentiated and relatively autonomous social spheres.[3]

Ministry in this context was construed as a kind of *public office*, more like a local magistrate than a physician or attorney. In both Virginia and New England, ministers in established churches were paid at least in part with public funds. Public compensation took various forms—including salaries, parsonages, goods in kind, and glebe lands—and it brought with it public duties, like preaching on publicly observed fast days or blessing local militias. And it invited public oversight. In New England the whole town—not just members of the congregation—often had some say in who would fill the office of minister. Ministry was so embedded in the standing orders of New England that ordination was not to service in some denomination, as it often is today, but to a particular congregation in a particular place. If a minister moved (and many did not), he was often ordained again to ministry in the new place. Ordination did not convey portable sets of credentials that individuals could carry wherever they went. It bound a person to a place, even as it bound that place to the person of the minister. Ministry was an office in a standing order. Individual competence and charisma mattered, of course, but the office itself, condensing all the power of the standing order, was the ground of pastoral authority.[4]

Just as the congregation and the office of minister were not confined to a distinctly religious sphere, theological education in the standing orders of colonial America happened primarily as general education in the undifferentiated institutional spaces of colleges. The earliest colleges in the colonies were founded to form leaders for the standing orders. The desire for an educated clergy was especially strong. Harvard was founded in 1636 as a generation of Puritan settlers found themselves "dreading to leave an illiterate Ministery to the Churches, when our present Ministers shall lie in the Dust."[5] Likewise, the College of William and Mary was founded in 1693 as Virginia Episcopalians contemplated the loss of a generation of priests trained at Oxford and Cambridge. People preparing for ministry in these standing orders did not attend a seminary that was set apart. Like Lyman Beecher, they usually received an education both general and theological in a college they attended with people who would go on to many different offices in the standing order. They learned the particular skills and wisdom necessary for ministry in apprenticeships to established pastors.

"Theological education" in colonial standing orders did more than form pastors. It is anachronistic to assume the narrowing of theological education to a special training for clergy that became the dominant form and then project that definition back in time to define theological education. A better reading is that theological education was practically undifferentiated from general education. Anyone seeking an office in a standing order would need to know theology—not as a specialized subject, but as the substance of the worldview in which all the offices and institutions of the standing order made sense. Theological education was for all who would hold office, whether in the church, the courts, or the civil government.

The nature of theological education as general education becomes clear from the trajectories of students. The curriculum of Harvard College in the seventeenth century might have been designed to form a literate ministry, but even in those earliest years, only about half of Harvard's graduates went on to become ministers.[6] Those who did often went on to hold other offices, including governor, judge, and college president. People who held these offices did not take different courses; there was nothing like the modern system of a "major" and "electives." All students took similar courses of study. The shared education mirrored a social imaginary in which the roles themselves, and the spheres in which they played out, were not strongly differentiated.

The 1701 charter of the Connecticut Collegiate School, which became Yale College, makes this broader purpose clear. It established the college as a place "wherein Youth may be instructed in the Arts & Sciences who through the blessing of Almighty God may be fitted for Publick employment in both Church & State." The General Assembly's charter of Yale College in 1745 celebrated the fact that the college "under the blessing of Almighty God has trained up many worthy persons for the service of God in the State as well as the Church."[7]

The undifferentiated education of early colonial colleges was thoroughly theological, and it was not only for ministers. For it was less about learning the distinct skills a congregational leader would need and more about imbibing the social imaginary that ordered the world. Colonial theological education formed people not specifically for pastoral ministry but for the broader category of office in a standing order.

Standing orders began to come unraveled even before they were fully established. Processes of disestablishment unfolded at different speeds in different places, but they were occurring all across the English colonies in the eighteenth century. Political and theological arguments about the need for tolerance played important roles, but ideas were often catching up with realities on the ground. It was difficult as a practical matter to assert a standing order across the large spaces of the colonies, especially when they had porous and contested frontiers. Moreover, many landholders sold land to the highest bidder, whatever that bidder's religious affiliation. Speculative markets in land helped create pluralism as a social fact. Changing, unstable relations with European powers further eroded standing orders. When the Crown revoked the charter of the Massachusetts Bay Colony in 1684 and appointed the Anglican Edmond Andros as governor, Congregationalists with Puritan roots gave up hopes of establishment and called instead for pluralism and tolerance. Soon Massachusetts was exempting Anglicans, Quakers, Baptists, and other minority traditions from the taxes that supported churches. The standing orders—always patchy, never absolute— were coming undone.[8]

Some of the most intense pressures on standing orders came from religious movements that started within them. Revivals split some congregations and produced many new ones, undoing standing orders that legitimated a single comprehensive congregation as the village church. Revivals also stressed the importance of personal renewal, providing grounds for people to challenge clergy they thought had not been sufficiently revived. Office alone had less power to secure authority. And revivals' stress on free individual decisions fit better with a world people understood themselves as making rather than a world given by standing orders.[9]

The Revolution brought the crisis in the standing orders to a head, for no single religious tradition could win support as an established church for all the colonies. As the imagined political community expanded from colony to nation, standing orders became impossible. The Constitution acknowledged this reality in 1787; the First Amendment made it explicit in 1791. The Constitution did allow standing orders to persist on the state level. The Congregational church was fully disestablished in Connecticut only in 1818, and held on in Massachusetts until 1833. But the hold of the standing order on the social imaginary was broken long before.

Elites certified by the old order railed against its collapse, declaring that the end of a standing order would lead to the end not only of the church but also of the state. Massachusetts Congregationalist Phillips Payson, preaching an election sermon in 1778, acknowledged the importance of liberty, especially of conscience. But the freedoms that liberty brought made internalized constraints all the more important, Payson argued. Those constraints came chiefly from religion, and religion depended on public establishment. Disestablishment would leave religion to "the humors of the multitude." The result entailed not only a dissolution of true religion but also a grievous threat to "order and government in the State." For a mind shaped by the givenness of a standing order, it was impossible to imagine church or state apart from it.[10]

It was not only elites who had trouble imagining a church apart from its relationship with a standing order. Roger Finke and Rodney Stark argue that by 1776 only 17 percent of free Americans were members of churches.[11] The number of people with some connection to congregations was probably larger, as high expectations of members kept many people on participatory edges of congregations they did not formally join. But it is clear that religious adherence declined throughout the eighteenth century to a low point in the years around the Revolution. Many factors contributed to this pattern, including a rising rationalism, but none more so than the fact that many churches—especially the most established—were yoked to a social imaginary that no longer rang true. When churches tried to continue in the roles they played in standing orders, they became badly out of sync with a world in which standing orders were losing legitimacy. If the numerical decline continued in straight lines, the disestablished church would wither away in a few decades. It looked as if the worst fears of a preacher like Payson might come true.

THE MOTHER SCIENCE

Many observers shared Payson's fear that the dissolution of standing orders would undo both church and state. When French aristocrat Alexis de Tocqueville visited the United States in 1831, he was surprised to see another dynamic at work. He wondered how people would come together apart from standing orders. "In aristocratic societies," Tocqueville wrote, "men do not need to unite in order to act, because they are held tightly together."[12] The legacies of standing orders bind people together and assign them their roles in collective action. "Among democratic peoples, on the contrary, all citizens are independent and weak; they can hardly do anything by themselves, and no one among them can compel his fellows to lend him their help. So they fall into impotence if they do not learn to help each other freely."[13] But, as Tocqueville saw, the people in the United States *had* learned to help each other freely. They had developed a social technology of voluntary associations that created and renewed social bonds. The old standing orders had made possible a set of social relations that made human life human, Tocqueville wrote. In the relationships standing orders make possible, "Sentiments and ideas are renewed, the heart grows larger and the human mind develops only by the reciprocal action of men on each other." But in democratic countries that have broken up the standing orders that assigned people to places in a larger connected whole, this kind of sociality is "almost nil," in Tocqueville's estimation. "So it must be created there artificially. And this is what associations alone are able to do."[14]

In truth, voluntary associations were no more artificial than the standing orders they displaced. It is part of the ideology of standing orders to appear given rather than made by conquest and subjugation, just as it is part of the ideology of voluntary associations to present themselves as the entirely free creations of the people who make them. But Tocqueville was right to see voluntary associations rising to do the work that standing orders could no longer do. He named explicitly the similarity in the ways standing orders and voluntary associations functioned: "Wherever, at the head of a new undertaking, you see in France the government, and in England, a great lord, count on seeing in the United States, an association."[15] Voluntary associations played a role like the king-sublimated-into-state in France and like nobles-blended-with-capitalists in England who could still call on legacies of standing orders in their societies. In Tocqueville's words, voluntary associations "take the place of the powerful individuals that equality of conditions has made disappear."[16]

Tocqueville saw Americans forming voluntary associations for all kinds of purposes. Whenever they saw some need, he wrote, they formed an association. "The art of association" thus became what Tocqueville called "the mother science" of the new kind of society.[17] He marveled at all the directions to which they turned this core social technology:

> Americans of all ages, of all conditions, of all minds, constantly unite. Not only do they have commercial and industrial associations in which they all take part, but also they have a thousand other kinds: religious, moral, intellectual, serious ones, useless ones, very general and very particular ones, immense and very small ones; Americans associate to celebrate holidays, establish seminaries, build inns, erect churches, distribute books, send missionaries to the Antipodes; in this way they create hospitals, prisons, schools. If, finally, it is a matter of bringing a truth to light or of developing a sentiment with the support of a good example, they associate.[18]

The voluntary association evolved into an open-ended social technology that could be turned to just about any purpose. The purpose defined and legitimated the organization. The voluntary association did not claim divine establishment from time out of mind, like a standing order might. It rather claimed to share in divine *mission*. That sense of mission charged the voluntary association with meaning.

That missional charge was especially powerful when connected to a nation that was seen as having a sacred role in world history. Contrary to nostalgic neoliberal tales of a time when voluntary societies were strong and the state was small, the two arose together in tight connection. As Theda Skocpol has argued, the state provided essential infrastructure that allowed voluntary associations to thrive, including not just rights of free speech and free assembly but also laws of incorporation, a sympathetic tax code, and a postal service that let people of common minds come together for causes in which they believed.[19] The network of voluntary associations, in turn, helped structure the state through political parties and advocacy groups. It created relationships across regions that cultivated national consciousness. Moreover, voluntary associations provided the social technology that made rapid expansion of white settlement possible, underwriting narratives of national expansion with both the institutions that let settlements take root and an ideology that justified expulsion of Native Americans and French and Spanish Catholics in the name of freedom. In this ideology, voluntary associations demonstrated white Protestant settlers' moral superiority, both in their high-minded aims and in the voluntary nature of their associations. They helped legitimate the expanding state that secured the differentiated sphere in which they operated. Precisely as voluntary associations, religious organizations were connected both to the imagined community of the nation and to the state that embodied it.[20]

The formal separation of church and state, then, made possible a new kind of connection between the two. The Swiss-born, US-based historian and theologian Philip Schaff began to diagnose this connection in two lectures he delivered in Berlin in 1854. Schaff told his German listeners about the extraordinary vitality of Christianity in the United States. The signature of the American church, he said, was "the voluntary principle."[21] The principle "follows unavoidably from the separation of church and state."[22] One might worry that a disestablished church would have neither the funds nor the social sanction needed to thrive. "But, on the other hand, the voluntary system calls forth a mass of individual activity and interest among the laity in ecclesiastical affairs, in the founding of new churches and congregations, colleges and seminaries, in home and foreign missions, and in the promotion of all forms of Christian philanthropy."[23] For example, people in Germany gave little thought to theological faculties, Schaff said. But people in the United States joined together to found and fund seminaries that trained pastors in the traditions they valued most. Because of the great outpouring of energy unleashed by the voluntary principle, the church was stronger than ever: "The nation, therefore, is still Christian, though it refused to be governed in this deepest concern of the mind and heart by the temporal power. In fact, under such circumstances, Christianity, as the free expression of personal conviction and of the national character, has even greater power over the mind, than when enjoined by civil laws and upheld by police regulations."[24] America, Schaff said, was "the Phenix-grave of Europe."[25] It was where the Christian traditions of Europe, formed in imaginaries of standing orders, died to establishment and rose to new life as voluntary associations in close cycles of mutual legitimation with a nation they defined as Christian.

Over time, the form of the voluntary association itself attained a kind of aura. The form became self-legitimating. The institutional form of a voluntary association marked an endeavor as powerful and purposeful. The form made membership meaningful and fit so well in the larger social imaginary that religious adherence in the United States doubled in the first half of the nineteenth century. After a plateau in the years around the Civil War, it shot up again and continued this upward trajectory long into the twentieth century.[26] A preacher like Phillips Payson was right that something was passing away with the disestablishment of the old standing orders. But he could not imagine just how vital religion could be in this new network of voluntary associations.

CHURCH AS A NETWORK OF VOLUNTARY SOCIETIES

The "mother science" of association informed the formation of a whole constellation of new institutions, including denominations, congregations, and benevolent societies. These were not just new institutions but new *kinds* of institutions, stamped with the worldview and practices of voluntarism. The rise of benevolent societies most clearly reflected this dynamic, as most were newly founded. But a related dynamic played out as already-existing institutions changed at deep levels, often without changing their physical locations or their names. Established and dissenting churches became denominations. Parish-like village churches became voluntary congregations. These new kinds of institutions required new kinds of leaders: not officers taking their places in a standing order but professionals with the skills and vision to lead voluntary societies.

Even as standing orders were evaporating, a flood tide of new *benevolent societies* was rising to fill the social spaces they left behind. In 1803, the Reverend Jedediah Morse founded the Massachusetts Society for Promoting Christian Knowledge to resist both Jeffersonian democracy and Unitarian theology. A host of other societies followed, including the New England Tract Society (f. 1814). Soon these voluntary associations aspired to national reach. Organizations like the American Education Society (1815), the American Bible Society (1816), the American Sunday School Union (1816), the American Tract Society (1825), the American Home Missionary Society (1826), the Society for the Promotion of Temperance (1826), and the American Peace Society (1828) exerted national influence. The institutional form fit the times. As Tocqueville and Schaff saw, it was native to a social world that separated church and state. The form also depended on funding from the new concentrations of wealth being generated through the rise of manufacturing and the rapid expansion of mercantile economies. The benevolent societies were funded not by the state but by donations, especially from large contributors. On a subtler level, the societies also seem to have fit with the hopes and ambitions of the times. People with many options chose to give their lives in service to them and found great meaning in doing so. Native to this new social world, benevolent societies thrived.

The benevolent societies undoubtedly extended an ideology of white Protestant "trusteeship" into a new era defined by disestablishment of religion and differentiation of social spheres. But the social control exerted was complex and incomplete. The network was no simple monolith. The institutional form of the voluntary society was open to different positions. The American Colonization Society (f. 1816) and the American Antislavery Society (1833), for instance, tugged in different directions around questions of slavery. Benevolent societies could also be formed by any free person who wanted to found one. In time free Black people, women, recent immigrants, and minoritized religious groups all founded societies of their own. Their work suggests the pluralism and contestation that came to mark the world of benevolent societies. It also suggests what all these founders and agents of benevolent societies had in common. People might have been striving for different purposes, but they channeled their strivings through the same kinds of institutions: voluntary societies. Thus the deepest social control was not through the conscious agenda of any one organization, but at the level of the institutional form and the social imaginary it incarnated.[27]

Similar dynamics played out in other institutional forms that came to define an age of voluntary associations. After the collapse of standing orders, both established churches and dissenting churches became *denominations*. Neither church nor sect, the denomination represented a new form of church life. Many traditions—Anglican, Reformed, Congregationalist, Baptist, Quaker, Methodist, and more—had older roots. But the denominational form was something new. It defined religious organizations in a nation in which no religious tradition was formally established, each tradition was supposed to accept the legitimacy of every other tradition that became a denomination, and all the traditions existed together in a religious sphere that was differentiated from other spheres of society.

That differentiation of spheres was essential to the political theology embodied by denominations. The political sphere might be contested, but it was singular and centered on the state. Differentiation allowed the religious sphere to be a space of plurality that was compatible with this political unity. Traditions that became denominations did not have to accept the beliefs, practices, or governing structures of other traditions. The denominational ethos simply accepted the right of other denominations to continue to exist and, crucially, believed that all the denominations could exist together within the same polity. The denominational form thus vibrates in cycles of mutual legitimation with the modern nation-state. Even as the nation-state authorizes denominations as legitimate and secures their freedom within a distinctly religious sphere, the denominations acknowledge the state's power to define the boundaries of the imagined community. Charles Taylor describes this "neo-Durkheimian" dynamic with precision, writing that "it is a feature of denominationalism that, just because one's own church does not include all the faithful, there is a sense of belonging to a wider, less structured whole which does. And this can find at least partial expression in the state. That is, the members of mutually recognizing denominations can form a people 'under God,' with the sense of acting according to the demands of God in forming and maintaining their state, as in the case of the American 'civil religion.'"[28] Denominations came to offer theological legitimation of the state not directly, as in the older pattern of standing orders, but through the mediation of a civil religion that includes many denominations and is identical to none of them.

The denominational form has absorbed an incredible variety of religious traditions. If the form has been open, it has not been neutral. The form felt relatively hospitable to Christian movements that had never been legally established on any large scale in the United States, like Quakers, Baptists, Presbyterians, and Methodists. Anglicans and Congregationalists made grudging but relatively quick transitions in the first decades of the nineteenth century. Catholic ecclesiology, especially when coupled with imaginaries shaped by establishment in other places, proved more resistant. That resistance was only compounded by Protestant slander, discrimination, and violence. But American Catholicism steadily moved toward a denominational form, in fact if not always in theory, through the nineteenth and early twentieth centuries. Mormon belief and practice initially resisted the differentiation of religious, economic, and political spheres that the denominational ethos required. But eventually the Church of Jesus Christ of Latter-day Saints took its place as a denomination, too. Judaism, Islam, Hinduism, Buddhism, and other traditions beyond Christianity have all made innovations in thought and practice that let them join the ranks of denominations, in this sense.[29]

The denominational form has accommodated differences not only of religion but also of race, ethnicity, class, and national origin. The form fit readily with Jim Crow, for instance, for it could promise "separate but equal" standing within a larger polity defined by whiteness. H. Richard Niebuhr decried these divisions in 1929, revealing their sources in social factors and dispelling ideologies that attributed them to theological convictions.[30] But in relativizing the significance of differences between denominations—making them temporal, not ultimate—Niebuhr's critique strengthened the deeper ideology of denominationalism. Later twentieth-century ecumenical and interreligious movements tended to work along the same lines, relativizing differences and emphasizing common connections in a civil religion that helped legitimate a national order.

As religious movements became denominations, congregations became *voluntary societies*. Some congregations retained their names, buildings, and pastors even as they underwent deep transformations in their institutional form, changing from parishes, village churches, or dissenting congregations—all forms defined in relation to standing orders—into the kinds of free associations Schaff and Tocqueville celebrated. Congregations as voluntary societies expected pluralism, even competition, in their towns and cities. They developed ways to fund themselves that relied more on donations of individuals than on direct support from the state. They did more to recruit members. They developed new forms of preaching and worship that led people to make decisions to join the congregation. They became more internally homogeneous, reflecting not the whole town but different segments linked to race, class, kinship networks, and other markers of identity.

In this new form, congregations multiplied even faster than a rapidly growing population. The number of congregations in the United States grew from less than three thousand in 1780 to almost eleven thousand by 1820 and then to fifty-four thousand by 1860.[31] The congregation-as-voluntary-society fit closely with the ideologies and institutions of the age. And it flourished.

Just as multiple religious traditions became denominations, the local gatherings of many different traditions became congregations that shared the form of voluntary societies. As R. Stephen Warner argued, the congregation-as-voluntary-society first gained traction among white Protestants. But even traditions that in other countries centered on very different institutions, like temples or cathedrals, developed congregational forms as they took root in the United States. The process of forming congregations and fitting religious practices to them exerted a strong shaping power that homogenized traditions as it brought them into the space marked for religion. But this dynamic process of "institutional isomorphism" is not simply a projection of an undifferentiated white Protestant hegemony, Warner argued. The congregation-as-voluntary-society is not an automatic fit with Episcopal, Lutheran, and other Protestant imaginaries formed by establishment. And it has affinities with other traditions, like synagogue culture in Judaism. The form was also expanded, especially by Black church traditions, to range beyond the religious sphere into education, business, medicine, and more. Immigrant communities in every decade also expanded the scope and mission of the congregational form to encompass more of life. These expansions brought new depth and complexity to relationships in congregations. Exactly in this elasticity, the congregation-as-voluntary-society came to define the normative space for religious practice in the United States.[32]

MINISTERS AS PROFESSIONALS

This network of congregations, denominations, and benevolent societies demanded and made possible a different kind of leadership. Congregations and other institutions that were embedded in a standing order with relatively little differentiation of religious, political, economic, and other spheres could define ministry as an office in that order. But these voluntary societies required a different mode of leadership, one that underwrote the "purpose-driven" nature of their organizations. It was not enough to occupy a place in a standing order with stability, constancy, and fidelity; deep in the self-understanding of the voluntary societies was an imperative for growth and a desire to transform the world. Leaders were instrumental to those ends. They needed to demonstrate not just "holiness" or some other virtue, but expertise in leading voluntary societies in growth and impact.

Voluntary societies also required visions of leadership that recognized the freedom of both members and leaders. Whether through exercising voice and vote or by leaving or threatening to leave, members could hold leaders accountable in new ways. Likewise, leaders faced fewer barriers to moving on and moving up. Ordination was increasingly understood as a kind of credential that an individual attained and could carry to new places. The promise of freedom for both pastors and congregants mirrored the ideology of voluntarism at the heart of the new congregational form.

Over time, these shifts in leadership joined with Protestant understandings of vocation and consolidated around the image of the *professional*. As Donald M. Scott argued, "By the 1850s the New England ministry had become a 'profession' in a modern sense. Just like a lawyer or a doctor, the pastor now offered a specialized service to a particular self-selected clientele, which would not hesitate to dismiss him if it was dissatisfied with the quality of his service."[33] A professional understanding of leadership fit with the social imaginary and the institutional forms of voluntary associations.

"Profession" was no more total in defining ministry than "office" had been. Disestablishment kept both state and national governments from playing a strong, direct role in defining the boundaries of the profession, as they would for, say, medicine and law. And the voluntary nature of the donations that supported congregations meant that only a few ministers saw salaries like those of other professions, especially as those professions consolidated their own places in markets of expertise. The drive toward a professional ideal also met significant resistance from many different directions in the first half of the nineteenth century. Episcopalians in New York and Catholics in Baltimore resisted the instrumental understanding of ministry for the sake of a more priestly vision. Many Black pastors and other Black spiritual leaders thrived beyond any system of professional credentials, even as some Black denominations moved toward professional ideals. Ecstatic revivals on the frontier argued for authority grounded in an outpouring of the Holy Spirit rather than that grounded in expertise and accreditation. Restorationist traditions rooted in the Cumberland resisted strong distinctions between clergy and laypeople by appealing to New Testament models of ministry. Hispanic and Indigenous Catholics in California were insulated from pressures to professionalize their religious leaders. Denied ordination in most traditions, women preachers appealed to other sources of authority and other ways to define their ministries. Vowed religious communities practiced forms of Catholic faith in which the professional ideal made little sense. Itinerant preachers in rural New York and New England kept older forms of lay exhortation alive. Even among urban Congregationalists and Presbyterians who embraced the professional ideal, legacies of the old authority of office endured.

With such resistance, plurality of practice, and structural limits, E. Brooks Holifield argues, ministry in the United States became "only partially a profession."[34]

But if the professional ideal was always resisted and never fully realized—indeed, if it has never completely described a majority of Christian ministers in the United States—it has still exerted great cultural, political, and economic power precisely as a normative ideal. It gained such power in part because of its close association with white, Protestant, urban, and Northeastern concentrations of cultural and economic capital. And it grew in power in part because it fit so well with the institutions of the rising social imaginary of voluntary associations. Professional clergy were formed and authorized to lead the new, voluntary, associational style of congregations and benevolent organizations. While not certified by state or national government, professional clergy were authorized by denominations that performed analogous credentialing functions, and on an increasingly national scale. The professional model's fit with other key institutions imbued it with new authority and touched off related processes of institutional isomorphism. Even religious traditions that had internal reasons to take different forms, and might do so in other countries, were pulled in the United States toward a constellation of congregation, denomination, and professional clergy.

The professional model for ministry fit not just with the institutions of the age of voluntary associations but also with the deepest values and assumptions that shaped the wider social imaginary. Like the Protestant understanding of vocation that flowed into it, the professional model was in principle equally open to all people. Even when this accessibility was restricted in practice to white men whose class made formal education possible, the promise of equal accessibility was essential for the legitimacy of the professional ideal. Legitimacy depended on belief that the profession was in principle open to all, so those who benefited from it were justified in their gains. The professional model construed people not only as equal but also as free. Broken out of a given place in a standing order, the white man that the professional model imagined was free to choose his career. He might even move to pursue this calling. Historian Burton Bledstein contrasted it with the older assumptions of the standing order. In the standing order, "The Lord's 'calling' had committed His servant to perform his duties in a single congregation and community for a lifetime. But the meaning of an organic ministry, slowly maturing in intimate and familiar surroundings in which social order was paramount, was disappearing. The profession of the ministry had entered competitive society in which unrestrained individual self-determination undermined traditional life-styles."[35] The free, equal individual presumed and formed by the professional model of ministry fit both the constellation of voluntary institutions and the social imaginary that knit them together into a meaningful whole.

Professional models of ministry helped pioneer a broader space in American society for professionals of many kinds. Denominational associations of ministers functioned something like the professional societies that were emerging in other fields. The American Medical Association, founded in 1847, was an early example. In the decades after the Civil War, the space of professionalism expanded and solidified, with new professional associations for lawyers (1874), social workers (1874), librarians (1876), and more. These same decades saw a steady expansion of state licensure not only for doctors and lawyers but also for dentists (beginning in 1868), pharmacists (1874), veterinarians (1886), and accountants (1896).[36]

The professions arose as a new middle class in the decades that saw an older middle class of artisans, small business owners, and small property-holders give way to industrialization and increasing economies of scale across all kinds of markets. The professional ideal promised to check the worst effects of expansive capitalism and machine politics, taming chaotic competition with self-regulated professionals and replacing a political spoils system with merit and expertise. It promised to reconnect the hurly-burly of modern life to some sense of the common good.

These promises of professionalism played key roles in legitimating the emerging space for workers who understood themselves as professionals—including ministers. The nascent professionals were neither labor nor capital. Unlike capital, their primary resource was their own expert labor. Professionals were paid for services they themselves rendered. But unlike labor, they depended less on means of production owned by others. Physicians and attorneys, for instance, tended to own their practices either as individuals or as partners with other professionals. Even those who did depend on institutions that were at least partially controlled by others—like teachers and, to varying degrees, ministers—exercised greater autonomy than other employees.

Professionals established themselves in this distinctive role through a dynamic that operated across many different spheres. In this dynamic they marked off some domain as an area in which they had specialized knowledge and so exercised unique competence. Professionalizing physicians claimed this unique competence in relation to health, as professionalizing ministers did in relation to the goods promised by their religious traditions. As those traditions became voluntary associations, the ability to lead a thriving voluntary association became especially important. But the sphere of pastoral expertise also included things like salvation, spiritual enlightenment, sacraments, interpretation of the Bible, and moral formation of young people. Different traditions prioritized different goods and combined them in different ways. What professionalizing clergy shared was this core dynamic in which they broke some domain out of the larger whole of life, asserted unique expertise in relation to it, and offered specialized services in pursuit of the goods it promised.

This dynamic of professionalization had several implications. If professionals had unique authority in relation to a distinct domain, then only professionals could evaluate the work of other professionals in their field. This autonomy distinguished professionals from even highly skilled employees. Professionals therefore tended to organize in associations that functioned more like guilds than like labor unions. Ministerial associations and denominational judicatory bodies—whether defined as dioceses, presbyteries, districts, conferences, or in some other way—pioneered the form that other professions adopted. In many cases states deferred to these associations or similar boards to inscribe into law the power of professionals to define their membership. States that did not directly underwrite this power still deferred to it when ministerial duties overlapped with functions of the state, as in defining who could sign marriage licenses, who could serve as chaplains, or which students qualified for federally backed student loans. Entirely beyond the state, ministerial associations had sufficient cultural capital to make their boundaries meaningful, especially as denominations asserted power on a national scale.

The core dynamic of professionalization not only let professionals mark the boundaries of their own guilds but also authorized them to define their services as incommensurable with the services of others. If professionals exercised specialized knowledge in a distinct domain, the logic ran, then no one else could offer what they offered. If you wanted the health physicians offered, you had to see a physician. This incommensurability insulated professional services from open competition in a boundaryless market. It kept professional services from becoming ordinary commodities for which a consumer might shop around, and so lifted professionals into a different kind of economy. At least in the ideal form of these economies, people seeking goods in them adopted a posture of trust that was mirrored by a professional sense of responsibility that placed the good of the client and the values of the profession above individual gain. That service ethos further charged professional status with a distinctive moral quality. Professionals were not only administering important goods—goods too precious to be left to the market—they were administering them in ways that prioritized the clients' interests over their own profits.[37]

The ideal of professional work offered not just a different position in the economy but a different life course. In contrast to the iterative work of farming for many years the same piece of land—or serving the same congregation, or saying the same daily office—a successful professional vocation promised opportunities for growing autonomy and responsibility. It promised a *career*. And in contrast to a mere series of jobs, or to making a living through one business deal after another, a professional career had direction, a sense of purpose and progress, that connected an individual life to the common good. In a time when people worried about the moral compromises of business and politics, a professional career reconciled desires for economic security, status in the community, autonomous self-expression, moral purpose, and a lifetime of progress. It offered a holistic, this-worldly salvation that seemed both a pathway to and a foretaste of a more eternal reward.

If ministry was more persuasive in its promise of moral purpose than in its promise of economic security, it was still attractive as something like a profession. Steady numbers sought ordination as growing churches sustained a dynamic equilibrium with the number of clergy. As late as 1966, almost ten of every one thousand first-year college students identified ordained ministry as a probable career.[38] Professionalized ministry lit up in a constellation that included benevolent associations, denominations, congregations, and other voluntary societies. As part of this powerful constellation, professionalization kept its promise for many ministers. They enjoyed careers marked by public trust, meaningful service, and relative economic security. And they gained access to these careers through education in theological schools that defined themselves as professional schools.

THEOLOGICAL EDUCATION AS PROFESSIONAL EDUCATION

A new kind of school arose in the first decades of the nineteenth century in the emerging constellation of voluntary societies. Andover Theological Seminary was founded in 1807 out of the disappointment that both Old Calvinist and New Divinity Congregationalists felt at the appointment of Unitarian Henry Ware to the Hollis Chair of Divinity at Harvard. They knew they could no longer trust Harvard with the education of their ministers. But they did not found a rival college. Instead, they founded a specialized school dedicated entirely to training people for ministry: a seminary. The differentiated school mirrored the differentiation of spheres that was happening with disestablishment. Just as the unity of the old standing orders gave way to separate spheres for religion, politics, and economics, the older pattern of theological education as general education in a college gave way to theological education as specialized instruction in a distinct kind of institution.

The new model fit perfectly with the constellation of voluntary societies. The seminaries were voluntary societies at their founding. In their form they were like the American Bible Society, the American Antislavery Society, and other benevolent societies, but with a distinct mission to form people for ministry. As voluntary societies, they were sustained more by denominations and donors than by tuition payments of individual students. Moreover, as Lyman Beecher of Lane Theological Seminary argued in 1834, seminaries were the hubs that trained leaders for other voluntary societies. They drew students from and contributed leaders to benevolent societies. They trained people to lead the new form of congregations. They enjoyed especially close symbiosis with denominations. As Philip Schaff observed in 1854, "Formerly it was customary for students to prepare for the ministry under some experienced clergyman, and some do so still; but since the beginning of the present century it has been found desirable to erect special institutions for this purpose, mostly in connection with a college. Now, almost every respectable denomination and sect has one such seminary or more of its own; and the tendency to multiply them is, in truth, only too strong."[39]

Denominations founded seminaries, and seminaries helped create the denominational form. They helped provide the substance of denominational connection. Indeed, seminaries were often the most significant collaborative efforts of early denominations. Beyond inviting this collaboration, they nurtured and transmitted the distinctive cultures of their denominations. They formed denominational identities through teaching distinctive approaches to doctrine and liturgy, of course, but also through forming the kinship networks and all the patterns of speech, dress, manners, and bodily movements that marked different denominational cultures.

Forming people for leadership in the emerging network of denominations, congregations, and benevolent societies meant providing them with an education that let them strengthen these voluntary societies and enhance their impact on the world. It meant giving students not just the cultural accessories that marked them as members of the standing order but also the tools to make a difference. Seminaries associated with revival movements were especially blunt in emphasizing this instrumental value of theological learning. Charles Grandison Finney, the revival preacher the Lane Rebels asked to be brought to Oberlin as professor of theology in 1835, argued that "Our theological schools would be of much greater value than they are if there was much more about them that was practical."[40] Finney worried that schools of theology would produce graduates who preached sermons that sounded like learned discourses—sermons suitable for a standing order that no longer existed. Proper practical training would let ministers preach in ways that won conversions, built congregations, and transformed society.

Finney gave voice to a vision he shared with many. In this vision, theological education had an instrumental value. It was not a good in itself. It existed to form leaders of congregations, denominations, and other voluntary associations. In this vision—this ecclesiology, this eschatology—those associations were not ends in themselves, either. They existed to transform individual lives and society as a whole. Theological education was a means to the means to those great ends.

Finney's call for theological education to emphasize useful training for effective ministry found many echoes in the decades that followed. Few of those echoing voices were stronger than William Rainey Harper, the energetic Baptist that John D. Rockefeller entrusted with the founding of the University of Chicago. Though he himself was a formidable scholar of ancient Near Eastern languages and cultures, Harper's functionalist understanding of theological education as professional education had no room for biblical languages that ministers rarely used in practice. Besides, Harper argued in 1899, students were not very good with the languages: "No greater farce may be found in any field of educational work than that which is involved in the teaching and study of the Hebrew language in many theological seminaries. It may be suggested that to make Hebrew an elective is to lower the standard of theological education. Those who know the facts connected with the study of Hebrew by theological students will not make this claim."[41] What mattered, Harper said, was what students would use in their ministries. If they weren't using Hebrew in leading organizations and changing the world, it could be made an elective, or even dropped entirely.

Moreover, Harper argued, theological education needed to prepare people for more than just congregational leadership. "The day has come for a broadening of the meaning of the word minister," he wrote, "and for the cultivation of specialism in the ministry, as well as in medicine, in law, and in teaching." Theological education needed to follow other professions in training people for multiple specialties, including medical missions, denominational leadership, and college and university presidencies. In Harper's vision, theological education could be the means to many different ministries with many different impacts. But its value was always instrumental.[42]

William Adams Brown, a Presbyterian minister and professor of systematic theology at Union Theological Seminary in New York, articulated the case for this instrumental understanding of theological education with particular clarity in an influential 1919 article:

> More even than it has been in the past the seminary of the future must be a training school for ministers, men, that is to say, who have given themselves to a definite task. All that we do must be

shaped to this end. No study must be admitted to the curriculum, no matter how attractive it may be, that cannot be shown to have some direct bearing on the minister's task. And conversely, no study must be omitted from the curriculum, however great the tax it may make on time and energy, which can be shown to be necessary for ministerial efficiency.[43]

What's the purpose of theological education? Brown knew: it was to train people who would serve as ministers, in the broadest sense of that word. Everything that served the end of "ministerial efficiency" should be included in their training. Everything that did not should be stripped away.

This rising vision of differentiated seminaries offering specialized instruction to help ministers lead organizations solidified in the institutional form of the professional school. Seminaries played a significant role in creating that form, but it emerged as part of wider reforms in higher education in America. In the early decades of the nineteenth century, it was far from obvious that professionals would be trained in schools. The apprentice model remained influential in forming people for practice in medicine, law, ministry, and other fields. An apprentice worked alongside an established practitioner and, crucially, had access to the practitioner's library.[44] Meanwhile, college enrollments stagnated as the general education colleges offered—a form suited to standing orders—ceased to resonate with the world that was emerging. The kind of education offered by seminaries pointed toward a more specialized and functionalist vision of higher education that stressed the preparation of students for careers. After the Civil War, more and more colleges broke up the singular curriculum of general education into majors and electives—and more of these courses were framed as functional preparation for something like a profession. New research universities like Johns Hopkins, Clark, and the University of Chicago made specialization the norm. The Morrill Acts of 1862 and 1890 directed proceeds from the sale of public lands to colleges that joined specialization to instrumental preparation for careers.

The practical norm found voice even at Harvard. In 1891 William James argued that the university should be oriented to "the fighting side of life . . . the world in which men and women earn their bread and butter and live and die."[45]

As colleges and universities oriented themselves more completely toward preparing students for careers, professional schools of every kind expanded. Theological seminaries led the way, with more than eighteen schools on the Andover model founded before 1825. Schools of law, medicine, and dentistry gained ground in later decades. Other fields sought to consolidate their professional status with schools of their own, and specialized professional schools emerged in pharmacology (1868), architecture (1868), teaching (1879), veterinary medicine (1879), accounting (1881), and even business (1881) in the second half of the nineteenth century. The expansion of the number of schools was paralleled by an expansion of the time people spent in schools. In 1875, only one law school required three years of study. By 1899 a majority of them did. No medical school required four years of study in 1875, but nearly all of them did by 1899.[46] Academic credentials came to be essential for licensure as a professional. As James Fallows notes, "Before the First World War not a single state required that its lawyers have attended law school, and fewer than a third of all North American medical schools required even a high school diploma for admission. By the Second World War professionals without advanced degrees were becoming an oddity."[47] Specialized education became a key marker of professional standing—including for ministers—and schools expanded to provide training and credentials.

Education as a marker of professional standing fit and helped form the larger professional ideal. As broader publics warmed to the professional ideal's insistence that the work of professionals could only be judged by other professionals, they came to assess professionals more by "inputs" than by "outputs"—more by their credentials than by their results.[48] Formal, specialized education emerged as an essential part of any respectable set of professional credentials. As Bledstein observed, "The public came to accept the middle-class article of faith that the regularly trained professional, however dubious his reputation and shoddy his record, however crude his technique and rude his behavior, however rigid his attitudes and inadequate his knowledge, was superior to the merely experienced operator. The difference was the role played by the school."[49] Schools evolved to credential professionals, and professional standards came to center on formal, specialized education.

The rise of the professional school as an institutional model reflected and galvanized theological education's movement toward specialized instruction that prepared people for effective service in more-or-less religious voluntary associations seeking to improve society. The model of the professional school exerted its strongest influence in theological schools affiliated with new or newly rebooted research universities inspired by the German model, like the University of Chicago (founded 1890), Emory (rechartered and relocated in 1915), and Duke (renamed and decisively endowed in 1924). The theological schools affiliated with such universities were explicitly defined as professional schools and were designed to be like schools of law and medicine. The norm of the professional school also tugged on theological schools affiliated with older universities, like Howard, Harvard, and Yale. Internal reforms at these universities increasingly identified the divinity schools as professional schools. The cultural capital of the university-based schools, especially when mediated and amplified by their role in training faculty for other schools, let the professional school model exert influence even on freestanding seminaries. Different schools responded in different ways, as always. But the whole field of theological education was pulled toward the professional school as a norm.

The model of the professional school stamped what was taught and learned in ways that further stressed the instrumental value of theological education in preparing effective ministers for leadership in churches that shared an understanding of themselves as denominations. While the University of Berlin (established in 1809) was an important model for American research universities, Friedrich Schleiermacher's case for the inclusion of theology in that university does not seem to have exerted much direct influence on American theological schools. But it does offer a kind of X-ray of the logic at work as theological education moved into professional schools that took their place in a wider sphere of higher education defined by the research university—whether the theological schools were formally affiliated with research universities or not.[50]

Following Immanuel Kant, Schleiermacher argued that theology could have a place in a research university, but that it should not be grouped with the "lower" faculties that did basic research. Theology did not (and should not) take the *wissenschaftlich* form of such knowledge. Instead, Schleiermacher argued, theology should be grouped with the "higher" faculties of law and medicine. It had a place in the modern research university as *applied* knowledge. A school of theology might therefore be framed as a set of *wissenschaftlich* disciplines—like history and philology—that found distinct unity and purpose in the formation of "princes of the church." Schleiermacher was cautious and ambivalent about what historian Thomas Howard has called the "Erastian modernity" that defined relations between church and state in Prussia at the time.[51] But Schleiermacher relied on that vision to make his case for theology in the university. He argued that the significance of the church as a social entity gave the state an interest in the formation of church leaders. And because the university served the interests of the state, at least to some significant degree, the formation of ministers was a legitimate function of the modern research university. Thus the study of theology could be included so long as it was oriented toward the formation of clergy who led churches in ways that promoted the health and vitality of the state.[52]

Formal disestablishment of the church in the United States meant that the German model could not transfer without significant translation. Theological schools as professional schools did not form clergy for direct service to the state. But they did form clergy for leadership in churches that understood themselves as denominations in the wider civil society that sought to reform and redeem the state. Again, William Adams Brown of Union explained the core logic with particular clarity. Theological education was for the sake of "ministerial efficiency," he argued. But ministry was not an end in itself. Ministry worked toward the formation of the church as an association of free individuals, a voluntary society that united people across lines of difference. And even this church was a means to other ends:

> To build a unified church on the basis of autocracy is not hard. It has been done again and again. To build a unified church on the basis of freedom requires a degree of intelligence and discipline to which as yet few of our churches have attained. It is the same problem which faces us in religion as in democracy itself. How can we who accept the principle of free determination as the supreme law of the State succeed in uniting men of different races and ideals in a single community of free peoples? Somehow it must be done unless all our struggle and sacrifice is to be in vain. But we shall not succeed in doing it in the State unless we succeed in doing it in the church, and to show how this can be done will be the supreme office of the seminary of tomorrow.[53]

The "supreme office" of the seminary Brown envisioned was the coming together of free people across lines of difference to form a unified state. Theological education formed ministers who led voluntary societies that anticipated that ultimate goal.

Brown was especially clear in stressing the significance of the state as a *telos* for theological education as professional education. But he should not be read as idiosyncratic. He was simply making plain the place of theological education within the prevailing social imaginary. That imaginary featured congregations and other voluntary associations that united free individuals for the sake of shared mission. Theological education, ministry, and even the church itself were instrumental for that mission. And the mission was framed within a denominational ethos that valued a pluralistic civil society within a shared polity defined by a nation-state. Theological education, in this model, served a public good—just as Schleiermacher promised it would in Germany. And that public significance helped justify the place of theology in the modern research university in the United States. Of course, the cultural establishment of Protestantism, some sizable endowments that were difficult to redirect, and the sheer inertia of institutions all have played significant roles in establishing theological education within modern research universities and within the sphere of higher education more broadly. But when an official rationale has been required, it has tended to follow the path sketched by Schleiermacher and Brown. Theology has been included because it contributes to the formation of leaders of socially significant institutions. This arrangement allowed for the bracketing of the question of the truth of theological claims. To the extent that theology schools taught something true—like history or philology—the teaching fit within the norms of *Wissenschaft*. But such teaching could happen in the other faculties of a university. The justification for the something more promised by a theological school was not its contribution to the pursuit of truth, but its social impact.

The institutional form of the professional school embodied this logic, even when people within the schools espoused other views. The form of the professional school gained further articulation—and discipling power—with the formation of the Conference of Theological Schools in 1918. Chaired by A. Lawrence Lowell, the president of Harvard University who made majoring in a discipline the norm for undergraduate education, the conference gathered leaders from fifty-three Protestant seminaries for conversations on the state of ministerial education. In the wake of a 1924 report by Robert Kelly, executive secretary of the Council of Church Boards of Education, the conference commissioned a team led by Mark A. May of Yale and William Adams Brown of Union to work with the Institute of Social and Religious Research to produce a more comprehensive study of theological education in America.[54]

The studies arose in the wake of Abraham Flexner's 1910 report on medical education. The Flexner Report had touched off a process that imposed new requirements for the education of physicians that swept away a number of smaller schools and practically required connection to a university. The Flexner Report established the professional school as the definitive institutional context for medical education.[55]

May and Brown's report contributed to a related process. After receiving the report, the Conference of Theological Schools transformed itself into an accrediting organization, the American Association of Theological Schools (AATS). In 1938 the AATS published its first list of thirty-seven accredited theological schools, all affiliated with traditions that shared a strong denominational ethos. AATS went on to merge with the American Association of Schools of Religious Education to form the Association of Theological Schools (ATS).[56]

AATS and then ATS standards helped establish the professional school as the norm for theological education. From the start they pressed schools to move away from courses of study that did not require an undergraduate degree and to locate theological education at the postbaccalaureate level. The standards defined an instrumental vision for this postbaccalaureate education. They aimed to harness different academic disciplines toward the goal of preparing leaders for religious organizations that made an impact. And in bringing together different Christian traditions, the accrediting agencies embodied the denominational ethos in a powerful way. The standards reflected that ethos, leaving matters of doctrine and liturgy to the discretion of individual traditions even as they insisted on the form of a professional school.

Attendees at the first Conference of Theological Schools were overwhelmingly white, male, and "modernist" Protestant in their sympathies. They set idealized versions of themselves and their schools as the norms for recognition as a professional school. More or less intentionally, they turned whiteness into code. The professional model was not the first model for theological education to bind itself to whiteness as a norm. The institutions of the standing order did, too. The professional model broke with these institutions in many ways, but the white supremacy that ran through them shifted shape to take root in the professional model, too. As Willie James Jennings has argued, "The church and the academy, theological or otherwise, have been bound to the same whiteness since the advent of colonialism and both have been made to aim at a work of building an institutionalizing life that lay in the racial world like sun-baked mud that carries ancient power to grow bitter roots and poison herbs."[57]

Theological education was not alone in binding itself to whiteness. The larger project of professionalization did, too. In the wake of the Flexner Report, for instance, five of seven Black medical schools were closed. Only Howard in Washington, DC, and Meharry in Nashville remained. The number of Black physicians declined with the closing of the schools, and it did not recover over the course of the twentieth century. In 1910, before the Flexner Report, 2.5 percent of US physicians were Black. Almost a century later, in 2008, the number of Black physicians was still at only 2.2 percent of the total. Wayne A. I. Frederick, president of Howard University and himself a physician, has criticized this amalgamation of whiteness and professional education. "The Flexner Report was a catalyst," he said. "It started us down a road that is hard to undo."[58] The effects were not as dramatic in theological education. The persistence of Black denominations under Jim Crow, coupled with the tight link between denominations and seminaries, allowed more Black theological schools to endure. But Black schools and students still faced the fundamental dynamic linking professionalization to norms of whiteness.

Other traditions also faced norms for professional education that were in some way alien to them. The cultural and financial capital that came with accreditation provided important incentives for schools to join—even if reasons internal to their traditions led them to resist the dominant vision of theological education as professional education. Evangelical schools, for instance, had many reasons to be wary of the model, not least the ways the denominational ethos allowed for pluralism in doctrine. But as the Second World War wound down, schools like

Calvin Theological Seminary (joining in 1944), Asbury Theological Seminary (1946), and Fuller Theological Seminary (1957) all joined. Catholic schools drew on traditions that differed from the professional model in ecclesiology, theology of ministry, and other core ideas. But after the Second Vatican Council, a number of schools moved to join ATS and to adopt the norms of professional education for clergy. The Aquinas Institute of Theology, Maryknoll School of Theology, St. Meinrad School of Theology, and Weston Jesuit School of Theology, for instance, all joined in 1968. Just one decade later, fully one-fourth of all ATS member schools were Catholic. The circles continued to expand. Neither Jewish rabbis nor Orthodox Christian priests fit easily with professional understandings of ministry, but the 1970s saw schools in these traditions accredited as professional schools. Schools founded to educate women and men as missionaries and educators, like Scarritt College for Christian Workers, gradually turned into professional schools that were more and more like other ATS institutions. Charismatic and Pentecostal traditions had long-standing suspicions of the role of formal higher education in the formation of church leaders, but by the 1990s these traditions were turning their older institutions into professional schools and founding new ones. The Assemblies of God Theological Seminary, for instance, won initial accreditation in 1992. More recent years have seen new growth among schools serving diasporic communities, like Logos Evangelical Seminary, a Mandarin-language school that earned accreditation in 1999. All these traditions have revised and reshaped the professional model. But its core logic of education as an instrumental good for the formation of leaders of religious institutions that share a denominational ethos has only deepened.[59]

It is too simple to characterize this process simply as a story of ever-expanding inclusion. Likewise, it cannot be reduced to a story of coerced conformity. It is rather a deeply ambivalent story of consolidation.

Theological education in the United States has consolidated around a professional model that promises to prepare people to lead more-or-less religious organizations that take their place in a pluralistic civil society that seeks to transform the nation. The formation and knowledge offered by this professional theological education are specialized, instrumental, and designed to work through voluntary societies. Through the education process this specialized knowledge and formation become the properties of individual professionals; they are credentials they can carry with them into many different roles. This professional model has shown great elasticity. It has expanded to hold many different visions of what kind of knowledge and formation mattered most, from liturgical leadership to biblical languages to community organizing. Likewise, it has been able to accommodate very different visions of what it means to make the world a better place, from resisting racism to catechizing believers to working for ecological justice to winning the world for Christ. But across these differences, the core structures and logic of theological education as professional education have endured.

Consolidation around this model has never been total. Some significant modes of theological education in America have remained at a distance from the dominant constellation, including the forms undertaken in Hispanic Bible institutes, vowed religious communities, religious colleges that have maintained a place for theological studies apart from preparation for ministry, and movement schools like Highlander Folk School and the Freedom Schools founded by the Student Nonviolent Coordinating Committee (SNCC). Some of these alternatives question specialization, seeing theological education as a more general good. Others question the framing of theological education as an instrumental good, seeing it rather as a good in itself. Still others see theological education bearing fruit apart from voluntary associations, perhaps in more individual ways or in ways that depend on other kinds of community. By a combination of choice and exclusion, real alternatives persist.

If the consolidation has not been total, it has been powerful. And it has been more powerful because of its fit with the interlocking network of benevolent associations, congregations, denominations, and ministry as a profession. Together these institutions shared a social imaginary in which free people connected with one another in voluntary associations to knit together a nation and change the world. That role gave the associations themselves a kind of sacred charge. Working to sustain them—even just being a member—could give meaning to a life. When the association was charged with this kind of meaning, even work on a committee could double as Christian discipleship.

Until it couldn't.

2

Individualization

I have met only a very few people—and most of these
were not Americans—who had any real desire to be
free. Freedom is hard to bear. It can be objected that
I am speaking of political freedom in spiritual terms,
but the political institutions of any nation are always
menaced and are ultimately controlled by the spiritual
state of that nation.

James Baldwin, *The Fire Next Time* (1962)

By now, in this third decade of the twenty-first century, the reports feel routine, like dispatches from a terrible war of attrition.
Every successive study seems to document greater declines in
religious affiliation. In 2018 "nones" passed Catholics and evan-
gelicals to become the most common identity in relation to religion. In 2020 the number of Americans affiliated with a church,
synagogue, or mosque fell below 50 percent for the first time in
eighty years of Gallup polling. These trends have been intensi-
fying in recent years, and the COVID-19 pandemic has probably
accelerated them. They cut across lines of race, ethnicity, region,
theological tradition, and political party.[1]

For growing numbers of people, joining a church doesn't make
sense in the way it did as the constellation of voluntary associations came together. It doesn't feel required in the same way for a

meaningful life. It might even seem like an obligation that gets in the way of a meaningful life. Simply denouncing these trends has had almost no effect on them. Nor has better marketing been able to reverse them. Not even intentional investments in the formation of young people have been able to bend the curve. The shifts run too deep for such remedies to reach. Whether we celebrate them, revile them, or simply try to stay afloat amidst them, they increasingly flood our shared social world. Navigating some faithful way forward will include making renunciations and taking hold of affordances. But these moves need to begin from a clearer understanding of what is happening.

SURFACE TENSIONS

While the direction of the numbers is clear and relentless, the causes of these trends are less clear and more contested. For decades conservative and evangelical leaders talked as if some particular failings of mainline Protestantism were causing problems specific to that tradition. In these stories, declining numbers might be attributed to the sociological consequences of a church accommodating itself to a dominant culture or to the more direct wrath of God on apostate bodies.[2] "The collapse of the Protestant mainline has been swift, steady, and self-inflicted," R. Albert Mohler, president of Southern Baptist Theological Seminary, said in 2008. But Mohler's own denomination has not been exempt from these broader trends. Since Mohler's comment, his Southern Baptist Convention has seen fourteen straight years of declining membership. The number of baptisms in the Convention is dropping at an even more rapid rate. Similar dynamics play out in theological schools. Mainline stalwarts like Episcopal Divinity School and Andover Newton Theological School embedded themselves in larger schools to continue their missions. But evangelical schools have had to make radical adjustments, too. Liberty University, for instance, recently made headlines for making significant cuts in the size of its faculty to offset decreasing enrollment. Parallel declines in enrollment have led historic Gordon-Conwell Theological Seminary to sell its campus. Different dynamics are at work in different theological traditions. But broad trends of declining belief and affiliation are affecting every kind of school.[3]

If declining numbers don't track readily with theology and politics, they do track with generations. As sociologists David Voas and Mark Chaves have argued, the twentieth century saw significant gaps open between generations on questions of belief and religious affiliation. "Among people born after 1975, declared affiliation in 2014 was a full 23 percentage points lower than among those born before 1935 (71% vs. 94%)." Differences in generational cohorts were relatively small before World War II but started to expand in the second half of the century. Some surges in affiliation cut across generational lines, like in the late 1970s and early 1980s, as some of the same tides that lifted Ronald Reagan's vision of America as a city on a hill lifted evangelical affiliation across generational cohorts. And some periods—like the 1990s—saw downturns across cohorts. But these period effects come and go without changing the long-term direction of change. So, too, immigration matters in complex ways but does not change the overall trajectory across denominations.

The most powerful dynamic is one that every pastor already knows: for almost seventy years now, each generation has been less likely to affiliate with religious institutions than the generations that preceded it. Churches did not feel the full impact of this generational shift for many years, as most members of the more affiliated generations were still alive and many could give even more time and money to sustain the voluntary associations they cared about. But now that these generations are passing, the differences in affiliation across generational cohorts cannot be ignored.[4]

Seeing the shifts in generational cohorts helps us to make sense of the wider phenomena. But it also invites further questions. *Why* do members of younger generations display less affiliation and belief than older ones? If cohort replacement is driving the data, what's driving the changes in cohorts?

Any adequate explanation of declining affiliation will acknowledge the swirling plurality of factors at work. Shifting notions of respectability begin to tell the story. For large numbers of people in older generations, being a respectable person meant being affiliated with a religious body. But the social sanction for nonaffiliation has been decreasing. Strong majorities of younger generations now believe a person does not have to believe in God—let alone belong to some religious congregation—to be a good person. The easing of this sanction has reduced what sociologists call "social desirability bias," which had led people to overreport religious beliefs and practices when talking to pollsters (and their neighbors). There are weaker reasons now to claim affiliation with a church you haven't attended in years. But it's not just self-reporting that has changed. As it becomes more socially acceptable not to be affiliated with a religion, more people are finding themselves in that space. And as more people are not affiliated, nonaffiliation becomes more normal. Social sanctions decrease further. Thus nonaffiliation provides fuel for its own continued expansion.[5]

Nonaffiliation has also expanded as churches across the spectrum—left, right, and center—have overlapped more completely with polarizing political movements. The overlap has grown as what we usually think of as "religion" and "politics" have each grown toward the other. As politics has become dominated by questions of culture, values, and identity—and as political discourse has turned everything into questions of culture, values, and identity—politics has moved toward what we think of as church life. A church might not have an opinion on quantitative easing, for instance, but when political struggles focus on how to receive people who arrive at the nation's southern border, more churches across the spectrum feel as if they have something to say. And there is no question which kind of issue can do more to mobilize voters. The movement of politics toward religion is not just a matter of ideas; it's also happening at the level of institutions, as political leaders and movements reach toward bases that are increasingly defined, at least in part, by attitudes toward religion.

Just as politics has grown toward religion, religion has reached toward politics. Churches have done more to stress ethics and politics in part because they can invest church life with meaning within what Charles Taylor calls an "immanent frame" of this-worldly concerns. The book of Deuteronomy might feel boring, irrelevant, and practically unpreachable, for instance, even among people who claim to believe that every word of the Bible is inspired . . . until it seems to be talking about same-sex love. Doctrines, texts, liturgies all come alive for contemporary congregations when they can be connected to politics. The full significance of politics for religious life is revealed not just by the fact that congregations and denominations are taking stands on a range of issues. It's revealed in the centrality of those political and ethical stands for church identities. The surest signs of the significance of culture-war political issues for church identities today are the waves of division that have rolled through denominations in the last fifty years. Churches split about what they care about most; the lines of fracture point to the core of identity as it is lived (however it is described in denominational history and polity classes). Churches in past centuries might have split over doctrinal questions, as the early centuries were riven by bitter disputes over Christology. But it is difficult to imagine doctrinal disputes dividing the church today, either at the national or the local level. As one beleaguered pastor told me, "I'm fairly certain that I could deliver a string of heresies from the pulpit on any given Sunday and hear nothing about it from worshipers. But a statement deemed 'political' leads to ten phone calls and a string of coffee listening sessions." Culture-war questions often get dressed up in doctrinal drag—saying that disputes about sexuality are really about the authority of Scripture, for instance—but the absence of doctrinal disputes in other contexts, the move by all sides to prioritize political goals over consistent patterns of interpreting canonical texts, and the mobilization of every available resource for arguments about sexuality suggest that differences in doctrine alone aren't the forces driving division.

The significance of culture-war politics for identity comes into sharper focus in comparison with tensions around liturgy over the last fifty years. Many church bodies have found ways to accommodate those differences, even though they would seem to go to the heart of a church's life as a worshiping community. Some congregations have "contemporary" and "traditional" services that let different modes of worship flourish within the same voluntary association. It is difficult to imagine many taking a similar approach to contentious political questions, with the 9:00 service denouncing critical race theory and the 11:00 service calling people to join a demonstration organized by the Movement for Black Lives. Such differences have proven difficult to sustain even within denominations. Difference around such culture-war questions can't be sustained because these questions have become even more central than the mode of worship to the identities of religious bodies.

This increasing overlap of religious and political concerns has had complex effects on affiliation, even within particular Christian movements. There is some evidence that people with conservative political views who did not identify as evangelical in the past are doing so now. In many ways, "evangelical" has become an important part of a cluster of markers of conservative identity that also includes things like support for gun rights, concern about immigration and assimilation, and opposition to strong public health measures to counter COVID-19. In some cases, then, the close alignment of church life with culture-war politics seems to lead people to report higher levels of affiliation. Within some conservative political circles, a social sanction for claiming affiliation is still in effect. But while a broader conservative identity might lead people to identify as evangelical, it is not leading to deeper patterns of piety and participation. Evangelical identity was once accompanied by high levels of regular church attendance. But now a rising number of people who identify as evangelical—currently over 40 percent—attend worship services once per year or less. As sociologist and Baptist pastor Ryan Burge argues, "The fusion of evangelicalism and Republicanism has buoyed the religious tradition, while also making it less religious at the same time."[6]

Even as the close alignment of evangelicalism with conservative politics has led some people to religious affiliation, it has led others to leave the movement for other churches or even to end affiliation altogether. It has left a group of evangelical, charismatic, and Pentecostal believers without a comfortable institutional home, adding to the number of people who believe in God but are not strongly identified with a congregation. And it has led some liberals to write off all Christianity—even all of religion—as problematic, providing reasons for renouncing affiliations that might not have been strong but still would have been claimed in the past.[7]

If some liberals feel alienated from churches that seem too political, others are drawn toward forms of activism that seem more fully political. A 2018 poll by the Public Religion Research Institute found higher levels of civic engagement among people who identified as Democrats and claimed no religious affiliation. These unaffiliated Democrats were more likely to have gone to a march or a rally, expressed political opinions online, donated to a cause or candidate, and changed their consumption habits by selecting goods and service providers in line with their values. Political scientist Eitan Hersh notes the expressive qualities of these actions. They are the kinds of things that mark a person's identity in a way that religious affiliation might have in the past. "This online world of political identity," he argues, "is basically acting as a replacement for people who maybe a generation or two before would identify as Catholic or as Jewish or as Irish or Italian."[8] The transition from religious affiliation to a secular political identity is especially smooth when congregations have already downplayed distinctive doctrine and ritual, making them instrumental to ethical and political commitments that are the real sources of identity. Some who are slipping away from mainline congregations are simply engaging in what feels like a purer form of the pursuit of the justice the congregations have been telling them is the real meaning of the faith all along.

Any account of declining affiliation also must consider the profit-driven encroachments on the time people have to sustain voluntary associations. These encroachments come from every direction, including the "greedy professions" that claim bigger chunks of the lives of white-collar workers and the irregular hours and multiple jobs that devour the evenings—and Sunday mornings—of working-class people. As Mennonite pastor-theologian Melissa Florer-Bixler observes, "For churches whose greatest need is time, an economic model that prizes those who work the longest creates an impossible competition."[9] Further encroachments come from a youth sports–industrial complex and a broader meritocratic Hunger Games for young people that knows no Sabbath. Still more encroachments come from digital technologies designed to capture as much of our attention as they can. Sustaining voluntary associations takes time. When whole economies are built on the ability to colonize the hours in our days, we should not be surprised to see markers of affiliation decline.

Accounts of declining affiliation must also reckon with the church's complicity in sexual abuse of children and adults. To cite only one example: a 2018 investigation by the attorney general of Pennsylvania found that over one thousand children had been victims of sexual abuse by Catholic priests in the state. The abuses involved more than three hundred priests acting over seventy years in six different Pennsylvania dioceses. The church hierarchy actively worked to cover up these patterns of abuse. The grand jury's report concluded that "Priests were raping little boys and girls, and the men of God who were responsible for them did nothing; they hid it all." It is difficult to trace direct lines of causation from sexual abuse to disaffiliation. But the effects are surely there. A 2019 poll found that 13 percent of Americans identify as "former Catholics," and many cite the persistence and cover-up of sexual abuse as a reason. Such abuse is not limited to Catholic churches. An investigation by the *Houston Chronicle* and the *San Antonio Express-News* found similar patterns of abuse and cover-up among Southern Baptist churches that involved hundreds of pastors and church officers. Those lines of abuse also run through mainline, Orthodox, and Pentecostal traditions— and through traditions beyond Christianity. A church that has yet to address its participation in these crimes cannot blame only external forces for declining membership.[10]

A list of the forces roiling the waters of religious affiliation could go on and on. All of these forces matter. But factors like abusive clergy, churches more concerned with their image than with the well-being of vulnerable people, cascading demands on our days, and complicated entanglements with politics are not new. And they have not always led to declining membership. But in our time it seems as if all kinds of events and trends end in disaffiliation. They might seem to move in different directions—like the desire for less politics or more politics—but they end up flowing into the same current that is moving away from affiliation with a religious voluntary society. The breadth and duration of this flow, even with a complex and contradictory froth of forces on the surface, suggest the presence of deeper historical currents.

INSTEAD OF SECULARIZATION

Attempts to trace the deeper historical currents at work often take the form of stories of "secularization" in which the rise of modernity brings a decline in religious belief and practice. These stories have been advanced from all sides—from religious critics of modernity, from modern critics of religion, and from wry observers who promise a kind of learned indifference.

Secularization stories have a certain parochial persuasiveness in describing a few centuries of Europe's history. But they can't make sense of wider sets of data. They might seem to work, even beyond Europe, when declines in religious belief and practice are taken as the very definition of "modernity." But then they are mere tautologies, with their conclusion built into the ways they define key terms. They falter when they try to give modernity more substantive content and reach across multiple contexts. Economic development, for instance, is often taken as a synecdoche for wider processes of modernization that track with it, like urbanization, industrialization, and the rise of scientific worldviews. But in countries like Kenya, Nigeria, Brazil, South Korea, and the United States, growth in gross domestic product per capita has seen not decline but *growth* in the number of people who define religion as very important in their lives. Similarly, secularization stories fail on both individual and global levels when linked to education. In many countries, higher rates of formal education have tracked with higher rates of religious affiliation. A secularization story defined by education might seem to hold true in the United States, though, as rates of higher education have climbed in recent decades as rates of religious affiliation have fallen. But this aggregated picture obscures the actual relationships between the variables. As Ryan Burge has demonstrated, while there is some link between higher education and declining religious affiliation in the early part of the twentieth century, since 1950 there is no evidence of correlation between the two. On the contrary, growth in the number of religiously unaffiliated people has been driven by disproportionate growth among those with the *least* amount of formal education. Thus, neither economic nor educational measures of modernity support secularization stories. It's not clear what definition of modernity *would* let these stories describe the world as it actually exists.[11]

Moreover, secularization stories that take affiliation to stand in for all of religion obscure the complex lived realities of practice and belief. Over 60 percent of those who identified as "nones" in 2014 said they also believed in God. And over a third of them said they prayed at least weekly.[12] A focus on affiliation alone will be insufficiently curious about these dynamics. It will miss the vitality of a whole host of religious-ish practices that take place within and beyond affiliation. Apps promoting mindfulness attract millions of dedicated users. Figures like Brené Brown,

Glennon Doyle, and Oprah Winfrey reach mass audiences with messages of connection and transformation that are not simply secular. Programs like CrossFit, SoulCycle, and countless yoga studios thrive by offering not just fitness but also community, discipline, and a sense of meaning and direction in life. Sales and readings of tarot cards are soaring. The uprisings in response to the murders of Breonna Taylor, Ahmaud Arbery, and George Floyd have developed powerful liturgies, even as many organizers and participants feel that it is important to keep their distance from organized religion. We may diagnose and evaluate these developments in different ways. But, whatever they are, they aren't signs of an enlightened modernity displacing all things spiritual, supernatural, or religious.[13]

An exclusive focus on affiliation misses not just religiosity beyond traditional religions but also the mobility and vitality of religious practices within those traditions. As sociologist Nancy Ammerman argues, blinkered attention to particular institutions can miss the dynamic quality of the larger field of religion.[14] As some institutions decline, new ones emerge. Some of these might look like new congregations, like those of the Redeemed Christian Church of God, founded in Lagos, Nigeria, and now planting congregations across the United States. But other new religious practices do not show up in surveys of congregations or membership. In the hundred-day St. Enda Retreat, for instance, Benedictine nun Margaret Funk and Catholic lay theologian Kathleen Cahalan send voice memos to hundreds of listeners that guide them in religious practices that draw on traditions that run back through John Cassian to the Egyptian desert. The practice is intense, sustained, and formational. It is not just "spiritual"; it's also "religious," even aligned with organized religion. Despite this alignment, measures of congregational affiliation would overlook it.

Looking beyond affiliation is especially important for seeing the religious lives of people not shaped primarily by the patterns of affiliation that consolidated to define normative religious life in the United States. Russell M. Jeung, Seanan S. Fong, and Helen

Jin Kim describe a Chinese American sense of ritual propriety in family relations—*liyi*—that provides a horizon of meaning, ethical norms for the conduct of life, and identities that place people in relationship to one another and to a wider social whole. Practices of *liyi* don't require a congregation or other voluntary association. They can be quite strong even among Chinese American populations in which many identify as religiously unaffiliated. People committed to *liyi* might therefore show up as "nones" in surveys. But a flat description of them as secular would miss important dimensions of their lives. The best description of this dynamic is not secularization but a waning of the powers of institutional isomorphism that pressed past generations of meaning-making into congregations, denominations, and other institutions in the network of voluntary associations.[15]

An exclusive focus on affiliation can also miss the growing significance of chaplaincy. One index of this rise, sociologist Wendy Cadge argues, is the rising number of references to religion, spirituality, and prayer in medical journals. Cadge also points to surveys in which majorities of both patients and health-care professionals report the significance of religious and spiritual beliefs and practices for their understanding of the work of healing. These energies increasingly find institutional form in chaplaincy. Chaplaincy is "organized religion," but it is not organized in the usual institutional forms. Most ministries of chaplains are not organized by or as voluntary associations. They are part of hospitals, prisons, businesses, military units, schools, or other bodies that have different funding patterns, governance structures, and relations with clients than a congregation. Moreover—and crucially—they are not located in a distinctly religious sphere. These shifts in institutional form seem to make chaplaincy a form of religious practice that fits the times: student interest in chaplaincy is increasing along with demands for the services of chaplains. And all this energy in chaplaincy runs beyond the usual measures of religious affiliation.[16]

A focus on declining religious affiliation misses multiple forms of religious life that don't center on membership in some more-or-less-religious voluntary association. It also misses a more general decline in voluntary associations that runs far beyond the religious sphere. Membership in the Boy Scouts of America is down almost 50 percent in the last fifty years. Rotary, Junior League, Masons, Elks, Shriners, and other fraternal, civic, and social organizations have all suffered significant losses in status and membership. New forms of sociality are emerging—just as Ammerman suggested they would—but they often don't take the form of voluntary associations. The struggle of voluntary associations of every kind coupled with the vitality of religious life beyond voluntary associations suggests that what is declining is not so much religion as the institutional form of the voluntary associations that have been so closely associated with religion in the United States for the last two hundred years.

The case of Sunday Assembly brings this contrast into bold relief. Sunday Assembly was founded as something like a congregation for people who wanted to get together with others, but not in the name of any god. It therefore provides a real-world control case for the variables in question: if people are moving away from religious belief and practice because it is religious, they will turn up at Sunday Assembly. But if what they are *really* moving away from is the institutional form of the voluntary society, then Sunday Assembly won't be any more attractive than, say, the Evangelical Lutheran Church in America. Indeed, after a burst of energy (and publicity) at its founding, Sunday Assembly has staggered along, struggling like any other denomination. We can't generalize too much from such a small case, but it fits a wider pattern of phenomena that suggests that the part of "organized religion" that is most out of sync with the times is not so much religion as the ways in which it is organized.[17]

Instead of stories of secularization, then, we need stories that help us make sense of the changes that are actually transforming our worlds. We are in the midst of an unraveling as significant as the one that unknotted the standing orders and created the conditions in which networks of voluntary associations could be knitted together. The changes are not from more religion to less, but from one dominant way of imagining the relationships of individuals, institutions, the state, and God to ... something else.

I pause with the modesty of an empiricist (or a mystic) before that "something else." I do think we are seeing the rise of a social imaginary centered on authentic individuals. But that emerging imaginary has not yet consolidated as the kind of stable constellation of voluntary societies that exerted such power over the last two hundred years. Whatever comes next will be shaped by lines of force we can trace in the present. It will not come from nowhere. But it will also be shaped by events—like a global pandemic—we can account for in retrospect but cannot anticipate in advance. It will further be shaped by the choices we make, both individually and collectively. And, I trust, it will be shot through with the redeeming love of God. If that love exceeds all that we can ask or imagine, responding faithfully to it still demands that we do what we can to understand its movement in and in spite of the unravelings happening in and around us. A better understanding begins, I think, not with secularization but with individualization.

HOMO OPTIONIS

In trying to make sense of this unraveling of voluntary associations, I depend on a concept of *individualization* that I adapt from German sociologists Ulrich Beck and Elisabeth Beck-Gernsheim. I use it rather than the more common "individualism" to highlight the forces at work in the process of producing individuals. Individualism is often used to describe a belief system that takes the individual as the most basic unit of society and valorizes individual autonomy, self-expression, and well-being above all else. Individualization, on the other hand, suggests something more than a set of beliefs and values we might hold. It is a historically contingent but powerful set of social processes that operate on us, forming us as certain kinds of individuals. Individualization is not just something we believe; it's something that happens to us, whether we believe it or not.

Beck and Beck-Gernsheim describe the present moment as a "second modernity" in which an individual undergoes a "disembedding without re-embedding" into new communities that take primacy over the individual. If prior eras made kinship networks, religions, classes, nations, or voluntary associations primary, they argue, "In the second modernity, the individual becomes, for the first time in history, the basic unit of social reproduction."[18] Broken out of communities that defined the meaning of individual and collective life, individuals in the second modernity have to make our own way. As Beck and Beck-Gernsheim write, "Pre-given biographies get torn up. Each person now has to construct her own biography from a much wider selection of elements. The small set of pre-given life trajectories is replaced by a much wider set of unknown ones. And the pre-given intermeshing of role-sets is replaced by a much more fluid situation wherein nothing is pre-given and everything has to be negotiated."[19] Stripped of ready-made biographies, the individual becomes *homo optionis*, a person defined by having choices—and bearing the costs associated with them—in every part of life. Fewer and fewer dimensions of the world have a self-evident quality: "Life, death, gender, corporeality, identity, religion, marriage, parenthood, social ties—all are becoming decidable down to the small print; once fragmented into options, everything must be decided."[20]

Beck-Gernsheim and Beck are hardly alone in naming this phenomenon. Something like individualization is one of the founding themes of modern sociology and remains a perennial topic in the field. Individualization is not exactly a revelation. Moreover, Beck-Gernsheim and Beck can be too sweeping in their claims, racing past significant differences in the kinds of choices different people face; overlooking the importance of race, class, and gender for shaping those choices; and overstating the difference of "individualization" from all that has come before. But the term has great power to illumine disparate phenomena. We can see processes of individualization at work in every sphere of society. It is present in politics when charismatic "outsiders" connect to other disembedded individuals directly, without relying on the mediation of a political party. Similar dynamics are at work in an economic sphere in which hope for steady employment in a single firm throughout one's life is replaced by exhortations to build one's personal brand. They even shape the sphere of sports, as talented players at every level switch teams rapidly and repeatedly, and growing numbers of fans attach their allegiance—and their fantasy sports betting—as much to these individual stars as to teams. (Academia's own star system is more like this than those of us caught in the economy defined by its aspirations might want to admit.) And, as I'll argue below, individualization shapes a full range of religious lives and institutions. The changes run deep and wide enough to vindicate Beck and Beck-Gernsheim's claim that we are in the midst of "one of those moments of history where difference in degree becomes difference in kind."[21]

Powerful material forces are at work in individualization. More than thirty years ago, William Julius Wilson began to name a "disappearance of work" in urban Black communities, as factory jobs and other work that gathered people in large collectivities—and so facilitated organizing—gave way to a gig economy of endless individual side-hustles. If these conditions followed lines of structural racism to find and create especially vulnerable populations, they have since expanded to become more general. Contingent labor has spread across lines that mark race, class, and sectors of the economy. The pattern extends not just to Uber drivers and day laborers but also to adjunct professors and supply pastors.

These individualizing forces shape more than work. A global run of neoliberal policies privatized national industries to individualize wealth; worked to break union power to individualize workers; and eased public regulation of industries to individualize costs of health, safety, and ecology. These policies also unhitched corporations from regions and nations with the globalization of labor, markets, and supply chains, weakening ties to any common good beyond the aggregated interests of individual shareholders; shifted health and pension benefits to individual accounts, unraveling a social safety net with the promise of little hammocks of individual responsibility; and cut public funding for higher education, passing costs instead to individual students with the argument that whatever came of the education was a private good that students should pay for themselves, like a new pair of shoes. These cases are united, Ulrich Beck argued, by a transfer of *risk* to individuals. The result is a YOYO society, one that tells people that, at the deepest level, "You're on your own"—and then seeks to render that ideology true.[22]

If individualization breaks us out of existing communities and collectivities, it does not then set us free—despite its promises—to be any kind of person we might imagine. It rather drills us to become particular kinds of individuals. At the most basic level, the processes of individualization form us as the kinds of people who understand ourselves as able (even *required*) to construct our own lives, the relationships in which those lives take shape, and the horizons in relation to which they have whatever meaning they have. More specifically, these processes operate as we become the kinds of entities that can be linked to a Social Security account, covered by an insurance policy, insulated from accountability by a limited liability company, invested in a retirement account that can move with us to another job, or credentialed by a degree. It operates powerfully in the process of taking on and carrying debt, which imposes a kind of continuity of individualized identity through time. These material processes help form the individualized individual who bears and performs all the other talismans of identity. Under individualization we might change our religion, our gender, or our name, but the identity that bears debt, owns property, and enjoys rights remains stable.[23]

This process of subject formation takes place not just in the imposition of responsibilities but also in the assertion of rights. The discourse of rights has entered more and more spheres of society, most notably the family. Children and married women, once subsumed by too much of law and culture under a patriarchal whole, are increasingly recognized as rights-bearing individuals. There is emancipation in this, and justice. There is also a deep discipline that forms all of us as rights-bearing individuals.[24] Similar disciplinary forces are at work in contemporary K-12 education. In the twentieth century, the overwhelming majority of American young people attended public or Catholic parochial schools that offered relatively little flexibility. With an array of optional clubs and a single shared curriculum, they formed students to take their place in a constellation of voluntary associations united under the umbrella of the state. But now there is an incredible proliferation of choice at every level. A record number of American students are being schooled at home. There are not just more private schools, but more kinds of private schools. Among public schools, there are magnets, charters, online options, and more. Students have more options for their paths through their schools—and even more options if they enlist in an individualized educational plan. All these options are stratified in ways that reproduce privileges of race and class. Less obviously, they also reproduce neoliberalized individuals who have to choose their own formation—and who are blamed for their choices if things don't turn out as they had hoped.

Political theorist Wendy Brown excavates deeper layers of neoliberal individualization that do more to explain what it is like to live as this kind of subject. Brown observes that neoliberalism involves not just a reorientation of the state to sustain markets, but the circulation of market principles into every part of society. These "saturating reality principles" drive what Brown calls, following Michel Foucault, a "reprogramming of liberalism." Classical liberalism—the worldview that fits most closely with the constellation of voluntary associations described in chapter 1—formed subjects for free exchange in pursuit of needs and desires that were largely taken for granted. But neoliberalism reprograms our relationships to ourselves, pushing us not merely to satisfy what we think of as our needs but to treat ourselves as human capital, always in need of investment and enhancement for the sake of competition in a meritocratic market. It's not enough to satisfy ourselves; we need to work on ourselves.[25]

Neoliberal individualization drives a culture of life hacks and productivity plans that runs far beyond formal employment. It ranges widely to gather all of life into a portfolio of human capital. It extends to diet, exercise, dress, décor, relationships, and more. It shows up in home improvement shows that teach us how to organize our spaces and in smart watches that help us optimize our sleep. It's there in the life coach who provides guidance for individuals who have been disembedded from traditions and communities that might have offered guidance before. And, I'll argue below, this drive to curate ourselves shapes the ways we approach both religion and education, and the theological education that happens at their intersection.

Processes of individualization not only shape us as particular kinds of choosers; they also connect us to one another. To be disembedded from certain traditional communities does not mean a person enters an empty, formless social space. Individualization creates dense, complex webs of connection between us. It's just that those webs take the individualized individual as their primary unit and ground of legitimacy. We are connected first of all by our common formation as particular kinds of selves. We are also connected by a shared matrix of individualizing laws and policies that defines the horizons in light of which we choose our lives. We might choose to exercise our First Amendment rights in very different ways, for instance, but it is no small thing to share the shelter of these rights, and the identity of bearer of those rights. Our choices are also entangled with one another in ways that often go unacknowledged. A bank might tell us that we're on our own when it comes to making payments on a mortgage, but the financial crisis of 2008 made clear that deep material connections bind us to one another. Similarly, social media both opens space for individual expression and creates a fairly narrow set of shared channels through which those expressions flow. It also creates significant connections in the background, as it joins users in networks of surveillance and advertising. We may be ambivalent about—even sharply critical of—these social networks, but there is no denying that they bind us to one another in some way. We are both more individualized and connected in new ways.[26]

If individualization is not just something we choose but something that happens to us, we might expect to see more pronounced effects among those with less cultural, political, and economic capital to resist them. And that is indeed the case. Lack of affiliation, for instance, is more common among poorer people. As Ryan Burge explains, "The typical none is someone who does not have a college degree and makes less than $50,000 a year. Many are struggling economically, socially and spiritually and are disconnected from society." The pattern holds across racial and ethnic groups. Among Black, Hispanic/Latinx, and white populations, wealthier and more highly educated people are *more* likely, not less, to be affiliated with a church. Those who identify as "nones" are poorer and have less formal education. Among Asian/Asian American populations, affiliation varies more closely with immigration status than with income, with newer immigrants more likely than others to identify as "nones." It's not just that these groups of variously marginalized people aren't going to church. They are less likely to get married or to connect with other voluntary associations. They are more likely to die what Anne Case and Angus Deaton have called "deaths of despair." Despite caricatures that run through sermons and pop sociology, the "nones" are not primarily wealthy white urbanites skipping church to sip mimosas at brunch. They are also young Black men denied access to steady employment, white women raising children by themselves in a shredded rural America, otherwise documented immigrants for whom affiliation would be risky, queer youth who have fled families for their safety, and overworked and overwhelmed people who can't imagine what it would be like to have time to go to church and worry that they would be looked down on if they did. Even in a time of unraveling, lack of affiliation is tangled with other marginalities in tight knots of mutual reinforcement.[27]

The disproportionate effects of individualization appear not just in patterns of affiliation but also in the practices of self-transformation that are a sign of our times. Sociologist Jennifer Silva heard traces of these practices in interviews she conducted with more than one hundred poor and working-class young adults in Lowell, Massachusetts, and Richmond, Virginia. For most of these young people, the traditional markers of respectable adulthood—starting a steady job, getting married, raising children with a partner, buying a house—are inaccessible. Instead of telling narratives defined by these traditional markers, the young adults with whom Silva spoke "are working hard to remake dignity and meaning out of emotional self-management and willful psychic transformation." They are crafting stories that make sense of their suffering, frustrations, and accomplishments as part of a journey to a psychically healthy adulthood. The narratives help discipline feelings and actions that let them do better both in service jobs that require emotional management and in what Silva calls a "mood economy" whose currencies are dignity, recognition, and a sense of self-worth. Success in the mood economy promises a place to stand amidst the constant flux of every other part of life. People might turn to various practices identified as spiritual or religious for help with this work, but "privatizing happiness" is extraordinarily demanding, especially for those whose employment, housing, and relationships are precarious. And—as in other neoliberal economies—failing to succeed in the mood economy is attributed to a failure of the individual. Struggling to narrate oneself into adulthood, and to manage one's inner life in accordance with that narrative, becomes a source of shame and a justification for further marginalization. Neoliberal individualization might press all of us into working on ourselves. But that work is harder, and the stakes are higher, when material forces are arrayed against you.[28]

This disproportionate impact makes clear two paradoxes at the center of individualization. First, the choices individualization offers are not themselves chosen; they are *imposed*. We find ourselves compelled to compose our own biographies, thrust into relationships with ourselves that we did not choose and cannot easily avoid. And second, the universal, undetermined identity promised by individualization—anyone can be whoever they want to be!—comes in very different ways to different people, and the differences follow lines of race, class, gender, sexuality, immigration status, and other identity markers that already structure power relations in our society. The unraveling is not evenly distributed.

INDIVIDUALIZED RELIGION

The paradoxes of individualization also shape the particular forms religion takes in our time. Before considering the ways individualization unravels the consolidation of voluntary associations, I want to explore two more general ways it shapes religious life and practice. In particular, I want to think through some ways individualized religion becomes an *identity* and how the practices associated with a religious identity take on an *expressive* quality.

Social theorists have sometimes said modernity relegates religion to the private sphere. The disestablishments described in chapter 1 *did* unhook religion from formal connections to the state. But they also channeled religious energies into voluntary associations that have had extraordinary political impact, influencing debates about everything from slavery to the gold standard to the New Deal to civil rights. Just as religion did not become a private concern with the erosion of standing orders, it is not becoming purely private with the unraveling of voluntary associations. Religion keeps bursting into public significance today, and not only as a holdover from the age of voluntary associations. It is also public in its emerging forms.[29]

A better description of the impact of individualization would stress not the confinement of religion to the private sphere but the transformation of religion into an *identity*. The same reprogramming of liberalism that presses us to cultivate ourselves as

86

human capital casts religion as a defining aspect of the selves we might create. In this it joins a list of other properties that acquire the special property of an identity. As Vincent Lloyd argues, "Race, gender, and sexuality become identity groups to which one may or may not belong, like an alumni association or a bowling league. To this mix we may add religion, reduced to an identity group—another color in the rainbow composing the American nation, another trait of the atomized subject, another niche market for corporate profit."[30] Not all qualities function as identities. Left-handedness, for instance, might matter very much for a person's daily life. But for most left-handed people it does not become an identity, except in the softest sense. Religion, on the other hand, joins a select group of other qualities that we collectively grant the potential to define the ways we think about ourselves, connect to others, and represent ourselves in public.

Like any identity, religion is profoundly personal. But it is never merely private. When an identity matters to us—when it is part of who we understand ourselves to be—it is social, connecting us with others with whom we share the identity. It is public, for public expression and public recognition are as essential to identity as water and sunlight are to plants. These publicly expressed identities are only growing in their political significance. It's not just that political parties are increasingly coalitions of identity groups, or even becoming identity groups themselves. It's that political speech across the spectrum increasingly takes the form of expressions of identity, and political interests are increasingly defined in relation to identity. Identity gives both structure and content to the lived stuff of politics today.

The power of identities can occlude the deeper powers that shape things like race, sexuality, and religion into identities in the first place. As I argued in chapter 1, the powers that defined the age of voluntary associations pressed religious lives into the institutional forms of congregations and denominations. In that institutional isomorphism, to be a believer was to be a member of some voluntary association. But what Foucault called the "governmentality" of the reprogrammed liberalism in which we live now presses religious lives into a different mold: not one of voluntary associations, but one of identities, in the distinct sense I have been trying to use that word here. As Lloyd sees it, transforming realities like race and religion into identities is a way of managing them—and the people who bear them and are defined by them. The promise of free expression of identity is the promise of great liberty. And the liberties it grants can be meaningful, even life-changing. But, Lloyd writes, together "with the rhetoric of freedom is the reality of management, the subtle technologies of control that create the horizons of possibility for both religious and racialized lives."[31] The physics of this age form religion as an identity, one of the elementary particles out of which individualized individuals might create ourselves.

Within this governing logic, identities define those parts of our lives in which individual autonomy is sheltered and secured. A state, a school, or other disciplinary institution might demand many things of us, but it cannot interfere with those ways we define ourselves. Even a prison is legally obliged to respect an inmate's religious identity and the practices that are taken to be constitutive of that identity.

But identity involves more than just the freedom from external coercion that philosopher Isaiah Berlin calls "negative liberty." It also involves a "positive liberty"—not just freedom from coercion but freedom *for* a particular kind of life. At the center of that life is a quality of authentic self-expression. As Charles Taylor describes it, "The expressivist outlook takes [autonomy] a stage farther. The religious life or practice that I become part of must not only be my choice, but it must speak to me, it must make sense in terms of my spiritual development as I understand this."[32] It's not just that a person is free to choose whatever religious tradition the person wishes from a menu of denominational options, as in the age of voluntary associations. In what Taylor calls this present "age of authenticity," what we choose needs to resonate with our deepest senses of who we are and who we long to be. It needs to feel like authentic self-expression. It needs to resonate with our identities.

While the values associated with authentic self-expression have become more powerful in the last fifty years as the powers of individualization have accelerated, they are not new. They were not conceived in the Summer of Love. Indeed, one reason individualization has gained such traction is its ability to tap into older flows of practices and ideals that weave in and out of Christian traditions across continents and centuries. Taylor traces expressive ideals at work in seven centuries of European history, from the Christocentric piety that flourished in the High Middle Ages through devotional movements like the Brethren of the Common Life in the fifteenth century to the theologies and practices of reformers and counterreformers in the sixteenth and seventeenth centuries. Running through all these movements, Taylor writes, are long, deep currents with "a steadily increasing emphasis on a religion of personal commitment and devotion, over against forms centered on collective ritual." These currents bubbled up in North America most visibly in Puritan dissenters like Anne Hutchinson, but they were also present in everyday Puritan practices of reading, journaling, and private prayer. In the nineteenth century, they infused not only Transcendentalist and New Thought groups but also abolitionist movements that insisted on the dignity of each individual person and revival movement that stressed what they saw as the authenticity of individual piety over the hypocrisy of institutional forms. They blended with African traditional practices to create the distinctively expressive forms of classic Black church worship, what W. E. B. Du Bois described as "the Preacher, the Music, and the Frenzy." They have continued in the expressive qualities not only of "New Age" movements but also of charismatic and Pentecostal renewal movements in the twentieth and twenty-first centuries.[33]

Even a quick gesture toward this long, complex history of expressivist beliefs and practices can help us understand more clearly how they function today. In particular, it presses us past definitions of "spirituality"—whether from researchers or practitioners—that define it as nothing more than the ideological fog that surrounds the narcissism of younger generations. Knowledge of this richer history of spirituality as expressive identity also undoes attempts to define it by its opposition to organized religion. The expressive practices of spirituality have shaped both the inside of religious institutions and movements that set themselves against those institutions. That remains true today. Anxieties about institutional health have generated a lot of interest in people who identify as "spiritual but not religious." This focus has led us to neglect the many Americans who identify themselves as "spiritual *and* religious." Thinking about spirituality as expressive practices of individuals can help us stay attuned to the full range of relationships between these practices and formal institutions. Some practices, like the Enneagram, might grow at the edges of orthodoxy. Others, like *lectio divina*, might have more clearly ecclesial pedigrees. Still others, like Cardinal Hans Urs von Balthasar's writing on tarot as a kind of Christian hermeticism, might prompt a double take. What defines these practices is not their relation to institutions or orthodoxies but their promises of intense individual experiences, authentic expressions, and heartfelt connections to God and to other people. In this they are signs of the times.[34]

RESISTANCE AND KENOSIS

The practices of expressive identities have received sharp criticism from people invested in the church structures that consolidated in the nineteenth and twentieth centuries. Historian, *Christian Century* columnist, and patron saint of the order of voluntary associations Martin Marty denounced "spirituality" as "misty, evanescent, wispy and, dare we say it, rich in appeal to narcissism."[35] He has hardly been alone in this criticism. Religious and secular critics from many different schools have tried to resist the effects of individualization. Communitarian thinkers have denounced the selfishness and anomie it can produce. Agrarians have lamented the countless costs of abstracting individuals from particular places. New traditionalists have argued that the epistemology of individualism dissolves rationality and reduces us to endless argument. Critical theorists have skewered the pretentions of authentic expression that occlude the loss of more meaningful kinds of individual freedom: a "Don't Tread on Me" avatar is poor compensation for the loss of actual liberty that comes with integration into systems of surveillance capitalism.

I have real sympathy with all of these critiques. As one who grew up downstream from Lane, in a Presbyterian congregation shaped by multiple generations of my family, I carried these arguments in my bones even before I met scholars who articulated them with precision and power. But I have also collided—again and again—with the irony of trying to live out these critiques. Because processes of individualization are not just chosen but imposed, they cannot be evaded simply through critique. Many Christian social critics, for instance, have denounced individualization as a damaging lie. Our lives are not determined by us, they argue. They are given to us by God. And we begin to come alive—really alive—when we find ourselves in the story God has authored. All of this is true, at least in some way. But those critics obscure the individualizing choice that is forced upon us, even in the rhetoric of their own critiques. They speak past the position that they presume for their hearers, for people asked to make a decision to find themselves in God's story are precisely the kind of choosers individualization produces.

Even if we choose an identity that rejects the idea that we are responsible for making ourselves, we have still chosen that identity, and it is transformed by the fact of being chosen. It is one thing to find life in a Latin Mass when it saturates one's world, when one did not choose it and could not really imagine life apart from it. That is: it is one thing to find life in a Latin Mass within a standing order centered on the Mass. It is a very different thing to find life in a Latin Mass today, when it can only be encountered as one of many options, and when choosing it defines one's identity and transforms the Mass into a kind of expressive action. The inner quality of our relationship to it, and the identity it bestows, are transformed by this choosing. Of course we do not make ourselves. Some of the deepest features of our lives are given in tightly entangled divine and human powers. It's just that what is given to us today, like it or not, is the identity of individualized chooser emancipated and constrained for self-expression.

Seeing that caught-ness suggests a shift in tone, from scolding to compassion and discernment. It is easy to slip into scolding "nones" when we imagine them as privileged people acting in selfish ways. But the realities—both of who the unaffiliated are and what their experiences are like—are very different. Moreover, scolding presumes a power to live otherwise that most unaffiliated people—even those with relative privilege—do not possess. Just as Beecher could not scold Connecticut back into the Standing Order, we can't scold people back into the Kiwanis Club, the International Brotherhood of Electrical Workers, and the United Methodist Church. Even if they do return, they'll be making these organizations into something new. We'll have to rebuild social connections from the pieces and with the people individualization shapes. And we'll have to articulate a place for theological education within this new ecology.

This task presses us to feel for the ambivalent fissures that run through the not-so-solid social world of authentic individuals. I find one toehold in the paradoxes of my own mainline Protestant tradition, which arose in inextricable connection with the world of voluntary associations. My home tradition's pieties have both provided ideological fuel for the individualization that now threatens all our core institutions *and* contributed to emancipations of people assigned by the powers of this age to subordinate, surrogate, constricted, or otherwise death-dealing roles because of their race, ethnicity, gender, sexuality, able-bodiedness, or citizenship. Those emancipations, to the extent they have become real, are the great moral achievement of our times. If one could imagine many genealogies for them, as social facts they came tightly tangled with processes of individualization. And those processes, as I argued above, drew important substance and shelter from the practices and beliefs cultivated in voluntary associations. There were many other sources, to be sure. But we cannot pretend that this was an assault by utterly alien invaders. Thus, in working toward the emancipations that are the highest goods it helped achieve, the world of voluntary associations also gave rise to the individualization that now unravels it. It amounts to a kind of kenosis, not entirely chosen, and with the potential to be faithful in spite of itself.[36]

3

Unraveling

The crisis consists precisely in the fact that the old is dying and the new cannot be born; in this interregnum a great variety of morbid symptoms appear.

Antonio Gramsci, *The Prison Notebooks*
(1929–1935)

Identity and expression are tightly braided together in contemporary religious lives and practices. Religions get pressed into the form of identities, and identities come to life in expressive practices. These practices feel authentic when they ring true with who we really are, a self increasingly defined as and by identities. And they don't merely give voice to identities that exist prior to them; they are also the means by which those identities are created and cultivated. We take on a certain kind of Christian identity in the act of lifting our hands in praise. We become activists when we link arms in the street.

The twin engines of identity and expression are driving changes that run through every institution that came together to form the constellation of voluntary associations, including denominations, congregations, and ministry as a profession. In some cases, the changes erode or even dissolve established institutions. In others, they produce new institutions, even new kinds of institutions. And in still others, they work transformations within existing institutions. Much as an Episcopal parish in the old imaginary of a standing order in Virginia might have held on to its name and building even as it became a voluntary association, so a congregation, denomination, or theological school today might retain key markers of its identity even as it becomes a very different sort of institution.

However these changes unfold, they create stress for all the key institutions that consolidated in the age of voluntary associations. Congregations across political and theological spectrums are seeing declines in members, money, and vitality. Exceptional congregations—and there are many—do not change the larger trends. Even if we can point to growth in this or that slice, the larger pie is shrinking. Denominations are struggling even more. Fractured by internal divisions, they face not only declining budgets but also a loss of legitimacy even among those who remain affiliated with them. Ministry in these institutions attracts fewer people than it did in the past. And ministry looks—and is paid— less and less like a profession.[1] It's not just the salary that makes ministry less like a profession in the classic sense. High attrition rates reflect the fact that ministry, for rising numbers of people, does not offer the arc of a career of expanding responsibilities over a lifetime that is a hallmark of the professional ideal. In this, ministry is not alone. Professions of every kind face threats, as the space for professionals that opened up in the political economy of the nineteenth century is increasingly colonized by finance capital. Amidst these changes, theological schools function less clearly like professional schools, however they define themselves in official communication. A growing percentage of students seek something other than preparation for professional ministry. And the proliferations of degrees and accreditation standards undermine—for better and worse—theological schools' role as gatekeepers to a profession. The entire ecology of voluntary associations is struggling.

The struggles of theological schools today must be seen as part of this larger process. The professional model of theological education arose in symbiotic connection with all these other institutions.

The wider ecology made this model of theological education materially sustainable, with congregations and denominations supporting schools, forming students to enter them, and then employing graduates. When congregations and denominations started to offer less support, individual student debt could be framed as a reasonable way to sustain a system that promised entry to the life of a middle-class professional. But that promise is less convincing now, as every part of this wider system faces intense stress. It is little wonder, then, that theological schools are closing, merging, selling their campuses, shrinking the size of their faculties, pouring more time and money into recruitment of students, starting a frenzy of new options, and scrambling just to stay alive.

The stress on this wider ecology of voluntary associations creates crises for theological schools that go beyond numbers to questions of meaning and purpose. For more than two centuries, the dominant *telos* for theological education has been the formation of leaders for these voluntary associations who work for the good of a wider social whole. Generations of faculty have expressed ambivalence about this stated purpose, often tugging classes toward a *wissenschaftlich* ideal of knowledge as an end in itself. These sentiments are only growing as the job market and tenure and promotion standards discipline faculty into identities that earn recognition from their guilds. At the same time, increasing numbers of students are hacking curricula in order to pursue more personal projects. They are passionate about theological learning—but not necessarily as preparation for ministry, even in a most expansive sense of that vocation. Despite this dissent, for the vast majority of theological schools, the official rationale—the kind given to provosts, boards of trustees, and accreditors—remains the formation of leaders for congregations and other more-or-less-religious voluntary associations. Thus crises in the network of voluntary associations create crises of meaning for theological schools that compound financial crises and afflict even schools whose endowments buffer them from immediate financial pressures. Indeed, some wealthy schools are likely to run out of meaning before they run out of money.

Those of us who care about the church often narrate this story as one of decline. And there are indeed many kinds of decline at work. Church membership, student enrollments, and charitable donations are all going down. But these numerical declines—as important as they are—should not be taken as signs of some kind of world-historical process of decline and fall. As I argued in the introduction, such narratives make both historical and theological mistakes. They forget that we've been in moments like this before. They forget the ways history surprised Lyman Beecher. Even more: they forget that Jesus promises not to leave bereft those he names as friends.

Instead of decline, I see this time between the times as one of *unraveling*. The consolidations of the age of voluntary associations are coming undone. Space is opening between the institutions, individuals, and ideals once woven so tightly together—not just with one another, but with the larger project of a white Christian America. There is judgment in this unraveling, as when God promised to unravel the plans of the Egyptians in the book of Isaiah. There are also losses worthy of lament. There is a kind of revelation, like the unraveling of a riddle or a mystery. And there are new, fragile possibilities. Picked apart from one another, individual threads can't carry as much weight as they did when they were woven together. But they endure. Even now, threads of the love of learning and the desire for God are available to be woven together with other threads into a fallible, faithful pattern.[2] A time of unraveling can feel like the end of the world. It can be a time for grief, penitence, and discernment. But it is not a time for despair.

THE UNRAVELING OF DENOMINATIONS

Practices of expressive identity have taken a toll on the denominations that connected congregations to one another, to people of other traditions, and to a national order. This change is reflected in the growing number of people who identify as nondenominational. Twelve percent of Americans so identify today, up from just 4 percent twenty-five years ago. Nondenominational identity is even more common among Protestants, more than a quarter of whom now identify as nondenominational. Within the shrinking set of Americans who claim affiliation with some religious tradition, a growing subset identify as nondenominational.[3]

Cynics within denominationally committed circles often joke that "nondenominational" is just another denomination. They are right to see "nondenominational" as a coherent identity. Indeed, it might even be more coherent than a sprawling, historically complex identity like United Methodist, Roman Catholic, or Southern Baptist. But the charge misses the depth of the difference in ethos of insisting on a nondenominational identity rather than joining a denomination or forming a new one. A nondenominational identity lets a congregation position itself as anti-institutional in significant ways. It signals the priority of individual projects of self-expression. It refuses the inherent ecumenism of the denominational worldview, which pictures different religious movements as equally legitimate members of a larger social whole defined by the nation. Just as the institutional form of the denomination fit with a social imaginary defined by voluntary associations, now nondenominational identities fit with the social imaginary driven by individualization.

These same forces of neoliberal individualization weaken denominations from the inside. Denominational offices across the board are facing losses in funding, staff, and prestige. In a mutually reinforcing cycle as familiar as it is vicious, denominational leadership is simultaneously more open to women and people from historically minoritized racial/ethnic communities even as it is increasingly devalued, disrespected, and defunded. Large congregations are more likely to go their own way, even in areas once defined by significant denominational resources and collaboration, like education and mission. And the ancillary institutions that reflected and sustained denominational identity—camps, retreat centers, colleges, conferences, and seminaries—are coming unraveled from one another and from their denominations.[4]

Denominations are not just coming unraveled, though. They are also being ripped apart. The mid-twentieth century—a peak moment for the social imaginary of voluntary associations—saw a number of smaller denominations consolidate into larger ones. Old denominational divisions felt less salient as European ethnicities were increasingly gathered into a single homogenized whiteness and as that whiteness came to feel more important than regional divisions dating back to the Civil War.[5] As these old divisions became weaker, a denominational ethos that emphasized the legitimacy of different religious groups under the same national umbrella became more compelling, enabling the consolidation of mainline denominations like the Evangelical Lutheran Church in America, the Presbyterian Church (USA), the United Church of Christ, and the United Methodist Church. Since that wave of consolidations, denominations have been racked by one division after another. These divisions break along the fault lines of culture-war politics, as those politics increasingly mark identities. In some cases, contemporary fault lines reflect the influence of older divisions that were overcome to form the larger denominations. Congregations from the old Southern Presbyterian denomination, for instance, have been more likely to leave the Presbyterian Church (USA) for more conservative Presbyterian denominations. But the divisions aren't simply a return to an older order. There is, as sociologist Robert Wuthnow saw more than three decades ago, a restructuring of American religion.

Wuthnow identified the rise of what he called "special purpose groups," movements within denominations that seek to reform denominational positions on core culture-war questions.[6] In the United Methodist Church, for instance, special purpose groups like the Reconciling Ministries Network connect people and institutions to reform denominational policy and recognize the gifts of LGBTQIA+ Christians with ordination. On the other side, special purpose groups like the Wesleyan Covenant Association and the Confessing Movement resist changes in ordination standards and help congregations, pastors, and laity leave to form a new denomination. Parallel groups have existed in nearly every denomination. These special purpose groups might oppose one another on questions of polity, but they share a common organizational structure. As special purpose groups, they raise funds, produce resources, maintain lists of supportive congregations and pastors, and hold regular conferences. They retain relatively light institutional infrastructures, especially in comparison to denominations. They feel more like movements. These qualities let them resonate with the expressive desires of the individuals who often find them more meaningful than the denominations they set out to reform.

In the decades since Wuthnow first identified special purpose groups, the groups have contributed to splits in existing denominations and provided seedbeds for new ones. The splits make both the older denominations and the newer ones more internally homogeneous, especially around the culture-war questions on which they divided. Because they are smaller and more homogeneous after splits, both older and newer denominations can feel less like large, complex voluntary associations and more like expressive movements. They have less need to craft careful positions that keep ideologically diverse constituencies together. They can speak and act in more partisan ways, ways that do less to sustain a large institution and more to express identities with what feels like authenticity. After divisions, denominations become more like special purpose groups.

This kind of inner transformation seems a more likely outcome than simple disappearance. Denominations have significant holdings in land, pension funds, and other resources that make them unlikely to evaporate. And they continue to be important for the identities of clergy, seminary faculty, and older generations of laypeople. Instead of disappearing, smaller and more homogeneous denominations are already functioning more like special purpose groups. This transformation can be energizing, especially for those most invested in the defining issues. It enables them to spend less time and energy on keeping everyone on board and more on speaking with clarity and boldness on issues of shared concern. Speaking with this kind of clarity and boldness aligns the denomination with the expressive projects of the individuals who remain part of it. It renews a sense of connection to the denomination, but on different terms: not as an institution that has significance because of its place with other denominations in the shared life of a nation, but as an expressive movement that feels authentic to its members. This transformation erodes the old denominational ethos that could imagine many different religious groups as legitimate, analogous actors under a shared sacred canopy defined by the nation-state. What Charles Taylor calls the "civilizational connection" of religion was sustained directly by established churches in standing orders. It was sustained in a mediated way by denominations in the age of voluntary associations. Now, in the wake of individualization, that mediated form of civilizational connection is coming unraveled, even among those who remain part of denominations.[7]

Expressive movements do not have the inner drive to ecumenism that developed with the denominational form. Instead of a shared national canopy, the expressive ethos prizes purity. A person or congregation seeking purity is less likely to value the larger voluntary association enough to remain in membership when they lose a vote. Rather, the expressive ethos demands an institution that reflects the identity and commitments of the individuals involved. And so special purpose groups on opposite sides might start out trying to reform their denomination, but the drive to purity that expression demands ultimately forces them to form separate denominations. All these developments are amplified when religious identities map closely onto political identities undergoing similar transformations (political parties, too, have become more like special purpose groups). Denominations made in the image of special purpose groups might be more vital today, for they are more in sync with the expressive currents of our times. But it is not yet clear how they can remain connected to other denominations, especially those with whom they disagree, in some larger social whole. As we see in the energetic polarizations that mark every sphere of society now, vitality and unraveling can go together.

CHAPTER 3

THE UNRAVELING OF CONGREGATIONS
AS VOLUNTARY ASSOCIATIONS

Related processes are at work in congregations. Decreasing rates of affiliation are producing decreases of many kinds. The median number of people affiliated with any given congregation has been decreasing for more than two decades. Median attendance in weekend services is also declining rapidly. One prepandemic survey found a median attendance in US congregations of 65 people—down more than 50 percent from 137 in 2000. Mainline Protestant congregations suffered the fastest rate of decline, down 12.5 percent in the last five years, to a median attendance of 50. But evangelical, Catholic, and Orthodox congregations all saw significant declines of their own.[8] Not surprisingly, financial contributions to congregations have declined as well. Charitable giving of every kind has declined since the financial crisis of 2008. And giving to religious causes has declined even faster than giving to other charities. At the turn of the millennium, 46 percent of all households in the United States donated to religious causes. By 2018, that number was down to 29 percent. The decline is general, crossing lines of race, region, and religious tradition.[9] Declines in affiliation, attendance, and giving begin to push congregations beneath the thresholds needed for survival in their present form. A recent study by the evangelical firm Lifeway Research found that the number of congregations closing significantly outpaced the number being newly formed. Data from thirty-four Protestant denominations showed 4,500 congregational closures against the planting of 3,000 new congregations in 2019.[10] And all of this was before the COVID-19 pandemic shattered existing patterns of affiliation, giving, and congregational life.

Yet changing patterns of affiliation are not only producing closure and decline. Even with the decline in overall affiliation, most large congregations are growing. Indeed, 71 percent of congregations with membership over 1,500 *increased* in size between 2015 and 2020.[11] The shrinking number of total members combined with the growing membership in large congregations translates to a striking concentration of members in a few large churches. As Mark Chaves's analysis of denominational statistics shows, the pattern holds across nearly every Protestant denomination, from the Church of the Brethren to the United Methodist Church to the Southern Baptist Convention.[12]

Numbers for one denomination, the Presbyterian Church (USA), make clear how these trends are intersecting. In 2016, the majority of Presbyterian congregations had fewer than 100 members. Fully one-third of all Presbyterian congregations had fewer than 50. The median congregation is getting smaller, and more congregations are small. At the same time, more than half of all members in the PC(USA) were concentrated in fewer than one-eighth of the congregations. And almost one-third of all members in the denomination belonged to just 4.3 percent of the congregations. There were only sixty-six congregations with over 1,500 members, or 0.7 percent of the total number of congregations. But this tiny fraction had over 10 percent of the total membership.[13] The numbers highlight the ways that macro-level declines in affiliation play out on the ground of congregational life: a few large congregations are getting larger; many medium-sized congregations are becoming smaller, often too small to afford full-time leadership; and growing numbers of small congregations are on the edge of closure.

These numerical changes reflect and extend changes in congregational cultures as well. Very large congregations that are growing tend to press toward institutional forms that differ from a classic voluntary association in significant ways. More of the work of the congregation—especially the work that sustains it as an institution, like accounting and maintenance—is done by paid staff. Governance is less participatory, whatever the polity of the church stipulates. Most members of a two-thousand-member Presbyterian church will never serve on its session. Even notions of membership can be elastic. As sociologist Ryan Burge observes, many large, rapidly growing congregations "don't even have membership as a concept."[14] People connect to the congregation not as members of a voluntary association but as participants in forms of community that facilitate their work on themselves, their desire for connection, and their hope for powerful worship experiences and authentic expressions of faith.

Small congregations that aspire to the remembered past of their lives as a big-enough voluntary association tend to struggle. The work of sustaining the institution falls on fewer and fewer people. And when joining the congregation means being swept almost immediately into that work, it is less attractive to individualized individuals who feel overwhelmed with other responsibilities but also eager to work on themselves. Endowments, older generations, and just enough young people who value the old associational ways might sustain a shrinking congregation as a voluntary society for a season. But many small congregations that are trying to sustain themselves in the older form of the voluntary society are caught in downward spirals.

Small congregations that are thriving seem to be finding ways to tap into the same expressive energies that run through very large congregations. Some of these thriving small congregations were once larger congregations. They have found ways to shift not just their signage but their institutional form away from that of a voluntary association and toward some kind of expressive community of individuals. Other thriving small congregations, like St. Lydia's Dinner Church in Brooklyn and other congregations in the "fresh expressions" movement, were founded to be a different kind of community from the start. Whatever their origin, small congregations that are thriving tend to share a light institutional structure that does not require a lot of money or volunteer time to sustain. And they tend to promote personal expression within a network of close relationships. The model will probably struggle to operate at a larger scale. These communities can't grow much without losing their distinctive form. And that is fine with many who attend. As one worshiper at a church of about thirty people said, "It's like a house church in a really nice setting or a small group. I'm not interested in a large congregation."[15] Like strong megachurches, thriving minichurches find ways to break with the model of a voluntary association for structures that make room for the expressive energies of individualized individuals.

These changes in congregational life suggest a subtler change in the imaginary through which individuals understand their relationships to institutions and to God. One way the differences become visible is in resistance to the emerging forms. As one venerable elder in a large Presbyterian congregation attempting to remake itself on the megachurch model said, "The consultants are saying we should shift from volunteers to staff. 'Oh, the staff should do that. The staff should take care of that.' But what does that do for people? If you're not volunteering, you're just a person in a pew."[16] In a social imaginary shaped by voluntary associations, volunteering takes on a sacred quality. The congregation is taken to be of almost infinite value. Whatever official theology is preached, the congregation in this imaginary functions to mediate people's relationship to God. A whole world of practices points to this dynamic, from commissioning commemorative plates that picture the congregation's building to making the congregation a primary beneficiary of a person's will. In the world ordered by and around voluntary associations—a world I know from the inside, like one circumcised on the eighth day, of the stock of Israel, of the tribe of Benjamin, a Hebrew of the Hebrews; as touching the law, a Pharisee—it is only a slight exaggeration to say that the church building is a like a sacrament, that committee meetings serve as divine liturgy, and that service to the congregation is the core of discipleship. But when the voluntary association loses its aura, it loses the power to anchor all these practices. And so individuals are compelled to try to relate to God in a way that feels more direct in the imaginary that is emerging now: not by working on a congregation but by working on themselves.

THE UNRAVELING OF MINISTRY AS A PROFESSION

There is a place for visionary leaders and wise guides in both very large and very small communities. But the bifurcation of congregational sizes creates a world in which a small number of ministers have great autonomy, financial security, and even celebrity, while a large and growing number of ministers serve in precarious and part-time ways. These conditions press more and more ministers to become either stars at the top of the pyramid, entrepreneurs who try to start ministries in which they will star, employees of organizations that have already achieved a certain scale, or tentmakers who pair ministry with other work that can pay the bills. Stars, entrepreneurs, employees, and tentmakers can all be faithful ministers of the gospel. But none of them are professionals, at least in the sense ministers enjoyed in the age of voluntary associations. In a dynamic that parallels dynamics in other parts of the economy penetrated by neoliberalism, dwindling numbers of mid-sized congregations make for a dwindling middle class in ministry, as well as dwindling numbers of full-time ministers who exercise relative autonomy in their work. A congregation of about two hundred members was in many ways the natural habitat of ministers as professionals. It was large enough to provide a full-time, middle-class salary with benefits, some staff to do work labeled as outside the profession, and resources for professional projects. But this mid-sized congregation is exactly the kind of congregation that is disappearing. As it does, the space for ministry as a profession is contracting.

Congregational structures are an important part of the story. The polarization of congregations into very large and very small sizes diminishes the number of openings for full-time, fully credentialed pastoral ministers. Very large congregations depend on economies of scale, employing fewer full-time ministers per member. Like hospitals and law firms, they also achieve savings by unbundling the profession and assigning specific tasks to paraprofessionals like youth pastors, worship leaders, and pastoral caregivers. To say that these ministers are "paraprofessional" is not to diminish their excellence or faithfulness. It is just to acknowledge that they are often credentialed and compensated in different ways, that they usually function more like skilled employees than like autonomous professionals, and that their lives often take different arcs than those promised by a profession in its classic form.

Working in a very small congregation can be very different from working as a member of a large staff at a megachurch. But this, too, is increasingly something other than the kind of full-time, MDiv-certified, pension-earning professional ministry that distinguished the era of voluntary associations. More small congregations mean more pastors who lead congregations on part-time salaries, often without full participation in denominational pension and benefits plans. Fully one-fourth of the congregations in the Evangelical Lutheran Church in America (ELCA) can no longer afford a full-time pastor with full benefits. A similar ratio holds in the nation's Catholic parishes, according to the Center for Applied Research in the Apostolate (CARA). Almost half of Episcopal parishes are led by part-time priests, supply priests, or laypeople. The numbers of small congregations served by people Catholics designate as lay ecclesial ministers, Methodists call local pastors, Presbyterians call commissioned lay pastors, and Disciples of Christ call commissioned pastors are all increasing. Congregations of diasporic communities and charismatic/Pentecostal communities have long been led by teams of bivocational leaders who blur the lines between laypersons and ordained professionals. These pastors often provide wise and faithful leadership. Indeed, they frequently live out their ministries at personal cost that puts to shame those of us who can't imagine ministry as anything but full-time work with middle-class salary and benefits. My point is not that ministry is declining in quality, but that ministry is functioning less and less like a profession.[17]

The unraveling of ministry as a profession has a significant financial component. Salaries for ministers have been declining relative to other professionals for decades. In 2020, the average annual salary for a full-time clergyperson was $56,650. Others classified as "religious workers" were paid substantially less, averaging $40,070. Of course, amounts vary widely according to denomination and kind of placement. Salaries are further distorted by systemic racism. A 2003 study found that 41 percent of Black pastors received less than $13,000 per year. On average, Black pastors make about two-thirds the salaries of their white counterparts. And pastoral salaries continue to vary by gender, as enduring sexism in the church drives dynamics in which women pastors are systematically paid less than men. Although the gender gap has been slowly closing in recent years, this is attributable less to female clergy being paid higher salaries and more to male clergy being paid lower ones. As in professions like teaching and social work, greater access for women has led to a decline in relative wages for the whole field. Systemic racism and sexism are like accelerants for all the other forces that already consume the professional status of ministers.[18]

The extent and significance of the decline in clergy wages come into focus with comparisons over time. When the political economy of the nineteenth century opened up space for professionals as a distinct class, mainline Protestant clergy offered a paradigmatic definition of that space, along with physicians and attorneys. The average salaries of doctors and lawyers soon outpaced those of clergy. But education, benefits, social status, job security, and quality of life allowed clergy with MDiv's to remain in roughly the same professional class as doctors and lawyers. Now, though, lawyers average about three times the salaries of full-time clergy, while physicians average around four times as much. Individual outliers aside, it strains comparison to include clergy as part of the same class. Closer comparisons for clergy today are to teachers and nurses. Elementary and middle-school teachers averaged $65,300 per year in 2020. Registered nurses averaged over $80,000, while licensed practical nurses made just over $50,000. This is good and honorable company. But it represents a significant historical shift. In 1890, pastors made about three times as much as schoolteachers and nurses. Now they often make less. If ministry is still a profession, it is a profession of a different kind.[19]

The unraveling of professional status also reflects deep shifts in the culture of ministry. In the constellation of voluntary associations, professional clergy were authorized especially by their con-nection to a network of institutions that included congregations, denominations, and seminaries. Seminaries and denominations each played a role in certifying ministers to assume an office in a congregation. That office was the real source of authority.

Now, though, as the social power of all these institutions erodes, authority flows more from a minister's ability to dis-play *authenticity*. Surveys underscore authenticity as the quality people prize most in a preacher. Shifts in practice also manifest the shift in authorization. Preaching that displays authenticity tends to feature practices that present a private self. It features not only more self-disclosure but also more casual language, ges-tures, and spaces. Distinctively clerical garb like a collar, robe, or stole might mark the authority of office. But the authority of authenticity comes through clothing or accessories that display individuality, whether that is a Hawaiian shirt, statement eye-wear, or skinny jeans with expensive sneakers. Even distinctly clerical clothing can become expressive. Especially when worn by those in traditions for which it is not a norm, a chasuble on Sunday or a collar at the march is more an expression of iden-tity than a badge of office. And pastors within traditions that re-quire distinctive clothing have more and more options at their disposal. Expression can come through the cut and cloth of what seems like a uniform. Through all these tropes, the authority of authenticity plays with or even actively subverts older norms of "professionalism."[20]

The deprofessionalization of ministry is part of a much broader unraveling of the professions from the classical form that emerged in the nineteenth century and solidified in the first two-thirds of the twentieth. That classical form stressed the self-directedness of a credentialed professional in a skilled practice that was oriented to the common good. The specialized skills of professionals have only grown more formidable. But finance capital has penetrated spheres of medicine, law, and accoun-tancy, transforming more and more of the institutions in which highly skilled work happens from practices owned by the professionals who worked in them into corporations owned by and accountable to shareholders. The shifts are perhaps clearest in medicine. Physicians are increasingly likely to work in a practice in which they do not have an ownership stake. In 2018, for the first time ever, the number of physicians who were employees passed the number who owned part of the practice in which they worked. The number of women who worked as employees was even higher. And the direction of the trends is clear: fully 70 percent of physicians under forty worked as employees of practices they did not own. These numbers describe changes at the top of the old professional pyramid in health care. Employee status is even more powerfully enforced on nurse practitioners, physician assistants, nurses, physical and occupational therapists, technologists, and other health-care workers. As professionals become employees, they exercise less power to direct their practices toward the common good, in accord with the older professional ethos. They also enjoy less autonomy in their daily work. As the distinctive space apart from both labor and capital that defined professional status erodes, professionals in every field are increasingly pressed to become either entrepreneurs or employees. Finance capital has not played the same role in church life. But ministry emerged as a profession alongside other professions, and their erosion decreases the social and economic space in which ministry might operate as a profession.[21]

These structural shifts have been accompanied by shifts in the ethos of professionals. Strong institutions have the power to shape the characters, habits, dispositions, relationships, and worldviews of individuals. But individualization rewires the relationships between individuals and institutions. Now, as social critic Yuval Levin has argued, institutions that once formed individuals become platforms on which individuals perform. The dynamic is visible across multiple spheres. Fewer politicians are formed by their parties as they rise through the ranks; instead, they treat their parties as stages on which they can perform. In an ironic transfiguration of their own value, universities establish standards for tenure, promotion, and salary that encourage academics to neglect schools as formative institutions that they help govern and to regard them instead as places to stand as they cultivate their individual brands, which then contribute to the cultural capital of the school. Similar forces invite pastors to shrug off the discipline of denominations to create congregations that serve as platforms. Pastors who make these moves might become not just entrepreneurs, but *stars*. As stars, they can attain greater prominence than the leader of a voluntary society ever could. But they start to look less and less like professionals.[22]

There is meaningful emancipation in this dynamic, as people systemically discounted by networks of voluntary associations can gain leverage on and apart from them. Rachel Held Evans, for instance, would not have been ordained to significant pastoral leadership in many white evangelical traditions, but her virtuosity in displaying authenticity let her speak good news through other means to people in and on the edges of those traditions. Her ministry thrived not in spite of her lack of professional status but because of it. At the same time, there are worrisome elements in this dynamic, as star systems disproportionately reward the already advantaged and congregations that serve as platforms for stars boom and bust, leaving spiritual body counts in their wake. Mars Hill Church, for instance, hitched itself to the bro-gospel of Mark Driscoll, rode his stardom up, and crashed as he came down, all in less than twenty years. He, too, was not bound by norms of professionalism within a strong institution. Indeed, for his followers, his transgression of those norms provided proof of his authenticity.[23]

The mixed quality of these developments should make us wary both of calls to restore professionalism and of celebrations of its unraveling. But even if we hold on to professionalism as an ideal, the large-scale social and economic forces at work in these changes mean that calling individuals to regain a professional ethos is unlikely to restore professionalism as a norm. Even ministers with a strong professional ethos will find themselves caught up in these dynamics. They will be hard pressed, for instance, not to engage in practices that display their authenticity, whether in the pulpit or on social media. *This* is the disciplinary apparatus that operates most powerfully today: not the discipline that forms a person for leadership in a voluntary association, but the discipline that drives a person to display expressive identities that transcend institutions. This unraveling of professional ministry is neither simply progress nor decline. It is the ambivalent space in which we live.

THE UNRAVELING OF THEOLOGICAL EDUCATION AS PROFESSIONAL EDUCATION

Theological education in the United States has never been purely professional education. But a professional model for theological education attained dominant status over the course of the nineteenth and twentieth centuries. It arose in close connection with denominations, congregations as voluntary societies, and ministry as a profession. Crises and transformations in these institutions put extraordinary pressure on theological schools that arose to train leaders for this world.

The few congregations that grow very large and the many that grow very small do not always look to theological schools for professional clergy. Whether because they can't afford a full-time pastor or because they prefer paraprofessional employees, they hire fewer ministers with MDivs from theological schools. Moreover, the same ethos that leads the largest of them to withdraw from denominations leads them to undertake theological education themselves. This might mean collaborating with other congregations in training programs like the Acts 29 network for church planters, or it might mean starting a pastoral training program within the congregation, as nondenominational megachurches often do. Mainline megachurches might be more inclined to bring an existing seminary into their structure. These congregational efforts have taken many forms and have had highly variable results. But they are unified in their move away from the theological school as professional school.

So, too, changes in denominations contribute to the unraveling of theological education as professional education. As an older denominational ethos is displaced by the expressive identities of special purpose groups, affinities with denominational schools give way to affinities with schools that share a position on culture-war questions. A conservative Presbyterian congregation, for instance, might be more eager for a pastor trained at Fuller Theological Seminary than one trained at one of the denomination's seminaries. Likewise, a progressive Episcopal seminary might prize strong activist credentials over deep denominational ties as it seeks new faculty. This loosening of ties extends to students. Prospective students often value pragmatic concerns like location and price, perceived prestige, and a school's relation to the theological and political questions that define identity today more than denominational connection. What this means is that more and more schools will have more and more traditions represented among their students, faculty, and senior leadership. Weaker denominational identities pair with genuine ecumenical commitments to help drive this dynamic. It is also driven by the need to attract every possible student in an era of declining enrollments. The result is a more general market in theological education, one in which schools and students are less connected to denominations.

This shift goes along with changes in funding patterns. As denominations contribute less, the costs of theological education are increasingly shifted to students. These trends unfold within larger individualizing forces that have shifted costs for all kinds of education to students. States across the country have cut funding for higher education, and federal dollars flow primarily to fund research or to loans for individual students. All of higher education has individualized costs, and theological education is no exception. Funding at theological schools has become more of a compact between schools, students, and whatever institution students rely on for loans. Schools might offer scholarships of many kinds. Some are relics of endowments tied to denominations. But a school's top awards today tend to be tied to judgments about individual merit. They therefore reinforce what students already know in their bones: increasingly in theological education, you're on your own.

That YOYO reality reveals how severely denominational ties have weakened. Cuts in funding are obvious, like the repossession of furniture from a living room. But the individualization at work in changing patterns of funding might have more profound long-term effects, like cracks in the foundation of the house.

These foundational fractures are both reflected in and driven by changes in student vocations. When congregations and denominations are no longer charged with significance, leading them becomes less appealing. In 1966, almost ten first-year college students per one thousand saw clerical leadership as a possible career. By 2012 the number was down to two per one thousand.[24] This reduces the number of prospective students for theological schools. Even among students who go to seminary, growing numbers are interested in vocational paths other than clerical leadership. They might have pressing questions about God, or they might be ready to make sacrifices to work for God's justice. But these drives and desires flow through channels of identity and self-expression rather than through voluntary associations. These shifts in vocation contribute to spiraling changes in funding patterns for theological education. As more seminary graduates seek vocations beyond institutional churches, stressed denominations and congregations find it more difficult to justify paying for education for people who do not graduate to serve in them. At the same time, individual students feel weaker bonds of meaningful connection and obligation to congregations and denominations that are doing less to support them. Shifts in vocations lead to shifts in funding patterns that underwrite further shifts in vocations, as changing flows of both money and meaning break up the social imaginary of voluntary associations.

Students in a YOYO world feel neoliberalism's pressure to work on themselves. There is an economic dimension to this, as students seek credentials that will count in multiple different contexts. They face extraordinary pressure to add value to the individual portfolios they will carry into a world less structured by a strong network of voluntary associations. But the desires of students with whom I work are not only—or even primarily—economic. In working on themselves, they don't just want to become more marketable. They want to craft authentic identities. They want to engage in practices that express those identities and join them to others engaged in similar work. They come alive in classes that prioritize that kind of work. They find ways to do it even in classes that don't. It's not just "spiritual but not religious" students seeking to do this kind of work, but also students preparing for ministries of all kinds. As those ministries unravel as professions, students are trying them on as expressive identities. Whatever our syllabi and curricula, students are already transforming schools from places that form them for professions to places where they fashion and refine sacred selves.

The expansion of paraprofessional roles and the urgency of self-making have combined to drive an incredible proliferation of degrees in theological education in recent decades. Asbury Theological Seminary, for instance, offers fifteen different ATS-approved master's degrees in addition to the MDiv. Students can choose among a master of biblical and theological foundations, an MA in mental health counseling, an MA in youth ministry, and other options. Freestanding certificates in things like Christian studies, pastoral care, and youth and family ministry add to the number. Other schools offer not only competing versions of these same degrees but different degrees entirely.[25] ATS now approves more than 250 degrees in addition to the master of divinity.

The proliferation of degrees—almost all of them shorter than the three-year MDiv—meets the needs that students identify for themselves. It fits with the shape of ministry for many people today and offers a more streamlined preparation for it. Moreover, the mass of degrees can open space for students to do the identity work that is most urgent for them. At the same time, these shifts contribute to the unraveling of ministry as a profession and theological education as professional education. A classic profession depends on strong barriers to entry. A "gold-standard" professional degree like the JD or the MD secures a whole network of other requirements. The free exercise and the establishment clauses of the First Amendment have created distinct dynamics around ministry as a profession. The MDiv (and its antecedents) never interfaced with state regulations to play the same kind of role as other professional degrees. But the MDiv did connect with national denominational standards to create something like the barriers to entry that marked off ministry as a profession. Those barriers are coming undone now. With more than 250 portals through them, they can't do much to define a profession.

Changes in standards for accreditation of schools magnify these shifts. Some of these changes are happening within ATS, as 2020 reforms created much greater flexibility for schools in meeting standards for accreditation. The new standards do more to recognize and affirm the deep diversity of schools. Even broader expansion is happening as other kinds of institutions accredited entirely apart from ATS are arising. As Justo González has noted, "The Association of Theological Schools and its member institutions no longer hold the near monopoly on ministerial education that they had just a few decades ago."[26] I think there is much to commend in this greater pluralization. ATS's flexibility enables schools to respond to the needs of more diverse communities. And institutions outside the ATS ecology are doing some of the most brave and faithful theological education happening today. Changing standards aren't necessarily leading to decline, but they are unraveling a model in which theological education functioned as professional education.

Further unravelings come from the neoliberal governmentality that makes it feel natural—and necessary—to treat education as an investment in the portfolio of oneself. These disciplinary drives push students and schools toward a "credentialism" in which having the certificate or degree is more important than the learning that takes place while getting it. In the language of an older Left, exchange value trumps use value.

Credentialism today drives at least two different dynamics, one more common at schools that depend on tuition and the other more common at schools with rich endowments of cultural and financial capital. Credentialism presses tuition-dependent schools to offer programs that strip away general professional formation for something more sharply vocational, even transactional. Students caught in this machinery need to get the credential that lets them get the job they want—and they want to get it with as little cost as possible. Schools trying to meet this demand feel pressure to reduce required hours, offer degrees online, cut costs by relying more on adjunct faculty, and more. Moves like these can make a kind of theological education more accessible. And accessibility matters for the sake of gospel justice. We might be able to imagine radically accessible forms of theological education that are *better* than professional education. But attempts to make the professional credential more accessible can end in a bruising race to the bottom that leaves the credential without much of the formation it used to mark.

Credentialism spurs different dynamics at schools that compete more for prestige than for tuition dollars. Historian of education David F. Labaree diagnoses a dynamic in which schools seeking elite status move away from vocational preparation and toward the learning-for-its-own-sake that is supposed to characterize the liberal arts. The rising importance of credentials in determining a person's position in today's winner-take-all job markets means that the status of the institution granting the degree is of great importance. This dynamic can be seen as Supreme Court justices come from a tiny number of maximally prestigious law schools and as senior pastors of large and wealthy mainline congregations and faculty with tenure-track jobs of any kind tend to come from more prestigious theological schools. Because greater status accrues to schools with more prestige, and because prestige within the academy attaches to the free, disinterested kinds of study associated with the liberal arts, education that minimizes attention to the actual practice of ministry ends up having greater exchange value in the employment markets students enter upon graduation. To risk candor: even if (or precisely because) an MDiv from a prestigious university divinity school does less to prepare a student for the actual practice of ministry, it might prove more useful in launching the student's career. Thus, Labaree argues, "Liberal education has succeeded in colonizing professional education, but credentialism has turned this liberal education back to vocational goals. The content is liberal, but credentialism means that the content doesn't really matter."[27] As this dialectic unfolds, professional education consumes itself.

Cynical accounts of the power of credentialism do not do justice to the full range of motives I meet in students and colleagues from many schools, nor do they offer a complete account of the little miracles that break out in classrooms with astonishing frequency. But these structural pressures are as present as the walls of the buildings in which we do our work. And they join a fun-house collision of other walls coming in from every angle to shrink the space in which the established model of theological education as professional education might find a place to stand.

A Different Jeremiah

The unravelings I have been describing unmake institutions, loosen ties between them, and snarl the meanings and purposes that animate them. They are general enough social conditions that they extend even to institutions and individuals that would resist them. They threaten the whole social imaginary of voluntary associations. That social imaginary has been so tightly linked to Christianity in the United States for the last two hundred years that its unraveling can feel like the end of the church. Reversing the changes and restoring the world of voluntary associations can seem like the most urgent task of faith. And the most common rhetorical form for that faith is the jeremiad: a narrative of decline and fall that culminates in a call to turn from sin and get back to the good old ways.[28]

More and less religious jeremiads have abounded in response to the unravelings of individualization. The greatest of these—

from thinkers like Wendell Berry, Alasdair MacIntyre, Stanley Hauerwas, and the team Robert Bellah assembled to write *Habits of the Heart*—have important insights. But some crucial misreadings of the present moment are built into the genre. As I argued in the previous chapter, it's not clear that we *can* turn from away from individualization to rebuild a lost world. The conditions that drive individualization have great power to co-opt denunciations as expressive identities. When Wendell Berry moved from Stanford, California, to Port Royal, Kentucky, he was not returning to the life of his great-grandparents. He chose his life there in ways they did not, and for reasons that would be difficult for them to imagine. His endless, glorious writing about that life makes clear the expressivism at the heart of that choice. Likewise, when a seminary promises formation in some ancient or medieval tradition, it is offering a particular kind of late modern identity. These can still be good and valuable options, but they don't escape the world in which we are required to choose between options as we piece ourselves together. We might make our own history, as Marx wrote, but we do not make it as we please. We make it under conditions we do not choose.[29]

Perhaps more deeply, the call to restore the kinds of community that flourished in the age of voluntary associations overlooks the idolatries that sustained that social world. Consider the everyday idolatries that run through stewardship seasons, capital campaigns, and ordinary-time invitations to give money. These appeals routinely conflate the congregation—or the denomination, or the school—with God. The request is to offer money to God; the check should be made out to the congregation. Or consider calls for volunteers who will do the Lord's work by sustaining the congregation. Of course, this work might be a response to the grace of God. The problem is not the work itself but that our rhetoric around this work leaves no daylight between serving the congregation and serving God. The conflations are not just rhetorical. Work in these voluntary associations is so meaningful because the associations themselves are charged with significance. Or, most insidiously, consider the thousands of decisions church leaders have made to value the voluntary association over the well-being of victims of sexual assault. The world of strong voluntary associations sacrificed children to the Moloch of the church's reputation. The crimes do not happen everywhere. But the idolatry does. The elevation of the association is a signature of the social imaginary.

The idolatry of this worldview extends beyond the voluntary associations to the nation-state that defines the larger society in which they have meaning. Charles Taylor points to the significance of belief in a providential role for the nation in the social imaginary of voluntary associations. In what Taylor dubs the Age of Mobilization or the neo-Durkheimian dispensation, people come together to create voluntary associations that are charged with significance as they are connected to some sacred national mission. In previous chapters I argued that leaders like Lyman Beecher made those connections plain, arguing that the seminary mattered because it trained the leaders of other associations, and those associations mattered because they would win the West for white Protestant America, and white Protestant America mattered because it would redeem the world. Echoes of that call to train leaders for institutions that will save the nation continue to sound through theological education. The chain of value at work is recognized not just with flags in sanctuaries and patriotic cant from the pulpit, but also in Christian speech that seeks to criticize, reform, and redeem the nation. In this worldview, congregations, denominations, and theological schools are important because they help save the nation's soul. And saving the nation's soul is so important because of the nation's sacred role. The chain of value connecting voluntary associations to a sacred nation operates even when it is not acknowledged, or acknowledged only indirectly, through critique. When that chain breaks—as it is breaking now—voluntary associations lose their aura. But we should not seek to restore that luster by reconnecting them to the refurbished idol of a sacred nation.[30]

The usual form of a jeremiad therefore will not do. Faithful prophets do not call people back to the altars of gods who are not

God. But what has become the standard form of a jeremiad has never done justice to the prophet Jeremiah. For Jeremiah does not just speak of some imagined, glorious past. He also speaks of the end.

The End

Therefore the Reign of God is not the *telos* of the historical dynamic; it cannot be set as a goal. From the standpoint of history it is not the goal, but the end.

Walter Benjamin, "Theological-Political Fragment" (1920–1921 or 1937–1938)

The unravelings of the last fifty years have created rolling crises for theological schools. It has been tempting for those of us committed to these schools and their missions to respond to unraveling with plans for better management. We (perhaps this particular first-person plural fits you, as it does me; if, by some grace, you have been exempted from this "we," then I ask your patience with my confession on our behalf) . . . we talk of enrollment numbers and funding models and relative position in various markets of money, students, faculty, and status. In moments of wider vision, we discuss long-term goals and mission statements. We might even, in Ron Heifetz's language, get off the dance floor to view the room from the balcony. These things matter. The work of a good manager deserves sincere respect. At a minimum, a good manager can help earthly goods to flourish. Even if these goods are not ultimate, they are real. The justice of our financial aid policies matters. Wise personnel decisions matter. Teaching in ways that help every student learn matters. Making payroll matters.

But I worry that our talk of managerial means is keeping us from conversations we need to have about the *ends* of theological education. When we concern ourselves with means, Thomas Merton wrote, we become "prisoners of every urgency. . . . Having lost our ability to see life as a whole, to evaluate conduct as a whole, we no longer have any relevant context into which our actions are to be fitted, and therefore all our actions become erratic, arbitrary, and insignificant."[1] We slip into the busy despair in which actions are means to other means in an endless regression that critical theorist Theodor Adorno called "manic pseudo-activity." I know this state from the inside. I know something of its cost. And so I have tried to frame this book in ways that hold it open to talk about the end. What is all this for? Why are we doing it? What are the ultimate ends of theological education?

This is an important but slippery set of questions. For the power of managerial logic in our time is so strong that it can permeate even what look like attempts to move beyond it. Church renewal literature sometimes borrows talk of BHAGs—big hairy audacious goals—a term coined in a classic *Harvard Business Review* article by James Collins and Jerry Porras for goals that involve "a huge, daunting challenge—such as climbing Mount Everest," or putting a man on the moon. BHAGs are audacious. But they are achievable. By us. In the horizon of history. As Collins and Porras write, "A true BHAG is clear and compelling, serves as a unifying point of effort, and acts as a catalyst for team spirit. It has a clear finish line, so the organization can know when it has achieved the goal; people like to shoot for finish lines."[2] A BHAG does not break managerial logic. It improves it. And many of the proposals for a goal or *telos* of theological education—whether in a book on the topic or the mission statement of a school—do not direct the school beyond the horizon of history. They still provide a finish line. Even if it is a mark we never quite reach, it is still the kind of thing to which we can aspire. These finish lines do not include ends that aren't even the *kinds* of things we could achieve, like the resurrection of the dead, a city so delivered from fear that its gates are always open, or saving knowledge of the living God. Instead, they offer big hairy audacious goals.

Managerial logic is wily. It can creep in even through language that seems theological. It surely infuses Lyman Beecher's hope that Lane might win the Mississippi watershed (and so the world!) for Christ. Downstream from Lane today, it might inform mission statements like "training leaders for Christ's church," "equipping prophets for God's justice," "raising up a generation of church planters," or, more subtly but no less surely, "forming faithful witnesses." All kinds of good things—like pastoral imagination, *theologia*, knowing God truly, to name some of the best recent candidates—can be inserted into the place of this goal. The problem is not with the content of the proposed goal. The problem is with the role into which it gets pressed in our thinking (a role that the authors of these terms might not intend). But when even these very good hopes get turned into big hairy audacious goals toward which we can manage institutions, then they have slipped from Christian hope into managementism, management made ideological, an end in itself. The problem is not the content of the goals but the temporal register in which they are considered. Such goals—even when they are dressed up in theological language—orient the institutions to the horizon of the immanent future. They propose the kinds of goods we could approach through curriculum reform, pedagogical workshops, diversity initiatives, and really vigorous five-year plans. But Christian hopes are not just goals. They live not in an immanent future but in an eschatological register that is both now and not yet.

We know how to design toward goals, even big goals. But what would it be like to think about theological education in this eschatological register, to see all our efforts as between the times, dependent on the victory of God's love that is present now, already accomplished, even as we yearn with all creation for a consummation of love that is not yet? The force of such questions cracks open the form of a theological essay, allowing a sermon to escape.

* * *

The days are surely coming, says the LORD, when I will make a
new covenant with the house of Israel and the house of Judah.
It will not be like the covenant that I made with their ancestors
when I took them by the hand to bring them out of the land
of Egypt—a covenant that they broke, though I was their hus-
band, says the LORD. But this is the covenant that I will make
with the house of Israel after those days, says the LORD: I will
put my law within them, and I will write it on their hearts; and
I will be their God, and they shall be my people. No longer
shall they teach one another, or say to each other, "Know the
LORD," for they shall all know me, from the least of them to
the greatest, says the LORD; for I will forgive their iniquity, and
remember their sin no more. (Jer. 31:31–34)[3]

Jeremiah's vision is not the telos of a long developmental process. It is not a goal, not even the biggest of goals. It is an end. It
is the end of theological education: "No longer shall they teach
one another, or say to each other, 'Know YHWH,' for they shall all
know me, from the least of them to the greatest, says YHWH."

The glory of this vision is in the details. God announces that
God will make this covenant—in God's own time, and for God's
own reasons. The people do not work their way there. God gives
them this knowledge out of loving covenant faithfulness. Speaking for God, Jeremiah says, "I will make a new covenant. . . . I will
put my law within them, and I will write it on their hearts." God is
the subject of every sentence that ends in redemption. God gives
people this knowledge because God desires to be known. And
God desires to be known because knowing and being known is
one dimension of what love is.

In case we miss the point, the prophet stresses not only the
agency of God but also the incapacity of humans. This is not because the people lack the cognitive capacities to think their way
there. The barrier is not mental ability in some simple sense; the
barrier, the prophet says, is sin. And because the sin is against
God, only God can forgive the sin. And it is the forgiveness of sin
that makes the intimate knowledge of the new covenant possible.

As verse 34 makes clear, for Jeremiah it is the forgiveness of sin, God's desire to reconcile us to Godself, even at great cost, that sets this whole process in motion. Sin keeps us from knowing God. God forgives sin, gives a new covenant. And this covenant bears fruit in the fulsome knowledge of God, knowledge so deep, so intimate, that it requires and accomplishes our transformation. We know, even as we are fully known, in the communion of divine love.

This knowledge of God has many dimensions. As Walter Brueggemann has argued, what the prophet describes as "knowing Yahweh" clearly has what we might call a cognitive dimension. In particular, it involves being able to recite the history of salvation. But it also has an affective dimension—it involves a disposition toward God, a fear of the Lord, a trust in the Lord, a deep assent to the lordship of God. And this knowledge has an ethical dimension. One could not know God in this way and fail to live by the Torah that God has inscribed in our hearts. Cognitive, affective, ethical—the knowledge of this new covenant is all-encompassing.[4]

God shares this knowledge with all, from the least to the greatest. Biblical scholars dispute whether "the least" here designates the smallest people—children—or the poorest and most marginal members of society. The question is interesting but not decisive. What is decisive is the "all" that governs this range. "They shall all know me." Whatever the end of theological education involves, it is not just expert knowledge for a select group of leaders. It is saving knowledge for all.

In Jeremiah's oracle, this knowledge is not a means to any other end. It does not even bring in the new covenant. It is the content of the covenant. It is the gift that God gives. It is not of instrumental value—not even for the saving of the world—for it is itself the very stuff of salvation. To know God is to be reconciled to God; to be reconciled to God is to know God, with all the cognitive, affective, and ethical dimensions that knowledge implies. And to know God is to be found in God—and so to be lost in wonder, love, and praise. This is not the means to some higher end. It is itself the end of all our hopes.

The end of our hopes is not the culmination of our efforts—not even as they might be supported by divine assistance. For the fulfillment of hope comes not with the perfection of teaching but with the end of teaching. "No longer shall they teach one another," God says through the prophet, "or say to each other, 'Know the LORD,' for they shall all know me, from the least of them to the greatest." Our efforts at theological education, then, do not approach the ideal asymptotically, getting closer and closer over time until finally God gives us a little boost to get us over the top. No. Jeremiah describes an end that is a real ending of all our teaching and learning. There is a meaningful discontinuity between effort and fulfillment.

The oracle therefore contains both negation and promise. It speaks a word of negation: our efforts to teach one another are not the means by which the covenant is fulfilled. The prophet's No shatters the diverse dreamscapes of our websites and the aspirational prose of our mission statements. Even our best hopes are not ultimate. The fulfillment of the covenant is not yet present in them. The oracle also makes a promise: even now the days are surely coming when all shall know God and be known by God, for this is what right relationship involves. God desires to be in right relationship with us, and God's desire—God's love—is stronger than all the powers that would defy it. That we have this hope shows that God is already keeping God's promise to be our teacher, even now. And this kept promise makes possible all the teaching and learning that we do in the meantime. Acknowledged or not, it runs through all our efforts. It lives in and in spite of distracted students, chattering professors, and classrooms whose maintenance has been deferred for decades. This angle of vision suggests a more intimate entanglement than even talk of treasure in earthen vessels, for our efforts at theological education are not just flawed containers that bear something precious. By the grace of God they are—in and in spite of our best efforts—made precious in themselves. And so we are called to relate to theological education as a fallen, fallible venture that is still illumined from within by God's promise to be known by all people. The light of that promise reveals both the failings and the glories of our work. It reveals both judgment and redemption. And it calls us to regard the theological school as a form into which we pour extraordinary effort as a sign of our hope for a promised day—O, great day!— when nothing like a theological school will be necessary, or even possible. That's not a BHAG. That's hope.

* * *

Christian hope hinges on an end that comes in the middle of the story. This can make it difficult to know how to go on. It makes impossible the postmillennial plans of Lyman Beecher and others who built theological schools designed to bring in the reign of God—or, in language that only seems more modest, make the world what God wants it to be. At its best, such instrumental reasoning posits a desired end and then devises theological education that helps attain that end. The end justifies the means, legitimating the institutions we create. But if the end has already come, what form should practical reasoning take? And if the end for which we long is not the perfection of our teaching but the cessation of our teaching, how can it inform our teaching? And why should we even try to teach in the meantime?

A better account of Christian practical reasoning begins not with our actions but with God's. It begins with the trust that even now God is loving the world back to right relation. This is not a smooth and simple process. It is met with violence, resistance, and rejection. But God meets rejections of love with a willingness to keep loving, even at mortal cost to God's own self. In meeting violence with love-shaped patience, God refuses the terms of engagement defined by sin and death. And so the love of God opens into a fullness of joy that is both more and less than mere victory.

Because we give so much of our lives to powers of sin and death, because we receive so much of what we call our lives from them, we often experience this joy as judgment. It meets us as a kind of negation, a negation not only of the imperfect actuality of our lives and institutions but also of the ideals to which we aspire. This negation is not an abstract declaration of the infinite distance between God and all that is not God. Such abstract claims leave no room for the image of God, marred but enduring in created life. They cannot describe a Creator who sustains the world, a Word that became incarnate in the world, or a Spirit who groans with the world with sighs too deep for words. Nor can they dream of a God who chooses to commune with us in and in spite of everyday commodities of bread, wine, water, and words.[5] Any meaningful sense of connection between God and the lives we live in history becomes unthinkable when negation is abstract.

The love of God performs instead a more *determinate* negation. Like a refiner's fire, it is differential in its effects. It consumes the power of sin and death to determine responses to love. It leaves behind—and so creates anew—creation that can respond to love with love. Because a response of love can only come from a place of deepest freedom, the love of God does not dictate the shape of free response.

As Acts 16 tells the story, the love of God is like an earthquake that shakes the foundations of an imperial prison. It breaks the chains and opens the doors. It makes freedom possible. But this is not the shapeless freedom to do "whatever" that would come from abstract negation. For it is not just any walls, or walls in general, that have been broken. The earthquake breaks the walls of a prison holding apostles—people who have been sent—who healed enslaved people in ways that set them free. When *those* walls come down, the collapse makes it possible for the apostles to take up that work again. The collapse of the walls does not dictate how or where the formerly incarcerated do that work. They might even stay where they are, as Paul and Silas do, resuming their healing, liberatory work in the ruins of the prison itself. Such is the freedom given in the determinate negations of divine love.[6]

Christian practical reasoning begins with discernment of the particular walls that the love of God has torn down. It begins with

a discernment of divine negation, and so of the shape of our freedom to respond. Living into that freedom involves *renunciation*, a
loosening of our hold on the powers whose grip on us God has already broken. The Bible is full of memories of renunciations. As
Exodus tells the story, God heard the cry of the children of Israel
and delivered them from slavery. Their saying yes to that freedom
involved renouncing the bread and fleshpots that slavery once
provided. So, too, the Gospels remember how Jesus looked with
love on a rich young ruler who came asking earnest questions.
Jesus invited the young man to follow him and promised him
treasure in heaven. He called the rich young ruler to sell what he
had and give the proceeds to the poor. Giving everything away
was not a means to the end of some greater treasure, like the
capitalist ascesis of an investment, but simply the first step along
the journey with Jesus that was itself the treasure. Because the
young man would not make this renunciation, he could not live
into the freedom Jesus's love opened for him.

Stories of renunciations made and not made roll on through
the centuries. They are each particular, concrete. For we are not
called to renounce everything in general. We are called to renounce that from which the love of God has delivered us. We are
called to renounce that which we need to leave behind to walk
with the one who set us free. Christian practical reasoning begins
with discerning these renunciations, tracing the contours of the
determinate negations of divine love.

In our time, there is no work more urgent than the renunciation of the white settler colonial project that was intertwined with
the justification for a whole network of voluntary associations
and the seminaries—like Lane—that would train their leaders.
That project has already been revealed as a lie. Its legitimacy has
already ended, even if too many of us continue to live as if it were
eternal. Renunciation is just our leaving behind of this world that
is already dead. For those of us who identify as white, renunciation involves long processes of telling the truth, relinquishing
power, and making reparations. But the work of renouncing the
project of a righteous white Christian America that will save the

world is not limited to those who have been most privileged by its formations. Vincent Lloyd calls the Black church to practices of "severing relationships and divesting capital, most importantly social capital."[7] And Tina Campt draws on Black experiences to define practices of "refusal" that involve "a rejection of the status quo as livable and the creation of possibility in the face of negation, i.e., a refusal to recognize a system that renders you fundamentally illegible and unintelligible; the decision to reject the terms of diminished subjecthood with which one is presented." This kind of renunciation becomes, Campt writes, "a generative and creative source of disorderly power to embrace the possibility of living otherwise."[8] Renouncing the power of the settler colonial project to animate a network of voluntary associations and infuse theological education with meaning opens up a new set of possibilities. It does not set us free to do anything at all, for much of what we might do—even in the name of antiracism—would only rebuild the very structures we say we have renounced. Real renunciation sets us free for teaching and learning otherwise. This is where any serious reimagining of theological education must begin.

In renunciation we acknowledge the determinate negation that the love of God has already accomplished. We relinquish our holds on that which does not give life. This frees our hands to take hold of *affordances* in the times and places in which we find ourselves. In speaking of affordances, I mean to describe historically contingent contours of institutions, beliefs, and practices. Like the cracks and crags of a cliff face, affordances have specific forms. But their forms do not dictate how we use them. Seeing a small knob of rock, for instance, we might grab hold of it with a hand, push off it with a foot, swing over it, use it to navigate, or even find ways to move past it as if it were not there. Affordances have a determinate shape, but they do not determine what we make of them.

Affordances arise in time. They are subject to social forces, worked and reworked by human hands, and weathered by contingencies of every kind. They can be relatively benign, readily available for all kinds of useful moves. They can also be scarred by sin. Affordances formed in violence can be treacherous, but they can also—even at the same time—offer handholds for faithful response. Even structures of domination have seams and self-contradictions that offer affordances for those with eyes to see.

We take hold of affordances trusting that God is creative and persistent, always finding ways to offer love to us, always opening anew the possibility of faithful response. But such faith does not suggest that affordances are simple and straightforward provisions of Providence, divinely given resources that are purpose-built for faithful use. Such a vision does too much to flatter the powers of this world. Not everything that offers some affordance is automatically aligned with God's hopes for the world. Such a vision misses the deep ambivalence of what affordances make available to us. They come from mixed sources. They can be used for good or evil or nothing much at all. They can cut our hands even as we make grateful use of them. We can try to use them and fail. The affordances I mean to describe are less like pennies from heaven and more like a crazy king who would kill to find someone who can interpret his dreams. In his violent madness the king creates a handhold by which the people can be saved and God's faithfulness can be displayed. But this does not mean that God appoints the king or underwrites his power. Affordances might also be found in a historically white seminary that starts to recruit students from minoritized groups in earnest when the number of white students who want to enroll is not enough to support the vocations of a mostly white faculty. We don't have to call this an unmitigated good to say that there might be hand-holds here for faithful response. Just so, a seemingly secular age might hollow out spaces of yearning in individuals in which new forms of theological education can take root. But this does not mean that we should accept those yearnings uncritically or conform to the self-understandings of our age. It means that when we try to respond in our time—for we cannot turn the clock back to another—we have things to work with.

Discourses on theological education often posit some time-less norm and then try to describe how it might be applied in the present. But God enters history not with a blueprint for our buildings but with a cross that cleaves the ground on which they stand. Christian practical reasoning does not try to apply a norm. Instead, it involves discerning the work God's love has done, renouncing the powers God's love has undone, and finding affordances that might be used in free and faithful responses. We do not marshal affordances to build a new temple, for they do not fit together in such grand ways. Besides, in the city for which we yearn, there is no temple, for the Lord God Almighty and the Lamb are its temple. Instead we put the pieces together to build tabernacles, portable shelters for our sojourns in the desert of the meantime. And God meets us there.

4

Renunciations

Renunciation—is a piercing Virtue—
The letting go
A Presence—for an Expectation—

Emily Dickinson,
"Renunciation—is a piercing Virtue"
(1863)

The story of the last forty years at Broadway United Methodist Church in Indianapolis starts like many others. Broadway was a historic congregation with an overwhelmingly white membership that had once been one of the most distinguished voluntary societies in the region. As the tides of the city shifted—churned by white flight and pulled, always, by the moon of racism in real estate markets—the neighborhood around Broadway became poorer and Blacker. White members found reasons to drift away, and neither people from the neighborhood nor people from around the city found many reasons to join, bringing processes of unraveling to Broadway even before they reached other voluntary associations. The established way of being a congregation was becoming unsustainable.

But then, in fits and starts, the story took a turn. Mike Mather, the pastor, first tried to shape the congregation as a voluntary society that would serve the neighborhood. This produced no systemic change, scant goodwill from the community, few new members, and many burned-out volunteers. After some time serving another congregation, Mather returned to Broadway. He did not know what the congregation needed to be, but he knew it could not be an enlightened, service-oriented version of what it once had been. The congregation decided to start paying attention to their neighbors neither as potential members of their church nor as potential clients of their service ministries, but as people among whom God was already at work. Lay leader De'Amon Harges inaugurated the role of "roving listener," going house by house through the neighborhood and holding open the question, "Where is the abundance lying in each house, in each block?" He knew that divine abundance was there, he said. "All I had to do was bear witness to it."[1]

That work of discerning what God was already doing involved listening, discovery, wonder, and thanksgiving. It also involved renunciation. Harges and Mather saw that the congregation had ministries, committees, and projects—whole ways of being— that it had to let go in order to grasp anything new. The ministries had been sources of meaning, assistance, even transformation. But trying to continue them now, under these transformed conditions, drained the people trying to sustain them and did little good for anyone else. Moreover, it kept the congregation and the neighborhood from living into the life abundant already within and around them. But it isn't easy to let go of ministries that fit with the ways we see the world and understand ourselves. As Harges remembers the story, there was a clear need for the congregation to grieve the closure of these ministries. And so the congregation took time in worship to grieve together, remembering what had been done and saying of each ministry, "Well done, good and faithful servant."[2]

The benediction was generous in the ways that reflect the hopes we bring to funerals. Of course the ministries had done good. Of course they had expressed and nurtured the faith of the servants involved. Of course they had brought people together. And of course they had also been streaked with racism, paternalism, and the everyday pettiness of congregational life. But in renouncing them, releasing the congregation's hold on them and their hold on the congregation, the congregation trusted them to the mercy of God, who makes good and faithful servants even of tax collectors for the empire. And so in renunciation they spoke a benediction not in praise of what they renounced but in praise of the God who redeems.

CONCRETE RENUNCIATIONS

In the sermon I argued that what had to be renounced was the white settler colonial project that animated the network of voluntary associations in which the theological school took shape as a professional school. It is tempting to think that our renunciations should be offered in a final and total sense. But that drive to total renunciation depends on abstractions, like giving up sin-in-general for Lent. And abstract renunciations too often tip into virtue signaling with little real content. They also tend to miss the ways racialized violence is woven through every aspect of an institution's life, and the ways it can return even in actions and statements meant to reject it. Racism and settler colonialism cannot be reduced to discrete items on a checklist of things we should renounce. They rather live in and across a thick tangle of historical forms. We have to attend to their presence in these forms and renounce them, again and again, in all their historical particularity. And we have to be mindful of the ways they can regenerate, like a hydra's head, even in our best efforts at renunciation.

Renunciation is not an abstract declaration but a concrete letting go of what determinate negation has negated. In the context of this book, I want to ask what it would mean to renounce the model for theological education that Lyman Beecher sketched as he made the case for Lane Theological Seminary, the model that consolidated a central position as part of a dominant constellation, the model that promised to train leaders for religious-ish voluntary associations for the redemption of a white Christian America that would go on to play a central role in redeeming the world. Simply naming this model precisely begins to reveal the racist and settler ethos that animates it. Accurate description opens the most important lines of critique. But critique does not exhaust adequate description, especially when offered in the grief, penitence, and hope of a final blessing. I have also tried to describe this model's role in the abolition of slavery and the establishment of democratic habits and institutions. And I can speak of it only in the implicated, complicated relationship that I have to it as my hometown, my native country, a land that has formed me so thoroughly that its soil is mingled with my flesh.

Processes of neoliberal individualization have torn through this land like Cyrus, subduing nations and stripping kings of their armor. They break yokes of oppressive orders even as they destroy beautiful, valuable, and sacred things. The Cyruses of individualization are not identical to the redeeming work of God. Their rampage is no story of the reign of God progressively realizing itself in history. The reign of God is rather like a seed growing secretly in and in spite of this wreckage. And so we do not worship Cyrus, and we do not welcome individualization as the herald of a new age of autonomous free expression. We simply reckon with the ambivalent terrain that its earthly conquest has shaped.

Part of that reckoning involves renouncing the professional model for theological education that arose as part of the constellation of voluntary associations that individualization has unraveled. What I am calling the professional model for theological education is related to the "clerical paradigm" Edward Farley critiqued in *Theologia*, his landmark 1983 book on theological education.[3] I use language of "professional" rather than "clerical" to expand the circle of reflection beyond intrachurch relations. I want to keep the wider social, racial, economic, and political dynamics in view. I also want to press toward a more fully material analysis that points to a more local and American genealogy than Farley's more idealist and more European narrative. But the deepest difference in our analyses is temporal. In the 1980s and '90s, Farley called teachers, students, and schools to leave the clerical paradigm behind. Despite the power of his argument, few did. But now the professional model is unraveling beneath us, around us, and within us, however we feel about it. The task before us now is not reform but renunciation.

Renunciation does not depend on critique of the model in its best form; it simply refuses to do all that would be required to continue an unraveled model under present conditions. Critical theorist Theodor Adorno describes the need for renunciation:

> Nothing is more degenerate than the kind of ethics or morality that survives in the shape of collective ideas even after the World Spirit has ceased to inhabit them—to use the Hegelian expression as a kind of shorthand. Once the state of human consciousness and the state of social forces of production have abandoned these collective ideas, these ideas acquire repressive and violent qualities. And what forces philosophy into the kind of reflections that we are expressing here is the element of compulsion which is to be found in traditional customs; it is this violence and evil that brings these customs [Sitten] into conflict with morality [Sittlichkeit]—and not the decline of morals of the kind lamented by the theoreticians of decadence.[4]

An unraveling social order creates a booming job market for theoreticians of decadence. Their narratives of decline give us ways to think about the losses we see all around us. They let us blame others and ourselves. And, crucially, they hold out the promise that we could reverse the changes with rigor and effort. But the signature of the present moment in theological education is not spiritual, moral, or intellectual laxity. It is rather the exertion of extraordinary effort to live in established forms and according to established norms even after those forms and norms have been hollowed out by changes in social life. The sign of our times is the effort to sustain undead forms with living bodies, hopes, and resources. This vampire dynamic is what we are called to renounce: not the professional model as we might remember it, at its strongest and its best, but the professional model as we encounter it now, hollowed out and hungry.

The nature of renunciation becomes clearer through contrast with three kinds of changes that do not renounce the existing model but seek to sustain it: sacrifices, rationalizations, and pluralizations. Any change can involve some loss, but the strategy I want to highlight as *sacrifice* converts things like endowments, land, buildings, air rights, and library holdings into funds that can sustain the existing model, at least for a time. These sacrifices can be painful for seminary communities. And they may be prudent, especially in the short run. They may buy a school enough time to discern next faithful steps. They might even fund the first of those next steps. But by themselves they should not be confused with renunciations of the professional model. They are often the opposite: a commitment to the existing model that is so strong that cherished parts of the community's life are sacrificed to sustain it.

So, too, *rationalizing* reforms like reducing degree requirements, offering programs online, and shifting to adjunct, part-time, and other contingent faculty do not necessarily renounce the basic structures of the professional model. They tend to push toward leaner, more efficient versions of it. In describing these reforms as rationalizing, I do not mean to stress a generic reasonableness. I use the term more as sociologist Max Weber did, naming a process of streamlining an institution's existence toward the values that are its goal. Again, these decisions can be painful. And they may land somewhere between necessary evils and positive goods—a space familiar to prudent managers. But neither their painfulness nor their prudence should lead us to confuse rationalizations with renunciation.

Changes that *pluralize* the people served or the positions for which the school prepares them can bring significant changes to a school. But these, too, do not necessarily break with the professional model. Enrolling students from more denominations, regions, nations, or racial/ethnic groups to prepare them for ministry is still working within the same familiar logic. Pluralizing the identities of people who enter does not automatically transform the model through which they travel. So, too, preparing people for work beyond congregational ministry—even beyond *any* kind of ministry—pluralizes but does not renounce the model that forms them as professionals. More kinds of people can be prepared for more kinds of service without transformation of a model that is defined by a *telos* of preparing people for professional leadership in service organizations that contribute to the common good. Like the sacrificial conversion of campuses to operating expenses, and like the rationalization of systems to offer professional formation more efficiently, pluralization of students and professions usually still operates within the professional model. These may be shrewd steps, at least for the time being, and at least in some cases—the kinds of things that let a school continue to employ people as it waits for God's call. But waiting on the Lord involves not just keeping the doors open but also making renunciations. And renunciations will operate at deeper levels.

PROFESSIONAL STATUS

As I tried to show in chapter 2, professions like ministry, law, and medicine consolidated as a new middle class late in the nineteenth century and early in the twentieth. Industrialization, urbanization, and new concentrations of capital swept away an older middle class of artisans, shopkeepers, and, eventually, farmers who worked land that they owned. In this new political economy, the professions staked out space that was neither labor nor capital. As Barbara Ehrenreich and John Ehrenreich argued in a 1977 article, this new "professional-managerial class" was distinguished not only by its social location between labor and capital but also by a shared social *function*. Early professionals applied the scientific and managerial reasoning cultivated in the worlds of research and manufacturing to the work of social and cultural reproduction. Professions consolidated around all the core tasks of social and cultural reproduction: education, child rearing, health, hygiene, nutrition, the arts, public opinion, the pursuit of justice, and more. In addition to the professions that arose to guide life beyond the workplace, professionalized managers came to play more important roles within the workplace. They first sought to shape the motions of employees toward efficiency, and then, as production shifted from manufacturing to services, they sought to shape the affective lives of employees toward likability, sincere care, customer service, and team spirit. As the management of consumption grew in importance, advertising and public relations professionals arose to work in this space, attempting to shape even the reproduction of taste and desire. Culture went from something people had and made to something that professionals in a culture industry made for us and marketed to us. All of this work, the Ehrenreichs wrote, played a significant role in the long-run stability of the American political economy.[5]

Standing apart from both capital and labor put the emerging professional class in what Barbara Ehrenreich has named an "objectively antagonistic" relationship with both.[6] Professionals' tensions with an ownership class showed up in the muckraking journalism that challenged monopolies and exposed methods of production that were hazards to employees and consumers alike. They flowed through the Progressive movement that was an early political expression of this class, the Social Gospel that was its native faith, and the settlement houses that were its iconic institutions. But if professionals often found themselves advocating for poor and working people, their social location put them in antagonistic relations with those they were trying to reform. Managing cultural reproduction meant telling poor and working people how to conduct themselves in every part of their lives, including how to raise children, how to eat, how to care for their bodies, and what they should and should not enjoy. Moreover, the role of *managing* cultural reproduction meant distinguishing oneself from those one was charged with managing. That not every professional acted in these ways does not change the larger pattern that emerged. The basic structure of this relationship has tended to produce a complex, layered pattern in which poor and working-class people regard professionals with a mixture of resentment and respect, even as professionals regard their clients with a mixture of sympathy, care, contempt, and paternalism.

All these class dynamics were intensified in their entanglements with patterns of racialization. Professionalization linked up with constructions of idealized whiteness as white professionals defined themselves in relations with Black people they framed as needing reform.[7] At the same time, professional status, membership in voluntary associations, and respectability came together in a tight cluster for some Black professionals in this period. That cluster reproduced class divisions within Black communities even as it provided for upward mobility, meaningful community service, and social networks that served as bases for movements against lynching and for civil rights.[8]

Of course, individual relations on the ground have always been more complex, both for better and for worse. But—as most of us who provide or receive professionalized social services know in our bones—the Ehrenreichs are right to name a certain antagonism that is built into the relations between professionals and the people professionals seek to help. And that antagonism extends to the most basic stuff of life, as management of cultural and social reproduction crosses into homes, intimate relations, and bodies. "Thus," the Ehrenreichs argue, "the possibility exists in the professional-managerial class for the emergence of what may at first sight seem to be a contradiction in terms: anti–working class radicalism."[9]

The Ehrenreichs' analysis extends with uncomfortable insight to professionalized ministers serving in congregations and other voluntary associations that share in the denominational ethos. It's not just the groups from which these congregations draw their membership (it is only a small distortion to say that mainline Protestantism took shape as the professional-managerial class at prayer). It is that the ministers themselves are formed for this professional version of their vocation. Professional ministers—like professional teachers, lawyers, physicians, home economists, social workers, and more—manage social and cultural reproduction. In particular, we manage the religious beliefs and practices of people in ways that direct them toward the flourishing of voluntary societies that in turn promote the reform of a nation invested with exceptional significance. We might, for instance, retain practices like ecstatic speech so long as they can be fitted into a narrative in which they produce some good like individual agency or democratic politics. We might steer people away from observing Lent by wearing a devotional scapular and toward a Lent marked by acts of community service. We might stress parts of our own traditions that give us reasons for respecting the faith of people from different traditions, thereby strengthening and expanding the denominational ethos. As experts in spiritual and associational life, professionalized ministers domesticate religious energies and make them compatible with enlightened citizenship. We manage our part of cultural reproduction in ways that align with the efforts of other professionals, often in explicit partnerships.

Professionalization pulls ministers into the politics and everyday relationships of other members of the professional-managerial class. "Anti–working class radicalism" has been an all-too-apt description of the politics baked into professional ministry since the latter part of the nineteenth century, when professionalizing ministers joined with other Progressives in the Social Gospel movement. Instead of a politics focused on solidarity and redistribution, we join other members of the professional-managerial class in advocacy for others who remain others. Instead of the messy work of democratic politics, we seek to turn expertized, Christian-inflected morality into policy. (The discipline of Christian ethics has many roots, but one of the most important is as the research arm of this kind of professional politics.) These overt, large-scale politics are reproduced implicitly in everyday interactions, as professional ministers both genuinely serve and seek to reform poor and working-class people. The ambivalence of these efforts is met with the ambivalent mixture of admiration, resentment, gratitude, and resistance that people rendered as clients offer even the best professionals. All of us caught in these structures, on every side, may strain against them. We may even find ourselves lifted out of them, in little miracles of divine love. But these experiences of grace are so powerful precisely because of the enduring power of the structures of the professionalized relationships from which we have been delivered.

The nature of these antagonisms becomes clearer as we attend to the ways professional knowledge is tied to professional status. As Barbara Ehrenreich said in a 2019 interview, the professional-managerial class comes into existence through "the expropriation of the skills and culture once indigenous to the working class."[10] "Client" populations might have thought they knew how to do things like prepare food, raise children, make music, and care for one another's bodies and souls, but the professional dynamic discounts this knowledge and insists that others know better. Contemporary theorists Fred Moten and Stefano Harney describe this as one more version of the primitive enclosure that is a hallmark of settler colonialism: "It is therefore unwise to think of professionalization as a narrowing and better to think of it as a circling, an encircling of war wagons around the last camp of indigenous women and children. Think about the way the American doctor or lawyer regard themselves as educated, enclosed in the state's encyclopedia, though they may know nothing of philosophy or history."[11]

The process of professionalization draws a circle around some body of knowledge, charges it with status, and then anoints a select group as its authoritative interpreters. It is not just specialization but a transformation of the commons of shared intergenerational wisdom into private property.

The structures of professional theological education reproduce a version of this dynamic. In the wild, contested commons of the work of the Holy Spirit, the professional school draws a circle around a very particular kind of knowledge, insists that this is the kind of knowledge that really matters, establishes the school itself as the authoritative interpreter of that knowledge, and then confers authority on those who meet its standards. In drawing the circle that defines meaningful knowledge, the school renders knowledge beyond the circle as irrelevant or misguided. It is not too much to say that the professional school *produces* ignorance. Its first lesson, as social critic Ivan Illich writes, is "the need to be taught." Even if a school grants credits for competency attained outside the school, it continues in the role of arbiter, and so perpetuates the deeper dynamic. The school then invests those it certifies with status that marks their membership in a professional-managerial class.

Consider the ways a professional model of theological education tends to regard the knowledge students bring with them. Knowledge that can be assimilated to the paradigm of a professional school—like the ability to write an academic paper or the insight gained from managing a nonprofit—might be recognized, valued, and extended. But other kinds of knowledge—like having Bible verses memorized, being able to play "nothing music" on a Hammond B3, knowing how exactly to hold the hand of someone you're praying with, or having gifts for discerning movements of the Holy Spirit—tend to be ignored as irrelevant, consigned to "extracurricular" activities, or rejected as problematic.[12]

This production of professionalized knowledge has interacted in complex ways with race and class over the years. It is not just that theological schools accredited as professional schools have historically drawn their students from the class of people who have bachelor's degrees—already a select group—but that the process of theological education as professional education promises to confer a kind of status in itself. As Glenn T. Miller has pointed out, until relatively recently, when a high school wanted a pastor to pray at the baccalaureate service, it usually asked a pastor with a professional degree from an ATS-accredited school. Professional education has both reflected and conferred status, and not only for individual ministers. For more than two centuries, American religious movements have marked their own upward mobility by requiring professional education of their clergy.

This status was never just a matter of book learning. It has also been inculcated into the bodily lives of students. Samuel Miller, one of the first faculty members of Princeton Theological Seminary, published a manual of clerical manners and habits in 1827 to help students behave in a manner commensurate with their emerging professional status. It was not enough to know theology, Miller wrote. Graduates had to be able to comport themselves like professionals, "in conformity to those habits of propriety and delicacy which are commonly established in cultivated society."[13] Miller's book promised to show graduates how to display their new status in their bodies, instruction that became more subtle but no less present in later decades. As professional schools, theological schools put a stamp of respectability in the flesh of their graduates that radiated out into the communities they served. They conferred not only knowledge but also status.

Habits of the professionalized body and mind have too often taken whiteness as their norm. Carter G. Woodson traced this process at work decades ago, in the wake of the Flexner Report and parallel professionalizing efforts in theological schools. In *The Mis-Education of the Negro* (1933), he critiqued schools of theology in which "Negroes are taught the interpretation of the Bible worked out by those who have justified segregation and winked at the economic debasement of the Negro sometimes almost to the point of starvation." Pastors educated in these schools derived their "sense of right" from this professional education that was overdetermined by whiteness.[14] This left them alienated from the communities they were called to serve, with little to offer besides whatever worldly status might come from proximity to their credentials. Woodson described one preacher who "had studied the philosophical basis of the Caucasian dogma, the elements of that theology, and the schism by which fanatics made religion a football and multiplied wars only to moisten the soil of Europe with the blood of unoffending men." But, Woodson wrote, this preacher "had given no attention to the religious background of the Negroes to whom he was trying to preach. He knew nothing of their spiritual endowment and their religious experience as influenced by their traditions and environment in which the religion of the Negro has developed and expressed itself." All such knowledge was outside the enclosure drawn by settler professionalism. The preacher knew nothing of it—or had learned not to value it—and so the people "knew nothing additional when he had finished his discourse."[15]

The deepest problems with this dynamic cannot be solved simply by sprinkling more diverse authors into syllabi. Even readings that are diverse in many ways can be pulled within the circle and turned into professional knowledge that marks distinctions in status. So, too, the dynamic cannot be undone simply by diversifying faculty and student bodies, as essential as those tasks are. As Woodson saw—and as books in this series by Keri Day and Willie James Jennings diagnose for today—the powers of professionalized whiteness are not simply a matter of demographics.[16] Even with a more diverse academy, whiteness can continue to overdetermine what counts as "academic," "professional," "rigorous," "brilliant," and other qualities that name the boundaries of the enclosure. Real renunciation will have to go deeper, to the heart of the process that promises that mastery of some particular body of knowledge justifies the distinction of professional status.

Jesuit philosopher, theologian, and martyr Ignacio Ellacuría made this kind of renunciation in the vision he offered as rector of the Universidad Centroamericana in San Salvador (UCA). Ellacuría argued that the university should find its life and purpose in relation to a world-historical struggle for justice for "the poor majority." "The most striking consequence" of this orientation, he wrote, "is that it negates the notion that the main objective of the university is to train professional people."[17] Ellacuría valued the healing, teaching, and building work professionals might do. But he worried that simply restocking a professional class with new members would not bring the systemic change that the poor majority needed. He rejected what historian and theologian Justo González has called the "trickle down" theory of social change: the idea that training a professional class with progressive ideals could bring real transformation. Even if the new professionals came from poor backgrounds, Ellacuría argued, the change would be individualized—privatized—rather than structural.[18]

Ellacuría insisted that renouncing education for professional status did not involve renouncing rigor. If anything, he argued, simply training people to lead existing institutions was the less demanding path. The task of structural transformation was more difficult, requiring critical analysis and real innovation. It "requires as much academic excellence as possible," he wrote, "for otherwise we would have little to contribute as intellectuals to such complex problems."[19]

As Ellacuría saw, renouncing professional status need not tip us into know-nothing populism. And it need not do away with all distinctions, treating wise people as if they were fools or dissolving differences between teachers and students. A more determinate negation calls for more specific renunciation. Renouncing the professional model involves disentangling theological learning from the specific kinds of social, economic, and political status that come with being a professional. It pushes us to reimagine theological study as a process that does not depend on differentiating graduates from poor, working-class, and minoritized communities. Differentiation in status generates alienation, both in relationships and within graduates' own selves. Renouncing professional status lets us dream of theological education that does not alienate students from communities that formed them and communities they are called to serve, but instead draws them more deeply into the lives of those communities.

That work is especially urgent now, when whatever professional status theological education can confer is eroding beneath our feet. We might try to shore up this status with more and more frantic attempts to perform it: More rigor! Higher standards! A tighter circle of what counts as knowledge! Or, more subtly: Incorporate awareness of the old exclusions into a new legitimation of professional status! Make fluency in the languages of movements for justice into the new shibboleth that distinguishes true professionals from those who need their help! But such attempts will only do violence to ourselves, our students, and the self-emptying, status-renouncing God we claim as both our Teacher and the living Word we teach. They will not undo the injustice and resentment that status differentiation brings. Ironically, they also will not secure professional status in any part of the wider ecology of theological education. They will not make ministers more like the imagined exemplars of professionalism: the autonomous, respected, wealthy-enough, common-good-seeking attorneys and physicians of yesteryear. Nor will they slow the steady deprofessionalization of academic labor, even for those of us who cling to tenured and tenure-track positions. When tenure is a rarity, rather than the norm, it no longer provides the kind of shelter from the market that sustains an autonomous profession. It becomes instead a perk that schools might offer as they compete for employees in a labor market that generates massive inequalities. "Raising" or changing the standards for what counts as a professional will not transform these underlying dynamics.

What if we stopped trying to defend the professional enclosure of theological wisdom and the status it once conferred? What might knowledge of God be if it were freed from the demand that it be a subject we can master to display our distinction from other people in the crowd around Jesus?[20] What new and renewed genres for declaring the goodness of God might open to us if they did not have to conform to the norms of professional respectability? What motives might be unlocked in students (and teachers!) if schools offered no promises that diplomas were tickets to middle-class respectability? How might we move as bodies, even in the act of study? Who might take up theological study if it were unhooked from formation for even the most expansive sense of professional ministry? What institutional forms could centers of theological study take if they did not have to squeeze themselves into the mold of a professional school? What could theological education be if we gave up the idea that it could mark entry into a professional class?

CHAPTER 4

PROFESSIONAL DEBT

In the logic of professional education, it can make sense to go into debt to acquire a credential that serves as a ticket to financial security, meaningful work, and relative autonomy. Educational debt gets classified with housing debt as "good debt," the kind of debt that even smart, disciplined, thrifty people take on as part of their entry into the middle class. Credit cards may lead us to pour money down the drain like so many of the lattes we are not supposed to buy. But student loans are investments in our future that promise life-transforming returns.

This kind of reasoning has helped to justify the rivers of debt on which theological education has floated since individualization began to unravel the ecology of voluntary associations in which professional education was sustainable. The debt begins to accumulate even before students arrive in postbaccalaureate theological schools. Students who borrowed money to pay for education in ATS schools in 2019–2020 each carried an average of $32,642 in debt before they even started to pay for their theological education, an amount that has increased more than 10 percent since 2013.[21] Of course, this debt is not the fault of any individual theological school. It wasn't incurred for payments to any seminary. But when the whole system positions theological education as postbaccalaureate professional education, it structures incentives for students to take on this kind of debt as part of their educational journeys to professional leadership.

Debt continues to pile up for many students while they are enrolled in theological schools. ATS data shows that in 2019–2020 students who borrowed incurred an average of $33,532 in debt over the course of their theological studies. The average for all students—borrowers and nonborrowers alike—is lower, at $14,195. These numbers have been trending modestly downward in the last decade, probably due to cheaper online offerings and a Lilly Endowment–funded initiative to raise awareness and encourage students to minimize borrowing. Some individual schools have taken significant initiatives to reduce debt for their students.[22] But the numbers point to a major issue, with more than 49 percent of MDiv students incurring at least some debt during their theological studies. It is not too much to say that the professional model of theological education has evolved to *depend* on student debt.

The problems become more acute because of inequities in the distribution of debt. In 2019–2020, student borrowers who identified as white and non-Hispanic incurred the lowest average levels of debt while in seminary ($31,200). Student borrowers who identified as Asian and Pacific Islander borrowed a little more ($31,900), and student borrowers who identified as Hispanic/Latino(a) took on even more ($34,000 average). The highest average debts were incurred by student borrowers who identified as Native North American ($42,700) and Black and non-Hispanic ($42,700). Similarly, women in 2019–2020 were more likely than men to take out student loans while in seminary and left seminary with higher average levels of debt. The burden of debt falls heavily on all kinds of students. But it falls especially heavily on students from minoritized communities and on women—groups who already bear the costs of systemic injustice and who are more likely to face discrimination upon graduation.[23]

Heavy and unevenly distributed burdens of debt are not peculiar to theological education but are part of wider processes of individualization that transfer risk from societies, corporations, and institutions to individuals. As state and federal governments cut funding for higher education, more of the costs of college fall to students and their families. And as denominations, congregations, and other church bodies pull back funding for theological schools, costs of theological education have shifted to students. At the same time, in a closely linked parallel, "opportunities" for borrowing have expanded. Italian theorist Maurizio Lazzarato summed up the dynamics, arguing that "Student indebtedness exemplifies neoliberalism's strategy since the 1970s: the substitution of social rights (the right to education, health care, retirement, etc.) for access to credit, in other words, for the right to contract debt."[24] Student debt is therefore not a problem peculiar to theological schools, and some of its strongest drivers originate far beyond the sphere of theological education. It is part of a larger dynamic that tells students, "You're on your own." It is a sign of these YOYO times.

The financialization of debt has supercharged this underlying dynamic. Debts of every kind—including mortgages, student loans, commercial real-estate loans, credit card debt, municipal debt, and more—are now converted into securities and then traded in speculative markets. More than a third of all student loan debts in the United States have been securitized in these ways.[25] Securitization lets debt generate profits not only as interest is repaid but also as bundling and transformation into a security create value, and as the prices of these debts-made-securities rise and fall. As debt gets converted into securities, it becomes not only more profitable but also less risky to the initial lender. And so the incentive to offer debt expands. The larger economy becomes dependent on debt, both as a way of fabricating demand in long decades of stagnant wages and as a source of growth in itself. As Tayyab Mahmud wrote, debt has ceased to be a "private choice" and has become instead "a structural imperative."[26]

Theological educators have known for many years that educational debt reconfigures the ways graduates see their vocational choices. A 2014 survey of alumni of ATS schools received an avalanche of testimonies to the power of debt in shaping what seemed possible. "I left the ministry," one graduate said, "at least in a large part, due to financial considerations." Another respondent called debt a "silent clergy-killer. Most parish salaries cannot even scrape the top off and provide relief." Other options come to seem like the *only* reasonable options. "I had to return to my previous profession," another respondent said, "in order to pay the student loan debts."[27] A separate study from the Auburn Center for the Study of Theological Education reported that 37 percent of graduates of ATS schools "said that debt had influenced their career choices."[28] Debt shifts the rationality not only of vocational decisions but also of everyday choices like whether to postpone health care. It alters the landscape in which people make the most important choices of their lives.

The disciplinary power of debt changes not only the choices, but also the chooser. Debt presses borrowers to relate to themselves as human capital, as a portfolio of risks, obligations, and resources to be maximized. It punishes those who fail to manage themselves well as human capital. It invites people into this relationship at a young age. And it provides rituals in regular payments that drill this worldview into the self through steady repetition. Debt is therefore a process of deep formation. As Mahmud argues, "Neoliberal rationality aims at congruence between a responsible and moral individual and an economic-rational actor: a prudent subject whose moral quality rests on rational assessment of economic costs and benefits of their actions." It seeks an "interiorization of the market's goal."[29] And debt as disciplinary ritual works toward this kind of formation. "What better preparation for the logic of capital and its rules of profitability, productivity, and guilt than to go into debt?" Lazzarato asks. "Isn't education through debt, engraving in bodies and minds the logic of creditors, the ideal initiation into the rites of capital?"[30]

The formational power of debt shapes not only our relations to ourselves but also our ties with others. Loans bind creditors and debtors to one another in economies of debt, rather than gift. Moreover, shared debts create powerful collective identities. The debt of the US federal government was $28.43 trillion in 2021—about $86,000 per person.[31] Of course, there are no serious plans to repay that debt, and not everyone will contribute equally to paying even the service required to sustain and expand the debt. But all those who live in this country—whether credentialed as citizens or not, whether paying taxes or not—share in the costs of carrying this debt. The identity of national debtor exerts disciplinary powers that make it hard to escape. We can take the flag out of our sanctuary, refuse the imagined community of America, or even storm the Capitol, but we will still be a member of this community of debtors. The relative power of the United States often makes this discipline less visible to us. But the imposed community of debt shows up vividly in countries forced to repay national debts owed to creditors beyond their borders. The austerity measures imposed at different times on countries like Argentina, South Korea, Kenya, and Greece touched every part of life with forcible reminders of a shared identity as debtors. Other collectivities that take on debt—like congregations—might be easier to leave. But debt still permeates the relations that constitute a shared identity for those who are members of the community.[32]

The formational power of debt extends even to our sense of time. As theologian Kathryn Tanner argues, "the discipline of debt makes present and future simple artifacts of a past promise; present and future collapse into a past that continues to make its demands and cannot be forgiven."[33] Debt incurred in student years can capture borrowers' present realities and sense of what is possible in the future. It can make the past not really past and rob the future of the possibility of newness. Debt therefore contributes to depression not only by limiting life choices but also by teaching us that we are bound to a past that is now an eternal present we can never escape. It is the materialization of a depressive view of time.[34] The problem is psychological; the problem is *theological*. A culture of debt forms us not to believe in the gracious disjuncture in history—Sabbath, Jubilee, Easter—that is the signature of eschatological hope.

Those of us committed to theological education often express our desires for education that is formational. I share in these desires. I think formation is at the heart of what we do. But to do more faithful work in formation, we need to take seriously the formation in which we are already engaged. The practice of financing theological education through debt shapes the ways students think about themselves, their vocations, their communities, even the horizons of time. This formation is not fleeting, like a passion for saying the daily office that might fade after graduation. Monthly payments are the liturgy of human capital. Their formational power extends—with force—for years after graduation, long enough to shape lives even after debts might be repaid.

The Auburn Center study cited above rightly called for a "team approach" to reducing student debt in theological education.[35] Congregations, denominations, schools, and students all have roles to play—including advocating for changes in federal policy and the creation of alternative economies that make sustained theological study possible. But too often the shared work of institutions has been diverted into counseling students toward fewer loans and greater thrift. Programs that guide students in making individual decisions that reduce their total borrowing can relieve some of the pressures that come with indebtedness, but they still lead students to relate to themselves as human capital. The programs teach them to make more prudent investments in themselves. It is not just that they try to address a systemic problem with individual solutions. It is that the kind of individualization at work in the solutions is the formation that needs to be resisted.

The need to resist the expansion of debt has particularly sharp bite now, when ministry, the professoriate, and other professions for which theological schools promise to prepare people are unraveling as professions. Studies of debt among theological students frequently worry about the borrowers' sense that, because God has called them to ministry and will provide for their needs, they can safely take on debt. This is the wrong kind of faith, the guides say. A magical realism. But the logic of "good debt" for professional education has its own sort of faith: the faith that a costly degree will "pay for itself" by punching a student's ticket to the professional class. Debt, as Walter Benjamin wrote a century ago, is the religion of capitalism. That faith is proving more and more misplaced, even as debts expand.

These dynamics are even more troubling when we attend to race and gender. As I showed above, in the aggregate, theological schools rely on disproportionately high levels of debt for women and minoritized students. And, again in the aggregate, the faculties and senior administrators of ATS schools remain stubbornly, disproportionately, white and male. From thirty thousand feet, then, the professional model of theological education involves a debt-fueled transfer of funds from female and minoritized students to white male faculties for credentials that offer access to a shrinking number of good jobs. Of course, individual people and schools break from this pattern in meaningful ways. Aggregations always distort important details. But they can also be revelatory, and they can press important and uncomfortable questions. They press me, as a white, cis-gender male faculty member, to ask what part of my working life—salary, teaching load, support, status, and everything else—depends on the debt of poorer and minoritized students whose diplomas do not necessarily guarantee them places in a professional class. Even more uncomfortably, they press me to ask what I am going to do about these processes. Your relations to these processes may be very different from mine. They will surely pose different questions to you. But none of us can ignore them.

I have filled this section with numbers and analysis, but numbers and analysis didn't make these questions urgent for me. The lives of individual students did. Their stories vary widely, but too many of them are distorted in some way by debt. Even when students graduate without debt, the work of avoiding debt often shaped their time in seminary. And, I should acknowledge, I have been insulated by the privilege of teaching in wealthy schools with generous financial aid policies. Even so, I see debt's formational power in students' lives, and so in mine.

To tell only one story: One of my advisees, a young Black woman I'll call Tamara, had a promising career in business when she decided to say yes to the call from God to ministry that she had been hearing for years. She left her job to come to seminary. She missed out on some scholarships because their donors had tied them to majority-white denominations of which she was not a member; she missed out on others because they rewarded the kinds of excellence cultivated in liberal arts degrees, and she had pursued excellence in business and church leadership. She was on her own. She burned through her savings pretty quickly, and the debt started to pile up. She worked long hours at an off-campus job to slow the accumulation of debt, and the work cut into her time for studying. It was exhausting. And it was painful: she wasn't able to give herself fully to the learning for which she was giving up so much. She persevered, though, slowing her studies and eventually earning her degree only a year after most of her cohort. She knew she would face discrimination within a church movement that imagined mostly marginal roles for women pastors. And so she pivoted to chaplaincy, taking on more debt as she pursued the additional training the shift required. She is thriving in that ministry now, tending some of the poorest of God's people in times of illness and suffering. And she is still making chunky monthly payments on the debt it took her to get there, debt that continues to shape her decisions and her sense of herself long after graduation.

Tamara fought her way to her vocation, and it would not honor her faithfulness, perseverance, and courage to tell her story with anything but the happy ending she worked so hard to achieve. At the same time, though, we can denounce the layers of inequity that made her journey so difficult. We can tell the truth about the debt that extends the sting of those inequities, even into a happy ending. We can acknowledge the ways in which that sting runs all the way through a person. Even as we celebrate Tamara's perseverance, we can say that no one should have to pay the price she is still paying off.

For years I have responded to individualization and its unraveling of professional ministry and academic work by doing all I could to help students "win" the scramble for a shrinking number of good jobs. But these efforts do not change the underlying dynamics. And attempts to reform the debt that fuels these dynamics often just inscribe them more deeply. I have come to believe that we are called not to reform this system of debt but to renounce it. It can seem impossible to sustain theological education without student debt, and it might well be impossible to sustain it in a professionalized form. But we should not mistake the professionalized present for the full range of possibilities. It once seemed impossible to Lyman Beecher to sustain congregations without tax revenue, but the church endured disestablishment, even finding new ways to thrive. And the church has found ways to shelter teaching and learning about God for centuries without forming students as debtors. Our recent decades of addiction to student debt are a historical anomaly. Even today, Bible institutes, monasteries, intentional communities, Orthodox Jewish shuls, and other kinds of institutions all provide for rigorous, intensive, life-changing theological study without relying on debt. Renunciation is difficult; it will change our lives, because it changes where we put our faith. But the faith required is not otherworldly.

And it can be exhilarating to contemplate. What kinds of theological study could the church support with the wealth we already have if we were not trying to sustain professional schools? Who might be interested who is not interested now? What kinds of lives would learners be free to live if they did not have to go into debt to undertake intensive theological study? How could church leadership be transformed if it were unhooked from the increasingly hollow promises of professional status? What kinds of renewal might be possible if serious theological study was not channeled into the formation of professional pastors? How might the learning itself be transformed if it came with no promise of a return on investment? What kinds of rigor would be fitting for this kind of learning? What could theological education be if we got out of the market in human capital?

PROFESSIONAL REASON

Professional status is tightly intertwined with the nature of professional knowledge. The professional ethos seeks to change the world from a position that is in some meaningful sense *above* the part of the world to be changed. This vision stamps the nature of professional reason both with a presumption of distinction and with a deeply instrumental quality. It is the kind of knowledge a person set apart for leadership exercises to reform some part of shared, social life. Theological schools might teach a huge range of subjects with an even wider array of methods. But the form of the professional school steers this deep diversity of learning into expert knowledge for making a difference. Strange things happen to the many varieties of Christian wisdom when they get pressed into this mold.

As I described in the chapter on consolidation, instrumental reason becomes central to theological education through the accumulation of layers that form theological schools as professional schools. An old layer features the homespun pragmatism of the revivals that rebuilt the church as it was being disestablished. For revival leaders like Charles Grandison Finney, the truth of theology was displayed in its effectiveness in winning souls and redeeming society. The purpose of theological education was to pass on theological practices and ideas that *worked*. That kind of pragmatism served as a congenial base for the German model for the modern research university that came to influence higher education in the United States through the late nineteenth and early twentieth centuries. Friedrich Schleiermacher's argument for including theology in this modern university positioned it among the "higher faculties," like medicine and law. These higher faculties were distinguished by their ability to generate and transmit knowledge that was useful for the flourishing of society. At the risk of a bowdlerized reading that passes over Schleiermacher's subtleties to focus on institutional realities, the argument for theological education as a higher faculty in the modern research university begins not with any argument about the truth of theological claims—which would be hard to win in a modern research university, almost by definition—but with a recognition that religious institutions are socially significant. Whether religious institutions do good or harm—or both—they *matter*. And so it matters how their leaders are trained. They need to be trained with the knowledge to lead these socially significant institutions in ways that promote the flourishing of the wider society in which they exist. This rationale for theological education allows the question of the truth of theology to be bracketed. What matters is not whether theology is true but whether it is useful.

The formal details of the Berlin model have had less direct influence on American theological education than some have supposed. And of course, the majority of theological schools in the United States are not officially part of universities. But the instrumental justification Schleiermacher developed stacked on top of an older layer of revivalist pragmatism to create a new foundation for the theological school as professional school. Schools built on these layers derive a significant part of their rationale from their positive social impact. And that rationale invites theological learning into the role of means, not end.

When theological learning becomes a means to other ends, what Michel Foucault identified as the governmentality of reprogrammed liberalism extends deep into theological education. This is problematic even on its own terms, for overassimilation to a dominant logic that stresses making a difference limits the kinds of difference we can make. It is even more problematic when we remember other threads of theological conviction. As Edwin Christian van Driel warns,

> If the aim of a theological school is to produce skilled professionals, then the thinking and speaking about God that we do in the context of our school becomes instrumental. Our gaining knowledge of God is not for the sake of God, but for the sake of our own professional development. In treating God instrumentally, our predecessors would hold, we are failing to do the very thing we set out to do: to speak about God truthfully. To treat God instrumentally is to deny the very being that God is: the one to whom all things are directed, not the one who can be directed at all things.[36]

Van Driel's analysis points to the regressive quality of instrumental reason. When theology is made an instrumental good, valuable because it is useful, then theological study is also instrumentalized, valuable because it forms professionals who know how to use theology for good. This chain of instrumental reasoning works an inner distortion in the heart of theology. It forgets who God is.

When we cast knowledge about God—even God's own self—as means, not end, our actions take on a different quality. The pedagogy of usefulness forms us to see all knowledge as useful for some other project. But then those projects, too—even the church itself—also take on an instrumental quality. When the social imaginary of voluntary associations was at its most powerful, that chain of instrumental goods was anchored by a trust that they were building up a nation through which the world would be redeemed. But when that kind of faith in the nation unravels—as I hope it will continue to do—our familiar chain of instrumental reasoning is left without an end. It becomes an endlessly instrumental logic, with means to means to means, and any promise of an end over the horizon.

The pathologies of unraveled professional reason show up in different ways in theological education. Sometimes the reduction of theological study to an instrumental good shows up in the ways study withers apart from an external disciplinary apparatus: when students cram for exams and then take breaks that leave theological study behind, when pastors stop reading the kinds of books they read in seminary after they graduate, when activists shift from theology to other kinds of reading that seem more useful, or when faculty lose the desire for theological study once they attain tenure or realize they never will. When theological study defined as a means attains some temporal end, or when it no longer seems helpful in securing that end, the professional model gives us no reason to continue studying.

The instrumental quality of professional reason can appear not only in the cessation of theological study, but also in the manic continuation of its forms. Such busy despair shows up whenever we are consumed in sustaining practices, institutions, and forms of life that have become disconnected from their ends. It's there in the days of faculty and administrators that are packed with quick-twitch responses to crises that get framed entirely in managerial terms. It's present, too, when students channel all their intellectual energies in pursuit of grades that are (at best) means to places most of them don't want to go.

When means become means to other means in an endless chain of instrumental reasoning, that chain can start to stand in for an end. The busyness itself becomes reassuring. (If we are working this hard, it *must* be for a good cause!) Our activities become a kind of fetish, something broken out of the pattern of ordinary use and ascribed a magical value.

The instrumental quality of professional reason can also appear in what critical theorist Herbert Marcuse called "repressive desublimation." When a religious or ethical system has authority, Marcuse wrote, it disciplines us to sublimate our drives and desires into acceptable forms. But when material and ideal processes of individualization break the disciplinary hold of those forms, our drives and desires are no longer subject to sublimation. Desublimation can be emancipatory, Marcuse wrote, especially when the systems are unjust. But desublimation can also take repressive forms as the powers of this world harness unrepressed desires for their own purposes. When we cast off the old repressions of thrift and modesty, for instance, capitalism is ready to make use of unleashed consumer desires. Likewise, the fascist state makes use of violent desires no longer sublimated into religious forms. Repressive desublimation makes emancipated affects into tools for the will to power.[37]

In a curious dynamic, individualization unravels the disciplinary power of religious systems without immediately extinguishing the strong feelings associated with them. Old tropes, symbols, ideas, practices, and mannerisms can still retain a luminous afterglow, even after their disciplinary power comes unraveled, that makes them useful resources for individuals. This dynamic appeared with blazing clarity when Donald Trump, a seething cauldron of desublimated desire, had military forces clear protestors from Lafayette Square so that he could stage a photo of himself holding a Bible in front of St. John's Episcopal Church. Trump had not been disciplined by the Bible he held. It had not formed him to sublimate his desires. On the contrary, a big part of his appeal has been the way he gives license to the expression of feelings that Christian morality and middle-class respectability had taught people to repress. Instead, he tried to make the Bible subject to his desires, a means to his ends. This is no ordinary hypocrisy. This is instrumental reason gone feral, first breaking the disciplinary authority of the Bible and then trying to put the affective afterlife of biblical authority in service of a will to power. Trump's photo op reveals the dynamic. But it does not exhaust it. Indeed, professionalized theological education too often looks for ways to mobilize once-authoritative sources for the projects we already have.

In critiquing the ways professional education turns Christian wisdom into instrumental reason, I do not mean to suggest that theological education should not be political. On the contrary, I worry that attempts to use the stuff of theological traditions for our causes is *insufficiently* political. I worry that our little efforts to turn theological plowshares into political swords will be overadjusted to the norms we already have, norms already shaped by the powers and principalities of this age. The risk of this is especially high in an era that struggles to imagine any alternative to the financial capitalism through which we are making the planet a difficult place for humans to inhabit. The problem is not just the content of our instrumental politics, but the form. For too often they seek exactly the kind of power Jesus renounced, first in the wilderness, repeatedly in his ministry, and ultimately on the cross. It is the power of the righteous professional, using instrumental reason to set the world aright from above. We need theology that is not just useful but revelatory. We need theological education that sings of the worthiness of the Lamb who has been slain and that gathers people in glad anticipation of the wedding feast of this Lamb. Such visions are not easily domesticated for immediate political projects. In the glare of professional reason, they are not useful. But they are all the more political for that.[38]

Moreover, renunciations of professional reason can combine with renunciations of professional status to enhance the politics of accountability that womanist, *mujerista*, feminist, and other scholars have long argued must be central to theological education. An idealist accountability imagines the effects of instrumentalized theological reason on imagined communities and assumes it knows what those communities want and need. A deeper, more material accountability is rooted in ongoing relationships and comes to life in critical conversations with people in the communities to whom one is accountable. Renouncing professional status and professional reasoning opens channels for those conversations.

Likewise, in critiquing the ways professional education turns theological wisdom into instrumental reasoning, I do not mean to suggest that theological education should not be practical. The challenge is to distinguish practical reasoning from instrumental reasoning, so that we can renounce the latter without losing the former. Making this distinction begins, I think, with refusing a model in which theoretical knowledge is "applied" to practice. This application model neglects the role of practice in *generating* theological knowledge. Ministers of every kind know this: the practice of ministry is not just a formless void to which one applies what one learned in seminary. It is itself a site of the redeeming work of God, and so a place where theological reflection is required and deep theological learning takes place. So, too, with prayer, and feeding hungry people, and locking arms with comrades in the streets. Practice *generates* theological insight. Remembering this generative role helps us renounce instrumental reason without renouncing practical wisdom.

I'm convinced that most people don't start out with this instrumental understanding of the purpose of theological study. Students, colleagues, and friends are more likely to describe themselves as working out of some piercing experience, some desire, even some trauma, that cannot be expressed in simply instrumental terms. That's the shape of my own story, too. But the deep curriculum of the professional school calls us away from these burning bushes and toward the instrumental reasoning of a professional.

What could theological education be if it gave up the promise of teaching us how to use religious resources to change the world from a professional position? What could theology be if it was not fashioned as a tool for control? What kinds of politics might a useless theology embody? How would we evaluate theological claims, or readings of the Bible, if not by their utility for professional and political projects? What justifications for theological education might we give to university provosts—and to higher education as a whole—if not the argument that we offered useful training for people to lead socially significant institutions? What would the daily lives of teachers and students be like if we were not caught up in professional reason? What joys and sorrows would fall away? What new joys and sorrows would emerge? What would stress us out? What would no longer be stressful at all? Who would want to study theology? Why?

* * *

We might not know the answers to these questions now. But we cannot wait to renounce professional status, professional debt, and professional reason until we develop a new master plan that renders them unnecessary. Thinking that we can give something up only as a means to some known end misses the basic demands of eschatological practical reasoning. In particular, it misunderstands the epistemology of renunciation. Renunciation does not follow vision; it precedes it. In the grace of God, the divine No to the powers of sin and death and the divine Yes to life and life abundant are an inseparable, single Word. But in our temporal attempts to respond to that grace, we often have to say no before we can even know the direction in which we must say yes. The children of Israel leave Egypt before they know how to get where they are going. Jesus says no to the tempter in the wilderness before his full mission comes into view, at least for readers. And in baptismal vows we renounce evil before we turn to God. The speed with which most baptismal liturgies move from one moment to the next can obscure the moment between renunciation of sin and resolution to follow Jesus in a new direction, the long moment in which we are now called to dwell. In renunciation we release our grasp on destructive forces and wait with open hands for what God will provide. We stop listening to the chatter of the world and wait in silence for a word from the Lord. We may not know what form theological education should take. But we do know we can't continue to build our common life on professional status, professional debt, and professional reason. And so we renounce them in an act of faith. And we wait.

In naming this time between the times as a time of waiting, I do not mean to suggest it is a time for doing nothing. Renunciation is an active process that can involve intense asceticism. Discerning summons all our powers of attention. Wandering in the wilderness, living by the daily provision of God, is more strenuous, on deeper levels, than a well-provisioned march toward a goal we can see. To call this season one of waiting, then, does not invite indolence or sloth. It rather redefines the inner quality of all that we do in this time between the times. Waiting acknowledges that our actions do not have the power to give ourselves the new life for which we long.

5

Affordances

In a time of drastic change one can be too preoccupied
with what is ending or too obsessed with what seems
to be beginning. In either case one loses touch with
the present and with its obscure but dynamic possibilities. What really matters is openness, readiness, attention, courage to face risk. You do not need to know
precisely what is happening, or exactly where it is all
going. What you need is to recognize the possibilities
and challenges offered by the present moment, and to
embrace them with courage, faith, and hope. In such
an event, courage is the authentic form taken by love.

Thomas Merton,
Conjectures of a Guilty Bystander (1965)

In the first chapter of this book I tried to describe the slow but
sure transition, about two hundred years ago, from a social imaginary centered on standing orders to one centered on voluntary
associations. I went on to describe the ways in which processes of
individualization have unraveled voluntary associations, and to
ask what of this unraveling order we might be called to renounce.
With less certainty, and more qualifications, I now want to suggest that a social imaginary centered on authentic individuals is
emerging in the wake of this unraveling. I hesitate in naming this

imaginary not only because reality is always weirder and more plural than any single term can describe, but also because whatever is emerging is contingent. Conditions might change. We might even change them ourselves. And so I do not want to speculate on the future of theological education. Instead, I want to try to describe the present in ways that support faithful action.

One way to respond to social change of this magnitude is with a *forecast*. Forecasters spot trends and call people to act in light of them. But simply calling people to get in line with the world made by individualization overlooks the alienation, loneliness, precarity, and racialized inequalities that have come with this YOYO world. This kind of forecasting misses the fallenness of the present and any future that is strongly continuous with it. There is no gospel in adjusting ourselves to a forecasted future. Such calls are simply a matter of baptizing existing trends, accepting the promises of the newly powerful that the way things are going is the way they will continue to go and the way they should go. Forecasters read the crowd in Jerusalem and head for the hills. They call churches to go with the flow of white flight and move congregations to the suburbs. They put their trust in branding campaigns that promise to appeal to expanding demographics of potential students. Forecasts might get dressed up in the language of Providence or progress. But figuring out how to side with history's winners has little to do with Christian discipleship.

Another way to respond to social change is by asserting *timeless norms*. Givers of timeless norms might distill some *telos*, rules, or set of virtues that they argue should be realized in every time and place, including the new context that is emerging. The model is appealing because it feels higher-minded than mere trend chasing. The appeal is broad, because the norms to be defined as timeless can come from any kind of theological or political movement. But such norms are so far from lived experience that they struggle to guide action in this world. We need another layer of norms to tell us which norms apply, and when. And then we need another layer to guide us in the application of those norms, in an endless regression that results in a groundless decision or, most commonly today, moralizing slogans that are not connected in meaningful ways to institutional reform or movements for social change. Moreover, this way of thinking is especially poorly suited to the needs of the present moment. It encourages us to apply norms to history that we treat like raw material, shaping it into what we think God wants it to be. This is exactly the mind-set of the white settler colonial project. It is the point of view invited by a position of professional status. We would find ourselves reproducing these things even as we claimed to renounce them.

Instead of forecasts or timeless norms, I want to try to describe *affordances* for eschatological practical reasoning.[1] Learning from a tradition rooted in twentieth-century phenomenology, I think of affordances as a set of concrete, historically contingent, morally ambivalent forms that can make possible a range of actions. They are not simply subject to our will—they have determinate contours—but they are open to engagement in many different ways. They invite but do not determine what we make of them. An account of affordances therefore seeks to avoid both a fatalism in which environment determines action and an existentialism in which the actor stands above and apart from any context in an abstract freedom that becomes actual by shaping the world to its will. Instead, an account of affordances describes subjects that are continuous with but not reducible to the ecological, cultural, political, and economic contexts in which we find ourselves.

This embedded subjectivity—this creatureliness—informs an account not only of action but also of perception. Instead of the Cartesian picture of a knowing subject using some concept to represent an alien world, phenomenologist Maurice Merleau-Ponty described the ways in which "a person's projects polarize the world, bringing magically to view a host of signs which guide action."[2] In Merleau-Ponty's vision, our commitments illumine the world in particular ways, letting us confront a world that is always already full of meaning—and of affordances for meaningful action. Faced with such a world, we engage in what philosopher

Hubert Dreyfus calls "skillful coping."[3] We do not act to realize the representation of some *telos* that we have in our minds; we rather act in a world already illumined by the *telos*. We do not see an inert world and then act on it to bring our projects into being. Instead, seeing by the light of the end, we encounter a world already alive with affordances.

A Christian hope that has learned from this tradition might understand affordances as arising in the wake of a redemption that is now and not yet. Such affordances come after the end in the middle: they are disclosed to those who see by the light of that end. They are what we can grasp when we renounce our hold on the powers and principalities whose grip on us has already been broken. They are the stuff we find in the desert to make tabernacles for shelter and worship in the long journey of deliverance. They make possible a wide range of free actions that are not arbitrary expressions of our wills but responses to redeeming love that has a determinate shape. In this combination of freedom and responsiveness, they take the shape of love. And like love, they are known in hope. Christian hope is not the wish that our projects will succeed in making the world the way we think God wants it to be; Christian hope is the light that illumines the world as already alive because of the love of God, already full of affordances for free and faithful response, even amidst the harm and suffering of this time between the times. Christian hope is the tone that tunes the ears of Roving Listeners to hear affordances in the world.

Such glad talk can make affordances seem like they must be good in themselves. But the redeeming love of God is wide and wily, able to make affordances even of exile, even of a cross. It would be profane to call such things good or even to frame them as "resources" in some kind of cosmic project management. But we would be thinking too narrowly, too moralistically, if we could not imagine them as caught up in God's great work of redemption, even if only in their negation. To see something as an affordance, then, does not require seeing it as good or useful. It simply involves seeing it by the light of redemption. In that light shine inseparable grace and judgment. "Perspectives must be fashioned," as Theodor Adorno wrote, "that displace and estrange the world, reveal it to be, with its rifts and crevices, as indigent and distorted as it will appear one day in the messianic light."[4]

Trying to see by that messianic light, I want to point toward a series of affordances for theological education in the landscape of the present. The list is incomplete. And it is particular, subject to the limits of my insight and my social location. But I hope this little list will spur others to see affordances I miss and suggest other ways of engaging the affordances I name. I give the most pages to what I see as a central value of the world individualization has made—authenticity—and thinking about what kinds of affordance it might offer. I offer briefer thoughts on affordances in changing demographics, ministries beyond professional leadership of voluntary associations, postprofessional solidarities, "leaderfull" movements, and complex institutions. I conclude with some reveling in the abiding love of God, not as a resource we can mobilize to strengthen our institutions but as a gracious affordance that makes all our teaching and learning worthwhile.

THE FELT URGENCY OF AUTHENTICITY

Authenticity has become a magic word, a word to conjure with. Outside of small circles of critical theorists and pop-culture savants, authenticity almost always has a positive valence these days. It carries that charge through many different meanings in many different contexts. A recent survey of hundreds of listeners to sermons highlighted "intense authenticity" as the quality they prized above all others.[5] Authenticity is deemed crucial for both individual and corporate brands, and the *Harvard Business Review* has featured multiple articles on how to cultivate it.[6] Many of Donald Trump's supporters prize Trump's willingness to "be real" and to say "what everyone was thinking but no one else would say." In survey after survey, they describe this willingness as "authenticity."[7] Trump is hardly alone in tapping into the cultural power of authenticity. Bernie Sanders, Stacey Abrams, and a host of other political leaders might prize very different qualities, but they share overlapping repertoires for displaying those qualities with authenticity.[8] Authenticity has power across spheres of society and across the lines that usually divide us. For better and worse, it is one of the defining affordances of our times.

Projects of authenticity feel so urgent for so many of us today because the processes of individualization have unraveled what Ulrich Beck calls "ascribed" identities. Lack of ascribed identity creates pressure for what he calls "achieved" identities. But this pressed freedom brings questions with it. What kinds of identities should we try to achieve? Who are we? What are we called to do? And if these answers are not ascribed to us, how will we know them? Questions like these bear down on us now. They create what philosopher Søren Kierkegaard called "the dizziness of freedom." Amidst that dizziness, authenticity promises a place to stand.

The social and literary critic Lionel Trilling began to clarify the nature of that place about a half century ago, as the transition from an age of voluntary associations to an age of authentic individuals was gaining strength. Trilling brought authenticity into view by contrasting it with sincerity. Sincerity, Trilling argued, described a state in which a person's private life aligned with her public role. This kind of sincerity is a cardinal virtue in the constellation of voluntary associations. It is one of the chief virtues professional formation is designed to produce. Authenticity, on the other hand, describes the alignment of a person's whole life—public, private, and otherwise—with an ideal, a true self, that is pictured as deep within the individual. This inner ideal is taken to be prior to and more basic than the nexus of market and social forces that presses people toward conformity. Trilling traced the roots of this shift to Romanticism, and he was surely correct. But as I argued in chapter 2, any genealogy of authenticity, especially for North America, must also include Christian practices like Puritan devotional reading, Black church worship traditions, and revivals that stressed the conversion of a "true" self and pioneered techniques for the public display of authenticity as a form of authority. The promise of that true self is the ground of prevailing notions of authenticity. It promises us a place to stand as we cultivate identities—or choose them from menus of options—in the space once filled by ascription.[9]

Preacher and mystic Howard Thurman discussed the power and depth of the ideal of authenticity in a baccalaureate address he gave at Spelman College in 1980. He encouraged listeners to attend to "the sound of the genuine." They would discern that sound deep within themselves, he said. And in responding to it, they would be free: "There is something in every one of you that waits, listening for the genuine in yourself—and if you can not hear it, you will never find whatever it is for which you are searching and if you hear it and then do not follow it, it was better that you had never been born. You are the only you that has ever lived; your idiom is the only idiom of its kind in all the existences, and if you cannot hear the sound of the genuine in you, you will all of your life spend your days on the ends of strings that somebody else pulls."[10] Thurman assured listeners that each of them was utterly unique. And he called them to express that uniqueness in an act of self-emancipation. He called them to authenticity.

Not every thinker was so warm to this rising ethos of authenticity. In 1985, just a few years after Thurman's address, Robert Bellah and his partners critiqued the rise of "expressive individualism" in their best-selling *Habits of the Heart*. The poster child for this brand of authenticity was a woman they called Sheila Larson. "I believe in God," she said. "I'm not a religious fanatic. I can't remember the last time I went to church. My faith has carried me a long way. It's Sheilaism. Just my own little voice."[11] Listening to one's "own little voice" not only produced a shallow and self-absorbed life, the *Habits* authors argued. It also unraveled the basis of social connection. As Bellah said in an address to the Association of Theological Schools, older forms of mysticism were disciplined by sects and other voluntary associations. But this modern, individualist mysticism was marked by an "inner volatility and incoherence." Moreover, it displayed "extreme weakness in social and political organization," undermining communities of every kind. And it was overconformed to the world in "its closeness to psychological man in his pursuit of self-centered experiences in preference to any form of social loyalty or commitment." The turn to authenticity in Sheila's style would dissolve desires to join voluntary associations and the discipline and connection that came with them. It would turn us into lonely narcissists.[12]

Bellah and his colleagues were right to recognize authenticity's power to unravel the network of voluntary associations. But in seeing this unraveling as ending only in narcissism, they paid too little attention to the ways authenticity could also ground different kinds of ethical commitments and social connections. They missed the affordance offered by authenticity. Curiously, the best way to bring authenticity into view as an affordance is first to sharpen the critique. For authenticity comes into view as an affordance not by realizing some hidden potential but through a process of mortification and redemption. It requires something like what what Jürgen Habermas describes as a "redeeming critique" (*Rettendekritik*).[13]

Theodor Adorno provided resources for this mortification more than three decades before *Habits of the Heart*. Adorno tore into the "jargon of authenticity" that he saw in the work of Martin Heidegger and already abroad in the wilds of Los Angeles. To translate Adorno into the idioms I have been trying to develop in this book, authenticity (*Eigentlichkeit*) is the ideological by-product of social processes of individualization that are dissolving both the remnants of standing orders and the network of voluntary associations. It can feel like a kind of compensation: I may be wrenched out of communities for an alienated existence, but at least I still have a chance to be authentic. What Adorno called the deep "untruth" of authenticity comes in its assumption that the self is somehow prior to and untainted by social relations. "What presents itself as an original entity," he wrote, "is only the result of a social division of the social process. Precisely as an absolute, the individual is a mere reflection of property relations." Such authenticity "is nothing other than a defiant and obstinate insistence on the monadological form which social oppression imposes on human beings." Authenticity not only mystifies structures of domination; it elevates their by-product to sacred status.[14]

The authenticity Adorno critiqued presumed the existence of some real, true self that was prior to any social relations. Just that prior status invested the self with all the authority that came with being really real. Adorno's critique helps us see the ideological quality of this vision. Redeeming authenticity begins with renouncing the illusion of this presocial self.

In an essay on the formation of Black subjectivity as a political task, bell hooks pointed the way to a more social sense of authenticity. "How do we create an oppositional worldview," she asked, "a consciousness, an identity, a standpoint that exists not only as that struggle which opposes dehumanization but as that movement which enables creative, expansive self-actualization? Opposition is not enough. In that vacant space after one has resisted there is still the necessity to become—to make oneself anew. . . . That process [of becoming subjects] emerges as one comes to understand how structures of domination work in one's own life, as one develops critical thinking and critical consciousness, as one invents new, alternative habits of being, and resists from that marginal space of difference inwardly defined."[15] The language of "creative, expansive self-actualization" and "the necessity to become" made clear hooks's intentions to move in the semantic range of authenticity. She was addressing people subject to dehumanizing processes of individualization that left them needing to piece together new identities. But hooks saw the ways in which this struggle was linked to larger social and political struggles. When she talked about "that marginal space of difference inwardly defined," she described the production of a subject that could differentiate itself from—and actively re-sist!—forces of domination that tried to define it. This was not the ideological authenticity Adorno critiqued and that Sheila Larson depicted, for hooks did not assume a "real self" prior to social relations that could serve as a positive foundation on which to build a life. On the contrary, she described the origins of the self in a negation—an act of resistance—that opened up space in which a person could begin to fashion a self. The Black subjectivity hooks described was not ahistorical, essential, and prior to social processes. It was not what Victor Anderson has called an "ontological Blackness."[16] It was rather something a person made in history, in the course of naming and resisting structures of domination.

Latinx practical theologian Patrick Reyes insisted on this social, political version of authenticity in his critique of the assumptions about privilege that too often haunt talk of vocation. "Sometimes," Reyes wrote, we think of vocation as "God calling us out of our present reality into some divinely purposed and infinitely better future. Unfortunately, life does not always allow this to occur. In fact, God often just calls us to survive. That's how it was for me." For Black and Brown bodies marked for death, Reyes argued, authenticity does not begin with the discovery of one's own little voice. It rather begins with survival that is a refusal of the powers of death to define a person's self and the shared social world. That refusal situates a person always already in solidarity with others. It is political, focused beyond itself, from the start. The self at the center of any truthful sense of authenticity emerges in the social, political space created by this refusal.[17]

I read Judith Butler's *Giving an Account of Oneself* as an elaboration of this process and the kinds of politics and communities that can flow from it. Butler deepened Adorno's critique of Heidegger and extended it to Jean-Paul Sartre's vision of a self that is forced to make decisions as it confronts moral structures. "The 'I' does not stand apart from the prevailing matrix of ethical norms and conflicting moral frameworks," Butler wrote. "In an important sense, this matrix is also the condition for the emergence of the 'I,' even though the 'I' is not causally determined by those norms."[18] The "I," produced as a person, to recall hooks's language, "comes to understand how structures of domination work in [her] own life."

In giving an account of this "I," Butler wrote, we find ourselves encountering formations and connections for which we cannot account. This profound opacity comes not just from incomplete sets of historical data, but from the nature of the task. Giving an account of oneself always involves a degree of alienation, as the narrating self stands apart from the self that is narrated. "There is that in me and of me for which I can give no account," Butler wrote. But this recognition "gives rise to another ethical disposition in the place of a full and satisfying notion of narrative accountability." There is, Butler wrote, "in this affirmation of partial transparency a possibility for acknowledging a relationality that binds me more deeply to language and to you than I previously knew."[19] In bumping up against those parts of ourselves that are alien to us, we discover ourselves as already connected to others. Giving an account of oneself engenders not just responsibility but relationship, community, and so the possibilities of collective political action. "When the 'I' seeks to give an account of itself," Butler argued, "an account that must include the conditions of its own emergence, it must, as a matter of necessity, become a social theorist."[20]

In giving accounts of ourselves, we become social theorists and, I trust, *theologians*. In making this claim I do not mean to pretend that Butler is doing a kind of crypto-theology. She would almost surely reject this claim. But I do mean to take seriously the project she describes, the work of narrating the conditions of one's own emergence. And as a Christian, I believe that telling the story of one's own emergence will always involve talk of God.

Christians affirm that all of life is lived *coram Deo*, in the presence of God. Former Archbishop of Canterbury Rowan Williams described something like this when he argued that ethics "is a difficult discovering of something about yourself, a discovering of what already shaped the person you are and is moulding you in this or that direction." This discovery of ourselves—this work of authenticity—comes not through "lonely introspection" on some presocial self but through "meditation on the relations in which we already stand." First among those relations is the relation to God. Authenticity involves knowing and being known by God, as Paul writes to the Corinthians. And being Christian involves learning to give accounts—testimonies—that describe ourselves not only in relation to social and historical forces but also in relation to God.[21]

Testimonies are always social, always offered in relationship. But they can take many forms and flourish in many different kinds of settings. Friedrich Nietzsche stressed the significance of testimony in juridical settings: his genealogy of morality depends on the reasons we give when we face a kind of trial. But, as Butler argued, testimonies are given and received as parts of many other language games. And they take many other forms. I think the canonical collection of psalms begins to suggest this depth and variety. Most psalms are some kind of testimony. In giving accounts of the psalmists' selves, they are both personal and corporate. Some of them confess sin and offer justification, just as Nietzsche imagined they would. But they also sing stories of deliverance. They narrate affliction and call for help. And they describe the wonders of the world they see—not least the singer's own self—and marvel at the glory of God. Learning to sing this fullness is what Christians believe is involved in giving an account of oneself.

What would it be like to orient theological education around the need to give deeply truthful and richly theological accounts of ourselves? What if—instead of preparing students for professional leadership in a network of voluntary associations—theological education acknowledged our shared need to form identities and connections in the wake of individualization? The work is difficult. My students' lives—and my own—show me just how difficult. What would it be like for theological education to help us bear the peculiar kind of freedom forced upon us in these times, and in ways that were faithful to God, connected to others, and life-giving for all?

Theological education oriented to this end would not be limited to those preparing for professional careers as stewards of voluntary associations. It would still be relevant for them—the shifting demands of professional life now require not just sincerity but also authenticity—but not *limited* to them. It would be for everyone seeking to fashion an authentic identity in relation to God. Theological education on this model would become, as Mark D. Jordan has said, "part of the ongoing exercise of Christian adulthood." That does not mean that we sweep everyone into MDiv programs—let alone into the one-year mini-masters that offer scaled-down professional education to laypeople with disposable income. It means we engage in a deep rethinking of the institutions and offerings of theological education on the way to creating what Justo González has called "an uninterrupted continuity between Christian education as it is provided in the local church and that which is available to more advanced students."[22] We need a full spectrum of offerings that ranges from free courses open to anyone, to courses held in conjunction with local congregations, to inexpensive certificate programs, to undergraduate courses that are fully theological, to traditional graduate and professional degrees. The spectrum would extend to prisons and jails, offering opportunities for study even to people who might never lead congregations. The work of authenticity would take different forms in different modalities. But the felt urgency of authenticity would animate the whole spectrum.

This full spectrum of theological education would need to be radically accessible, for the demands to form authentic selves bear down on all of us. That's true for people with some measure of privilege, like Sheila Larson. Or me. And, as I argued in chapter 2, those powers tend to bear down even harder on people already marginalized by poverty, racism, sexism, nativism, and more. Those powers and principalities might deny any ascribed identity, making family formation, steady employment, and other traditional markers of adult identity difficult to attain. Or they might ascribe an identity that licenses violence against a person, like "inmate," "deviant," "debtor," or "illegal." Either way, the need to form authentic identities runs deep and wide in our society, and it is especially acute for those who are least likely to enter professional master's degree programs. Given the breadth and depth of this need, theological education that takes hold of the affordance of authenticity must not become a luxury good, one more expensive offering that promises "wellness" and delivers distinction from bodies rendered unfit. It must not become the mere "moral ornament" that intellectual historian Chad Wellmon worries the humanities could become, a means of self-enrichment and status for people who are already comfortable.[23] Instead, it must grasp the groaning for authenticity at the center of so many lives today.

With this need to shift institutions and offerings comes a need to shift pedagogies. The question always lurking in the seminary as professional school is the question of utility. Sure, it's great to read Mechthild of Magdeburg, but will it preach? Or, more broadly, how can I use this knowledge in serving as a chaplain or leading an NGO dedicated to the abolition of the death penalty? Such questions may be irksome to faculty formed for *wissenschaftlich* pursuit of knowledge, but they are built into the instrumental logic of theological education as professional education. An education of authenticity would be animated by a different set of questions. Not: Will it preach? But: What does this mean to me? To us? What does it help me understand about the historical currents that shape the world in which we find ourselves? About the forces of domination that try to define me? About the content and direction of my hope? About who God is in relation to me, and what it means to live in relation to God?

Students are already pressing these questions, hacking both *wissenschaftlich* and professional courses toward projects that let them explore them. And students are doing it not only in theological schools but also in undergraduate classes in religious studies, history, literature, philosophy, politics, and more. The affordance of these questions and the energy around them are already there.

If questions of authenticity are pursued in ahistorical ways, they will slip into serving the ideological form that Adorno diagnosed and that Bellah and his colleagues criticized. Pedagogies that try to "help students find their voices" by imagining those voices as solitary and deep within each individual are so appealing precisely because they replicate the neoliberalism that is a dominant ideology of our time. Pedagogies that mortify and redeem the prevailing sense of authenticity, on the other hand, will stress genealogies. They will help us understand how we came to be the ways we are, and how we might want to live otherwise. They will bring us up against the opacities in ourselves and help us discover the ways we are already connected to others, and to God. They will frame authenticity not as dwelling in an inner starting point we take up practice to express, but as that which practice helps us make.

Biblical studies, in this model, would not seek to perfect a method that could deliver what the author of the text really intended. It would instead trace histories of interpretation that help us understand and reflect critically upon why we read a text in the ways we do, whom those readings have benefited, and how we might risk reading in more just and faithful ways. It would involve students in practices of reading and reading together. Above all, it would hope for fresh encounters with God in the text. Theology and ethics would not present learners with a series of moral and doctrinal options and ask them to choose their favorites and give reasons for their answers. They would instead help learners think historically about how particular doctrines and ethical visions came to exert power. And they would help learners think theologically about the worlds of faith and action in which they are already enmeshed. They would invite students to explore these genealogies not just as critique, but on the way to refined testimonies of their own. History courses would not obscure the present situation, promising to offer students formation in a venerable tradition that they then grasp expressively in projects of authenticity. That is, history courses would not satisfy the consumer demands of shopper-students seeking appealing intellectual and material artifacts with which to decorate their ancient-future worship spaces. They would instead offer histories that lead all of us to clearer understanding of how we have come to be in the situations we are. They might even risk talking about how this history relates to God's work of redemption. Classes in the arts of ministry would not scramble for relevance by stretch-

ing themselves to apply to more professions, turning homileti-
cians into public-speaking coaches for leaders of nonprofits and
pastoral caregivers into generic counselors. Instead, they would
celebrate the ways in which Christian practices of testimony and
caregiving have been broken out of the domain of professionals
and returned to the whole body of Christ. They would help students understand their own default modes in relation to these
practices and consider how they want to revise and refine those
modes. They would embrace the demands of these practices as
a kind of ascesis that had the happy side effect of making selves.
For instance: most of the time a person does not start off with
great depth as a reader of sacred texts and then learn skills for
expressing that depth in preaching (as the ordering of courses
in many schools' curricula presumes). Instead, the steady discipline of preaching—done with all the insight, attention, and love
a person can muster—more often gives a preacher depth, even
as and precisely because it blesses others. So, too, in practicing
care for others we find ourselves formed in new ways. In teaching we become new kinds of people. As professional skills, the
arts of ministry might be less relevant for the growing number
of students who do not desire to become professional ministers.
But as spiritual disciplines, they can give learners at every level a
chance to do the work they most yearn to do.

Pedagogies of authenticity involve more than critique, at least
in the colloquial sense of dispelling ideology. They require, as
hooks, Butler, and Williams saw, a more constructive and connec-
tive process, for they take us to the opacities that bind us to others in ways we could not choose. They are therefore more like the
"critical fidelity" Tyler Roberts described as "less a matter of inter-
rogation and autonomous 'choice' than the ability to give oneself
to others, to causes, to meanings. It requires vulnerability, dependence, and risk. It even requires certain kinds of passivity and the
discernment that enables one to negotiate complex interrelation-
ships between activity and passivity."[24] Pedagogies that took hold
of the affordance of a mortified and redeemed authenticity might
begin in critique. But they would go on to engage in connection,
construction, and conviction by the light of their end.

CHANGING DEMOGRAPHICS

What year it will happen is in dispute, but demographers are united in declaring that at some point in the next three decades people from historically minoritized groups will make up a majority of the population in the United States. As Juan Martínez has argued, these demographic changes are coming even sooner for theological schools.[25] A growing number of schools—like my own—that long served predominantly white student populations now serve students in which the majority identify as members of minoritized groups. These changes are moving at different speeds in different contexts. But they run throughout the whole ecology of theological education.

The diversity of student bodies is not only racial and ethnic. Working more anecdotally, I feel confident that theological schools are attracting more students formed in more traditions, and especially in charismatic and Pentecostal communities. I am equally confident that students are proud to claim a deeper diversity of sexualities and gender identities than they could in past decades. And, in a shift that is even harder to measure, I am convinced that more students bring greater consciousness of having been harmed by churches than their predecessors did. I meet more and more students at many different schools who are pursuing theological education not to become certified for vocations as professional leaders of congregations but to make sense of past harm in ways that let them move forward with other vocations. And of course, all these identities and more can tangle together in complex and wondrous ways.

There are many reasons theological schools are changing more rapidly than the general population. Students are significantly younger than the median age, and younger cohorts are more diverse. But this demographic change in theological schools is also connected to the processes of individualization I described in chapter 2. Commendably, those processes have delegitimized discriminations on the bases of identities of many kinds, making more schools open to more students. Less nobly, but still with great effect, processes of individualization have created imperatives for schools to recruit more widely than they did in the past. This increasing supply is met by a "demand" side of the market in theological education in which individualization leaves students more willing to attend schools that are not affiliated with the communities that have formed them. Moreover, the upward mobility of at least some members of historically minoritized communities makes more students ready for professional education even as the constellation in which it has normative power is unraveling. Growing numbers of Black, Indigenous, Hispanic/Latinx, and Asian/Asian American students have undergraduate degrees that open the doors to graduate and professional studies. And as evangelical, charismatic, and Pentecostal communities have eased some old ambivalences about professional theological education for clergy, they have also generated more students who are eager and prepared. For almost four centuries Christians in North America have expanded theological education as they have gained social and economic security. The present is no exception.

The most cynical appropriation of this diversity would simply recruit students from ever wider groups to support schools that change as little as possible. Schools might offer peripheral certificate programs or hire just enough faculty from minoritized groups to signal some interest without changing in any fundamental ways. Students in these schools would endure curricula designed with other people in mind and come out with whatever they could learn studying against the grain and whatever social and cultural capital a theological degree might confer. As I argued in chapter 4, these problems get supercharged by debt.

Changing demographics can and should invite deeper change. Schools that engage these developments as gospel affordances will shift their faculty, curricula, and pedagogies in ways that learn from student contexts and respond to student callings. They will not only expand access to cultural capital to select individuals but will also use their toeholds in higher education to transform what counts as cultural capital. Theological schools that are part of universities are often the most diverse units within those universities. Freestanding schools have parallel relations to higher education as a whole. Theological education thus is positioned to provide both intellectual leadership and little foretastes of a more deeply diverse future for the wider sector of higher education.

The list of necessary transformations is long and goes to the core of our practices and institutions. Whole books have been written on the changes that are needed, and I have tried to attend to dynamics around race in every section of this book. But one structural change can have wide-ranging effects: the need to connect not only with individuals but also with communities. Theorist Jodi Melamed rightly denounced a "neoliberal multiculturalism" that celebrates itself for welcoming diversities of individuals but fails to form wider solidarities that work for social change. Stripped of relationships that make material interests beyond the school relevant, diversity can descend into hollow gestures of recognition.[26] Former executive director of La Asociación para la Educación Teológica Hispana (AETH) Fernando Cascante prescribed the crucial antidote to such empty politics of recognition, calling schools to relationships of accountability with minoritized communities. Cascante exhorted one school to do work that was "not just good for Spanish-speaking students, but also good for Spanish-speaking *communities*."[27] Cascante's call comes from a clear perception of the ways power operates. Student activists have brought significant changes to schools across the country. But it remains true that schools hold most of the power in relation to individualized students. Relations with communities can hold schools accountable in new ways—just as they have long held schools accountable to denominations, donors, and other key constituencies. Relations with communities also open new channels for the fundamental levels of learning that schools need. Developing deep, just, accountable, and durable relations with minoritized communities is a first step for historically white schools in learning how to see changing demographics as an affordance illumined by redemption.

CHAPTER 5

MINISTRIES BEYOND PROFESSIONAL LEADERSHIP
OF VOLUNTARY ASSOCIATIONS

The unraveling of voluntary associations and the growing urgency of authenticity point theological education to wider work than preparation of ministers. But preparing ministers still has a place within that wider vision. The ministries at the center of the unraveling order—professional-ish leadership of more-or-less religious voluntary associations—may be contracting. But there is an affordance in the expansion of other modes of ministry. Some of these involve leadership of congregations and other voluntary associations without full professional standing. Observers disagree on whether the number of bivocational, covocational, and part-time pastors is increasing. The number has always been significant. What is clear is that this mode of ministry is becoming increasingly common in mainline Protestant denominations that did so much to make professionalized ministry a norm. Among United Methodists, for example, 27 percent of congregations were served by part-time leaders in 2000. Nineteen years later, the number had risen to 42 percent.[28] Some of these part-time and covocational pastors have MDivs, but growing numbers of them are commissioned as local pastors after completing a shorter Course of Study. Parallel developments are unfolding across other mainline denominations. Lindsay Armstrong, executive director of new church development with the Presbytery of Greater Atlanta, named three subgroups within this growing number of what Presbyterians call commissioned lay pastors. Some serve long-established but shrinking congregations in rural and urban areas; others serve new immigrant communities; and still others serve church plants whose entrepreneurial ethos fits better with a certificate program. All these developments are driving an expansion of lay pastors across mainline traditions. When they are coupled with traditions that have long histories of part-time and bivocational ministry, the number of people needing formation for ministry that does not involve a full professional degree is significant.[29]

Educational offerings for this group vary widely across the landscape. Some are educated in regionally consolidated programs, like the United Methodist Course of Study. Others enter forms that are more ad hoc, done in many cases by regional judicatory bodies. As a Disciples leader said, these regional bodies are already working at capacity. They have neither the resources nor the expertise to train lay pastors. Moreover, he said, trying to offer pastoral education complicates their core relationships of collegial accountability with these pastors. Even in the best cases, the resources devoted to educating lay and bivocational pastors are a fraction of those devoted to professional education.[30]

Seen as a gospel affordance, rather than as second-class exceptions, lay and bivocational ministries can offer rich modes of pastoral and ecclesial life. To say they are not fully "professional" is a comment about status, wages, career, and class, not about faithfulness or effectiveness. Seeing the full significance—and enduring status—of these ministries should lead seminaries, congregations, and denominations to devote much greater shares of their theological education resources to forming people to do them well. The best versions of this formation will not happen in cut-down professional degrees. They will require greater intentionality, including pedagogies that treat both current pastoral work and work in a learner's "other" job as affordances for learning.

If one sign of the times is the deprofessionalization of congregational ministry, another sign is the growing number of professional ministers who serve outside of voluntary associations. They are two dimensions of the same dynamics that are decoupling congregational ministry and professional status. Professionalized ministries are expanding in institutions that are not voluntary societies. That's practically a definition of chaplaincy—ministry in some institution that is not in the specifically religious sphere, and so is most likely not a voluntary association. And, as I argued in chapter 2, chaplaincy roles seem to be expanding, and interest in serving as a chaplain certainly is. Entities that employ chaplains in the health-care, military, education, and business sectors are rarely voluntary associations. They are founded, funded, and governed in very different ways. But increasingly employees in these sectors navigate their religious lives within these institutions instead of in congregations and other voluntary associations. They come as individualized individuals, and chaplaincy promises not doctrine but assistance with projects of authentic meaning-making. Moreover, chaplains typically serve not in an older model of professionalism that stresses self-employment and autonomy but as highly skilled and formally credentialed employees of large organizations with large concentrations of capital. Chaplaincy is a form of ministry that fits the times in which we live. Seeing it clearly as ministry outside voluntary associations brings its presence in many different kinds of institutions into sharper focus.[31]

Chaplaincy requires extensive professional education in and beyond schools. Theological schools are already shifting resources to attract students interested in chaplaincy and do more to prepare them for this work. But these moves exist in some tension with moves to form and support lay and bivocational pastors. The one follows professional ministry beyond the congregation; the other focuses on congregational ministry as its professional status fades away. A large and wealthy school might be able to sustain moves in both directions, but it would be difficult. As the model centered on professional leaders of voluntary associations unravels, it is not yet replaced by a new whole. It is not clear that it will be. In this time between the times, affordances invite movements in different directions.

POSTPROFESSIONAL SOLIDARITIES

As I argued in chapter 4, professional status invites a politics that sets pastors and theological educators apart from poor and working-class people. Even when we write books or make statements that stress racial justice, a preferential option for the poor, or other progressive language, material realities tug against anything like politically meaningful solidarities. Too often the politics of progressive, professional, white theological educators like me consist too much of empty slogans and virtue signaling. The draw of this mode only becomes more attractive as politics becomes more connected to expressive identities than to material change. We slip into what Eitan Hersh calls "political hobbyism," what Jodi Dean identifies as "performative allyship," and what Charles Taylor calls a "politics of mutual display." And too often professional theological education forms students for exactly this work, like a Christian ethics class that teaches students the right language with which to express the right commitments without cultivating the practical, political, theological know-how that comes in the discipline of long, on-the-ground struggles for justice.

Deprofessionalizations of ministry and the theological academy create hardship, precarity, and the intense frustration that comes with following the rules only to find that the game has been changed. They also offer an affordance for a different kind of politics. As historian and activist Gabriel Winant argues, "For the precarious academic, the overworked nurse, or the underpaid teacher [or, we might add, the pastor paid less than all of them], the contradictions between official ideologies of professionalism and the material reality of existence have become so vivid as to create a chasm. Through this gap, it is possible for a member of the [professional managerial class] to glimpse broader solidarity with the working class, even to imagine self-redefinition within it."[32] Deprofessionalized ministers and theological educators can find new kinds of common ground with people they once set out to help. Such alliances were visible in Chicago, as teachers went out on strike alongside members of the Service Employees International Union. They are also emerging between tech workers and the low-wage laborers, often on outsourced contracts, who clean the buildings and make the food on gleaming corporate campuses.[33]

In naming these potential sites of solidarity, I do not want to blur the real distinctions that endure. Meaningful distinctions exist between different kinds of work and even within jobs that seem to be in the same field. Nor do I mean to ignore the privileges of my own position. I do mean to describe the unraveling of a class, the ways a status marker like tenure changes as it signals exception rather than membership, the loss of confidence that my students (and, all the more, my children) will enjoy the weaving of meaning and material security that professions once offered, and the new possibilities for solidarity these dynamics make possible. As Movement for Black Lives organizer Alicia Garza said, solidarity is not "a blurring of our experiences and our unique conditions for the sake of peace," but is "a standing together in the muck of our differences and declaring that we refused to be divided by the people who are responsible for our collective misery."[34] Solidarities and alliances do not require identical conditions. They do require common ground for shared political projects. Deprofessionalization opens up that common ground for ministers and theological educators in a variety of situations. Theological education can be a tool for cultivating that ground and connecting with others who know it better than we do.

"LEADERFULL" MOVEMENTS

Perhaps the greatest moment for the constellation of voluntary associations came on August 28, 1963, as Martin Luther King Jr. stood at the Lincoln Memorial, facing the Capitol, preaching a dream for the nation before a crowd that was a composite of many hundreds of voluntary associations: unions, congregations, denominations, fraternal orders, and more. It's not only that most people who came belonged to some voluntary association. It's also that they came with the voluntary association, maybe even on a bus organized by the voluntary association. And they came to hear speakers who were listed as credentialed leaders of similar voluntary associations: the Very Reverend Patrick O'Boyle, archbishop of Washington; A. Philip Randolph, director, March on Washington for Jobs and Justice; Dr. Eugene Carson Blake, stated clerk, United Presbyterian Church of the USA, and vice chairman, Commission on Race Relations of the National Council of Churches of Christ in America; John Lewis, national chair, Student Nonviolent Coordinating Committee . . . on to the Reverend Dr. Martin Luther King Jr., president, Southern Christian Leadership Conference. The associations signal the speakers' legitimacy. Women were largely denied major leadership roles in the voluntary associations that came together for the march. But they still appeared on the program. They are listed as Marian Anderson, Mrs. Medgar Evers, Eva Jessye, and Miss Mahalia Jackson, all without any named connection to an association. Their presence was authorized in different ways. But every man on the program was identified in relation to a voluntary society.

The voluntary associations legitimated the speakers. When they spoke, they wore the mantle of their association, and the whole network of associations that joined together that day when civil society was made visible. The act of addressing the nation, even with sharp criticism, was charged with meaning because of a shared sense that the soul of this particular nation was of world-historical importance. That sense of sacred purpose then flowed back through to the voluntary associations represented in the march. They had sacred purpose because they shared in this work of redeeming the nation. This moment is the defining icon of the faith in which I was raised. Most of the voluntary associations in which I serve are still sustained by the half-life of the March.

In relation to the podium at the March on Washington for Jobs and Freedom, the role of theological education was to form and certify leaders of voluntary associations. At least Patrick O'Boyle, Eugene Carson Blake, John Lewis, James Farmer, Uri Miller, Joachim Prinz, Martin Luther King, and Benjamin E. Mays had some kind of theological education. That education was part of why they could lead the organizations that were listed with their names. It was part of what authorized their appearance on the podium.

Fifty summers after the March on Washington, in July 2013, a jury in Seminole County, Florida, found George Zimmerman not guilty of the murder of Trayvon Martin. Leaders of voluntary associations denounced the verdict. But opposition caught fire when Alicia Garza, a community organizer in California, wrote a post for social media that concluded with the insistence that "Our Lives Matter, Black Lives Matter." Her friend Patrice Cullors turned those words into a hashtag that raced around the world.

This movement was different from the one that marched on Washington in 1963. It spread through social media. Its organization was more fluid. Mainstream press struggled to understand who was in charge. Its style displayed a wariness of the respectability politics that came with voluntary associations and marginalized many young, queer, and nonprofessional activists.[35]

These marchers did not rely on churches or unions to give them rides to the action. They got themselves and one another where they needed to be in less centrally planned ways. The significance—the charge, the aura, the meaning—of the movement depended less on saving the soul of a redeemer nation and more on the immense value of asserting the dignity of individual Black lives in the face of domination. The movement connected with people's desires for self-expression that then linked with the expressive energies of other individuals. "Part of my motivation for organizing," Garza wrote, "was a desire not to feel alone in the world."[36] And she succeeded, sparking a movement that linked the protests of authentic individuals and charged them with a shared sense of sacred significance.

The movement wasn't leaderless, as some wrote when they were unable to locate the new movement's King. It was, Cullors said, calling on the legacy of Ella Baker, "leaderfull." The movement did not spring spontaneously from a hashtag. It built on years of organizing. Organizers were decentralized, Garza wrote, but "Decentralizing leadership . . . is not synonymous with having 'no leaders.' Decentralizing means distributing leadership throughout the organization rather than concentrating it in one place or even a very few people."[37] Movements need some kind of organizations to sustain themselves, Garza wrote. But people don't have to be part of organizations to be part of movements, in this vision. Movements like this are not voluntary associations, or even composites of multiple voluntary associations. They are, Garza wrote, "how we come together when we've come apart."[38]

The Movement for Black Lives has been one of the pioneers of this "leaderfull" form for movements, which have arisen in Hong Kong, France, Haiti, Chile, Bolivia, Turkey, Iraq, Lebanon, and other countries. In one notable example, the hundreds of thousands of people who gathered in Cairo's Tahrir Square to protest President Mohamed Morsi sparked connected protests across the country. Soon millions of people were in the streets. In time the Egyptian military intervened to overthrow Morsi and install a new president. Like the Movement for Black Lives, the movement in Egypt was not strongly mediated by voluntary associations. At its core were masses of individuals who came together to express demands for dignity. Movements like these, grounded in the dignity of individuals and driven by the expressive actions of individuals, activate the values and practices of the individualized individuals we have become. They fit the times.

Leaderfull movements have strengths and weaknesses compared to older styles of social organizing. My point is not to advocate for the form so much as to name its resonance with our times. One sign of that ascendance is the breadth and variety of the causes for which people take up the form: the "Freedom Convoy" of trucks that blockaded Ottawa in 2022 in protest of public health restrictions designed to curb COVID-19 had a structure like that of #BlackLivesMatter, even if participants held very different political positions. That openness to move in many directions suggests the power of the form itself.

If theological education helped form and authorize the leaders of voluntary societies who appeared on the podium in Washington in 1963, how might it relate to this new kind of movement? Schools might try to turn community organizing into something like a profession and train people for it. That effort could have some value. But it misses the deeper transformation at work in leaderfull movements.

Leaderfull movements invite modes of education that do not presume to trickle down from leaders to people. And the education might come *after* the protest, not before. As Atlanta rapper and activist Killer Mike said, the new movements need something like a "house of refuge" where people can go after the protest to "plot, plan, strategize, organize, and mobilize." In 1963, theological education prepared and legitimated leaders who disseminated knowledge at the march. In the leaderfull movements of today, the protest energizes people who then need a place to gather with others for study and connection. Leaderfull movements sometimes struggle to endure for longer than a single rally. They sometimes struggle to name practical objectives and develop strategies for attaining them. This kind of work takes time, space, and study. It is hard to do in the streets. But it could happen in theological schools. Thus theological schools that feel called to support leaderfull movements might think of themselves less as professional schools credentialing the next generation of movement leaders and more as safe houses that give people already involved in movements space and resources to cultivate the study and social connection they have already begun.

COMPLEX INSTITUTIONS

The transition from standing orders to voluntary associations showed that congregations and theological schools were durable, malleable institutions that could change their rationale even as they retained a kind of continuity. A state-supported Congregational church could become a voluntary society without changing its name or its building. And Yale College endured disestablishment to offer theological education in the new modality of a divinity school. This elasticity makes congregations and theological schools into affordances.

In megachurches, cathedrals, house churches, and other fresh expressions, congregations are finding ways to live as something other than voluntary associations. They are also finding their way to new relationships to theological education. They are not just sending students and donations to seminaries and receiving pastors in return. They are increasingly involved more directly in theological education, and in a myriad of ways. First Presbyterian Church in Atlanta nurtured TheoEd Talks that have reached thousands of people. Saddleback Church in Orange County seeks to offer the education their members need for whatever ministries they are involved in, including planting and pastoring congregations. They generate much of this education within the congregation and partner with a seminary for the subjects that require a different kind of expertise. St. Paul School of Theology joined with Church of the Resurrection in Leawood, Kansas, in an experiment that brought the school onto the congregation's campus. Trinity Wall Street, an Episcopal congregation in New York, absorbed the Church Divinity School of the Pacific in ways that let the seminary retain a great deal of autonomy even as it functions as an educational ministry of the congregation. These experiments all involve large and wealthy congregations. But the base communities of Latin America and Orthodox Jewish shuls around the world offer examples of smaller congregations with fewer resources that sustain intensive study.

Few congregations have done more in theological education than Holy Trinity Brompton, an evangelical megachurch in London. The congregation sparked study around the globe with its Alpha Course for lay Christians. When people worked through this, they wanted more. And so the congregation developed St. Paul's Theological Centre to offer additional opportunities for study. And when some students at St. Paul's found themselves called to the priesthood, the congregation supported local dioceses in creating St. Mellitus College, which forms people for ministry in partnership with congregations in which they serve throughout their course of study. The result is a full, connected continuum of offerings in theological education with congregations playing central roles at every step along the way.

Experiments like these have had mixed results. And they have not yet consolidated into solid institutional forms. But what is clear is that congregations seem to be rivaling or even displacing denominations as the most important church bodies in relation to theological education. The consolidation of money and members in a smaller number of congregations helps drive this shift. Whether doing the education within themselves, partnering with schools, or doing both at once, strong congregations are offering real affordances for theological education. In a prophetic call, Justo González underscored the value of these partnerships, stressing the need "to return theological education to its proper place, which is at the heart of the church—particularly of the church in its local expression, the congregation."[39]

Like congregations, theological schools can be complex, malleable institutions, able to sustain continuities even as they change in fundamental ways. Schools have the added advantage of having left the form of a voluntary association behind many decades ago. This gives them freedoms congregations often must struggle to attain. As schools, they also have some cultural capital. They can award degrees that are still meaningful in some ways. And some schools, like some congregations, carry significant endowments. The nine seminaries affiliated with the Presbyterian Church (USA), for instance, together have more than two billion dollars in endowments. Individual schools may experience scarcity as they try to sustain a professional model in the face of declining enrollments. But there are significant affordances in the overall support already given to theological education.

Schools might stretch their imaginations to see new affordances by considering different metaphors for their next iteration. A school could think of itself as a house of refuge for movement leaders, as Killer Mike proposed. It could reanimate Saint Benedict's image of the monastery as a workshop, casting itself as a kind of makerspace for projects of authentic faith, providing shared tools, expert guides, and coworking friends for people's diverse efforts to give theological accounts of themselves. Or it might follow the lead of modern monasteries in becoming sites of hospitality for pilgrims. In this model, a small, highly committed group sustains old, demanding traditions of practice and welcomes visitors to join in ways that are appropriate for their own vocations. This can lead to a shallow spiritual tourism, as visitors vibe on their proximity to authentic faith and then move on. But academic degrees don't guarantee deep rigor or transformational learning, either. And many monasteries have found ways for a relatively small group of "members" to play important roles in sustaining faith for much larger populations in this season of authentic individuals.

Schools could also center their efforts around events that offer the "higher times" that Charles Taylor identifies as especially resonant with individuals seeking authenticity. Events like the Samuel DeWitt Proctor Conference, Catholic World Youth Days, and the Wild Goose Festival attract thousands of participants. They create intense centers of energy and social connection. One could imagine significant education happening before, during, and after them. Schools might partner with existing festivals or create their own. The festivals would need to be different from the alumni and continuing education events schools now host. They would be more open to people with no previous affiliation. They would seek to gather masses. They would be oriented less to the institution and more to self-expression. That is: they would feel less like homecoming and more like Burning Man. Events that tap into the urgency of authenticity at that level could ground wider educational work on many levels. People might undertake intensive projects to get ready. They might participate in extraordinary experiences of learning while they are together. And they might form covenants for action and reflection with friends they meet at the event.

Schools also offer affordances for study as they open up space in which other communities of learning can flourish—perhaps in spite of or even in opposition to the school. Fred Moten and Stefano Harney limn these spaces as the undercommons in which Black study can thrive. They describe how "the subversive intellectual . . . disappears into the underground, the downlow lowdown maroon community of the university, into the *undercommons of enlightenment*, where the work gets done, where the work gets subverted, where the revolution is still black, still strong."⁴⁰ The undercommons can find a place to live in study groups, informal networks, and even classes that escape notice. It treats the school always as an affordance for study the school does not condone and cannot imagine.

House of refuge, makerspace, late-modern monastery, center of higher times, witting or unwitting host of undercommons: these just begin the list of institutional forms theological schools could take in an age of authentic individuals. Some might involve giving up accreditation or even the whole idea of degrees. Others might involve running an existing model in parallel with a new one, even for a long time. Most of the models on my fever-dream list will probably not be sustained as part of whatever constellation consolidates in the coming years. What will become part of that consolidation might not be on my list at all. But my hope is not to predict the next new model but to invite attention to the school as an affordance for something more than vending credentials to individuals investing in themselves. That model could fit these times, too, after all. It's already on the rise. But it's not the only possibility.

THE ABIDING LOVE OF GOD

It is a paradox of authenticity that we cannot work on it directly. Like many of my generation, I learned the hard way that nothing is less authentic than trying to be authentic (somewhere there are pictures, perhaps, but you will not get them from me). Like humility, authenticity is a virtue that emerges only as we give ourselves to something else. And so, even in an age that demands authentic individuals, authenticity cannot serve as the goal of theological education.

Given how deeply formed many of us are in the instrumental reasoning of the professional model, it can be tempting to graft the ends of authenticity onto that logic, such that once the purpose of theological education was to form professionals to lead voluntary associations that redeem the nation and so the world, and now its purpose is to achieve the state of knowing and being known that constitutes authentic being. But such thinking forgets the wisdom of centuries of Christian study that have revealed, again and again, the limits of study. It forgets Gregory's description of Benedict as *scienter nescius et sapienter indoctus*, knowingly ignorant and wisely unlearned. It forgets Julian's raptures and Juan's dark night of the soul. It forgets the longing the spiritual "Deep River" expresses for a home we cannot get to on our own. It forgets that the peace for which we yearn passes understanding. It forgets the depth of our need for the grace of God. There is an infinite discontinuity between even the best study and the knowing and being known by God that are the substance of authentic life. The beatific vision is not something we can list among the outcomes for a course. Study is not simply a means to the end that matters most.

Remembering this wisdom can lead us to a second set of temptations as we overcorrect for instrumental reason. We might throw study out completely in a celebration of ignorance that we wrap in piety. People who claim to follow Jesus have done things like this for centuries. But such moves are only more deeply in thrall to instrumental reason, just as antinomianism is still in thrall to legalism, for they cannot imagine a good for study if it is not a reliable means to the longed-for end.

More subtly, we might insist that study is already the end in itself. But this overlooks the very real experiences we have of learning over time, the struggle and delight of coming to know. There is a dynamic quality to study that gets lost when we treat it as a good with no purpose beyond itself. Seeing study as an end in itself can also make us too satisfied with our studies. It can lead us to make a fetish of our efforts, as if simply studying hard were salvific. That satisfaction can shift our focus to ourselves. It can leave us hoping for too little. It can cut the tense cord of longing by which God so often draws us into knowing and being known.

We need some way to think about theological study as oriented to an end beyond itself but not merely instrumental to that end. Perhaps it can be helpful to think of study as what Aristotle called a *motion*, an action that is incomplete in itself, seeking an end beyond itself, like walking to town or building a house. "For it is not the same thing which at the same time is walking and has walked," Aristotle wrote, "or is building and has built." These are "two different things; and that which is causing motion is different from that which has caused motion." The perfect tense and the present tense—the process and its end—are distinct. Just so, he went on to say, learning and being learned are two different things. Learning is a motion in this sense.[41]

Aristotle contrasted this sense of motion with what he called an *actualization*, which he described as a "process which includes the end" in itself. Actions like seeing, understanding, and thinking all are actualizations, in this sense. For, Aristotle wrote, "at the same time we see and have seen, understand and have understood, think and have thought." Actualizations hold the perfect and the present tenses together in a single moment.

Under the pressure of lived experience, a simple contrast between motion and actualization starts to break down in fruitful ways. We see the ways in which theological study does and does not fit the category of motion. It *is* a kind of motion whose end is outside itself, like walking to a town, but with this difference: in theological study we cannot achieve the end we seek. Even as we walk our way to pleasant towns of reading Greek or learning the real story of Azusa, our yearning stretches toward a City that is always past the towns. Our home lies over Jordan.

Moreover, as Aristotle went on to argue, the distinction between motions and actualizations is not absolute. In seeking ends beyond themselves, motions exercise capacities. The exercise of those capacities is good in itself, like an actualization. As the philosopher Aryeh Kosman writes, commenting on this passage in Aristotle, "a motion is the realization of what is able to be . . . qua able to be; it is the [actualization] of being able to be."[42] Just so, in theological study, we exercise our capacity to learn. There is a difference between learning and having learned, and so it is still a kind of motion. But in study we are also being the kinds of creatures who can study, which is to say, the kinds of creatures who can know and be known by God. And in being those kinds of creatures, in saying yes to the grace that makes and remakes us as such creatures, we are engaged in an activity that has its end within itself. In studying we are coming to know. Indeed, we study because we do not know. We are in motion, learning. But exactly in the process of coming to know, we are actualizing the selves—living as the selves—we are created, redeemed, and called to be. In walking along the way, a walk that makes sense only because we are not at our destination, we find ourselves receiving the gift of the end toward which we walk. In learning what we do not know, even in yearning for what we can't know in this life, we find that the love of God abides, always already in the present tense.

As the disciples walked to Emmaus, they moved toward a town that was a place to spend the night. It was not their ultimate destination; they had given up hope for that back in Jerusalem. It was just a place to stop along the way. But it was still worth getting there, like a paper at the end of a long semester, or the end of one of many books on a nightstand. They walked toward Emmaus as an attainable destination. As they walked, the risen Christ met them on the road and taught them in a long, peripatetic seminar on sacred texts. They were learning, in motion toward more perfect understanding they did not attain on the road. But exactly in the motion of their learning, Jesus was walking with them. In walking with him, they were already dwelling at the end of their journey. Even before they broke bread with him—even before they realized what was happening—they were sharing in the activity that was the meaning and destination of their lives, and ours. The great end of knowing and being known by God is not only over the horizon of our walking, but also present, in resurrection grace, all along the way.

Do not our hearts burn within us, even now?

For Further Thought

The Theological Education between the Times series ranges widely, but it is inevitably and self-consciously incomplete. Authors in the series share hopes that the books will spark many more critical, theological reflections on the meanings and purposes of theological education. And so they end—like all good worship services downstream from Lane—with invitations.

I hope readers of this book will gather with colleagues and comrades for sustained study. I hope that study will involve reading widely. I would commend the other books in this series to you. And I have tried to leave breadcrumbs in the endnotes that will make it easy to follow up on anything that interests you in this one. I hope you will read beyond works that are marked as officially about "theological education." Working on this book has only deepened my conviction that we have to think about theological education as caught up in much larger social processes—and in the much, much larger work of God in redeeming the world.

As you read together, I hope that you will also write together. I cannot overstate how much writing together has mattered for each phase of this project. Writing involves risk; it creates new possibilities for connection; it is a technology for the care and construction of selves. The stakes need not be high, the passages need not be long. The main thing is to enter into writing together.

I hope that the colleagues and comrades in your study group will become your friends, and that friends in your group will become better friends. Friendships have transformed both the books and the lives of the authors in this series. Bonds of friendship, especially across the lines that usually divide us, let us think better together. But friendship is not just a means to smarter writing. It is a joy in itself.

As you read and write with your friends, I hope you will frame your time not as strategic planning but as a set of spiritual exercises, including confession, renunciation, and discernment. Give time to worship. The strategies will come. There are principled reasons for this hope: exercises like these are partially constitutive of Christian life. They have value in themselves. There are also pragmatic reasons: we need more than strategic planning to do the work demanded by this time between the times.

Most of all, I hope that your gatherings for prayer and study are marked by a lightheartedness that recognizes that it is not all up to us. If it were, all our teaching and learning would be a series of empty gestures. We of all people would be most to be pitied. Theological education will continue not because we figure out the next model but because Wisdom seeks us out: on the way, at the crossroads, beside the gates, even in our individualization. She seeks us out wherever we are. Theological education will continue because God longs to be known.

> Does not wisdom call,
>> and does not understanding raise her voice?
> On the heights, beside the way,
>> at the crossroads she takes her stand;
> beside the gates in front of the town,
>> at the entrance of the portals she cries out:
> "To you, O people, I call,
>> and my cry is to all that live." (Prov. 8:1–4)

Notes

Introduction

1. Lyman Beecher, "The Building of the Waste Places" (sermon delivered at Wolcott, Connecticut, September 21, 1814), in Lyman Beecher, *Sermons Delivered on Various Occasions* (Boston: John P. Jewett and Co., 1852), 139.

2. Beecher, "Building of the Waste Places," 115.

3. Beecher, "Building of the Waste Places," 140.

4. Lyman Beecher, "The Memory of Our Fathers" (sermon delivered at Plymouth, Massachusetts, December 22, 1827), 2nd ed. (Boston: T. R. Marvin, 1828), 5.

5. Beecher, "Memory of Our Fathers," 14–15.

6. *The Autobiography of Lyman Beecher*, ed. Barbara M. Cross (Cambridge, MA: Belknap Press of Harvard University Press, 1961), 1:252–53.

7. *The Autobiography of Lyman Beecher*, 2:167.

8. Lyman Beecher, *A Plea for the West* (Cincinnati: Truman & Smith, 1835); see also Aziz Rana, *The Two Faces of American Freedom* (Cambridge, MA: Harvard University Press, 2010).

9. See Beecher, *Plea for the West*, 42 and passim.

10. Arthur Joseph Stansbury, *Trial of the Rev. Lyman Beecher, D. D. before the Presbytery of Cincinnati, on the charge of heresy* (New York: New York Observer, 1835), 27.

11. For a nineteenth-century account of the founding of Lane that seeks to claim the school for New School Presbyterians, see *History of the Foundation and Endowment of the Lane Theological Seminary* (Cincin-

nati: Ben Franklin Printing House, 1848). Excellent twentieth-century accounts appear in Vincent Harding, *A Certain Magnificence: Lyman Beecher and the Transformation of American Protestantism, 1775–1863*, Chicago Studies in the History of American Religion, ed. Jerald C. Brauer and Martin E. Marty (Brooklyn, NY: Carlson Publishing, 1991), and Lawrence Thomas Lesick, *The Lane Rebels: Evangelicalism and Antislavery in Antebellum America*, Studies in Evangelicalism (Metuchen, NJ: Scarecrow, 1980).

12. Theodore Dwight Weld, "Letter to James Hall, Editor, The Western Messenger," reprinted in the *Cincinnati Journal*, May 30, 1834, https://tinyurl.com/59vjfuu9.

13. For an account of Bradley's speech at the debate, see "Debate at the Lane Seminary, Cincinnati. Speech of James A. Thome, of Kentucky, delivered at the Annual Meeting of the American Anti-Slavery Society, May 6, 1834. Letter of the Rev. Dr. Samuel H. Cox, against the American Colonization Society" (Boston: Garrison & Knapp, 1834), 4. For an account of his life that was attributed to him, see Lydia Marie Child, ed., *The Oasis* (Boston: Benjamin C. Bacon, 1834), 106–12.

14. This account is drawn especially from *The Autobiography of Lyman Beecher*; Harding, *A Certain Magnificence*; and Lesick, *The Lane Rebels*.

15. On the Cincinnati Sisters, see Lynne Marie Getz, "Partners in Motion: Gender, Migration, and Reform in Antebellum Ohio and Kansas," *Frontiers: A Journal of Women Studies* 27, no. 2 (2006): 102–35.

16. Lesick, *The Lane Rebels*, 93.

17. See Stephen Middleton, *The Black Laws: Race and the Legal Process in Early Ohio* (Athens: Ohio University Press, 2005).

18. Lyman Beecher, "Dr. Beecher's Address," *African Repository*, November 1834, 280. Beecher's address to the Cincinnati Colonization Society of June 4, 1834, was originally published in the *Cincinnati Journal* on June 13, 1834, and was reprinted in the *Repository*, the journal of the ACS. See https://tinyurl.com/37cemes7.

19. "Debate at the Lane Seminary," 11. Samuel Cox's letter, reprinted as part of the account of the debate, contained extended excerpts from a letter from Samuel E. Cornish, dated December 4, 1833. See also Albert Raboteau on "Africans in America," PBS, accessed June 30, 2022, https://tinyurl.com/2huuc5ju.

20. The letter is quoted in *The Autobiography of Lyman Beecher*, 2:242.
21. *The Autobiography of Lyman Beecher*, 2:244.
22. Harding, *A Certain Magnificence*, 515n49.
23. Beecher, *A Plea for the West*.
24. Lesick, *Lane Rebels*, 132.
25. Quoted in Lesick, *Lane Rebels*, 142.
26. Lesick, *Lane Rebels*, 134.
27. On the deep ideological connections between civic republicanism and the project of white settlement, see Rana, *The Two Faces of American Freedom*.
28. George Yancy, "Tarrying Together," *Educational Philosophy and Theory* 47 (2015): 26.
29. Willie James Jennings, *The Christian Imagination: Theology and the Origins of Race* (New Haven: Yale University Press, 2010), 7.
30. See especially Glenn T. Miller's excellent three-volume history of theological education: *Piety and Intellect: The Aims and Purposes of Antebellum Theological Education* (Atlanta: Scholars Press, 1990); *Piety and Profession: American Protestant Theological Education, 1870–1970* (Grand Rapids: Eerdmans, 2007); and *Piety and Plurality: Theological Education since 1960* (Eugene, OR: Cascade, 2014).
31. For profound meditations on established forms as both blessing and burden, see Keri Day, *Notes of a Native Daughter: Testifying in Theological Education*, Theological Education between the Times (Grand Rapids: Eerdmans, 2021).
32. When referring specifically to the form establishment took in Connecticut before 1818, I follow the vernacular usage and capitalize the initial letters in "Standing Order." When speaking about the social imaginary more broadly, I use the lowercase "standing order."
33. Many historians and social theorists have proposed something like these three models for interpreting US history. I have been especially influenced by Andrew Delbanco's proposal that three "predominant ideas"—God, nation, and self—have defined three different eras in US history. See Andrew Delbanco, *The Real American Dream: A Meditation on Hope* (Cambridge, MA: Harvard University Press, 1999). I have also learned much from Charles Taylor's threefold typology, which he defines as the *ancien régime* (paleo-Durkheimian), the Age of Mobilization

(neo-Durkheimian), and the Age of Authenticity (post-Durkheimian). See Charles Taylor, *A Secular Age* (Cambridge, MA: Belknap Press of Harvard University Press, 2007). As the pages that follow make clear, I break with both Delbanco and Taylor in multiple ways. But they have been essential conversation partners.

34. For more on what I mean by "eschatological memories," see Ted A. Smith, "Eschatological Memories of Everyday Life," in *Explorations in Lived Theology: New Perspectives on Method, Style, and Pedagogy in Theological and Religious Studies*, ed. Sarah Azaransky et al. (New York: Oxford University Press, 2016), 23–43.

35. On *Uncle Tom's Cabin*, see Saidiya Hartman, *Scenes of Subjection: Terror, Slavery, and Self-Making in Nineteenth Century America* (New York: Oxford University Press, 1997), 26–28.

Chapter 1

1. On social imaginaries, see Charles Taylor, *Modern Social Imaginaries* (Durham: Duke University Press, 2004), esp. chap. 1. On the particular imaginaries settlers brought with them to North America, see Sidney E. Mead, "From Coercion to Persuasion: Another Look at the Rise of Religious Liberty and the Emergence of Denominationalism," *Church History* (1956): 317–37.

2. Luther S. Cushing, *Reports of Cases Argued and Determined in the Supreme Judicial Court of Massachusetts* (Boston, 1854–1860), 8:187.

3. E. Brooks Holifield, "Toward a History of American Congregations," in *American Congregations: New Perspectives in the Study of Congregations*, ed. James P. Wind and James W. Lewis, vol. 2 (Chicago: University of Chicago Press, 1994), 23–53.

4. See Donald M. Scott, *From Office to Profession: The New England Ministry, 1750–1850* (Philadelphia: University of Pennsylvania Press, 1978), and E. Brooks Holifield, *God's Ambassadors: A History of the Christian Clergy in America* (Grand Rapids: Eerdmans, 2007), especially 52–65.

5. *New England's First Fruits; In Respect, First of the Conversion of Some, Conviction of Diverse, and Preparation of Sundry of the Indians. 2. Of the Progresse of Learning, In the Colledge at Cambridge in Massacusetts Bay. With Diverse Other Speciall Matters Concerning the Country* (London: Printed by R. O. and G. D. for Henry Overton, 1643).

6. Holifield, *God's Ambassadors*, 53.

7. Quoted in David W. Robson, *Educating Republicans: The College in the Era of the American Revolution, 1750–1800* (Westport, CT: Greenwood, 1985), 14.

8. See Mead, "From Coercion to Persuasion."

9. See Ted A. Smith, *The New Measures: A Theological History of Democratic Practice* (Cambridge: Cambridge University Press, 2007), chap. 3.

10. Phillips Payson, *A Sermon Preached before the Honorable Council, and the Honorable House of Representatives, of the state of Massachusetts-Bay, in New-England, at Boston, May 27, 1778: Being the Anniversary for the Election of the Honorable Council* (Boston: John Gill, 1778), 20.

11. Roger Finke and Rodney Stark, *The Churching of America, 1776–2005: Winners and Losers in Our Religious Economy*, rev. ed. (New Brunswick, NJ: Rutgers University Press, 2005).

12. Alexis de Tocqueville, *Democracy in America*, ed. Eduardo Nolla, trans. James T. Schleifer, vol. 2 (Indianapolis: Liberty Fund, 2012), 898. Available at https://tinyurl.com/4txp4wh2.

13. Tocqueville, *Democracy in America*, 2:898.

14. Tocqueville, *Democracy in America*, 2:900.

15. Tocqueville, *Democracy in America*, 2:896.

16. Tocqueville, *Democracy in America*, 2:901.

17. Tocqueville, *Democracy in America*, 2:902.

18. Tocqueville, *Democracy in America*, 2:896.

19. Theda Skocpol, "The Tocqueville Problem: Civic Engagement in American Democracy," *Social Science History* 21, no. 4 (Winter 1997): 455–79.

20. On this "civilizational connection" in what he calls a "neo-Durkheimian" social order, see Charles Taylor, "The Future of the Religious Past," in *Religion: Beyond a Concept*, ed. Hent De Vries (New York: Fordham University Press, 2008), 200.

21. Philip Schaff, *America: A Sketch of the Political, Social, and Religious Character of the United States of North America* (New York: C. Scribner, 1855), 93.

22. Schaff, *America*, 115.

23. Schaff, *America*, 94.

24. Schaff, *America*, 91.

25. Schaff, *America*, 124.

26. See Finke and Stark, *The Churching of America, 1776–2005*.

27. Here I am both drawing on and arguing with a number of scholars who have seen the benevolent societies as vessels of "trusteeship" and "social control." See, inter alia, Clifford S. Griffin, *Their Brothers' Keepers: Moral Stewardship in the United States, 1800–1865* (New Brunswick, NJ: Rutgers University Press, 1960).

28. Charles Taylor, "Religion Today," Institute for Human Sciences, accessed July 5, 2022, https://tinyurl.com/yrsr6kda.

29. On Judaism's transformation into denominations, see Steven R. Weisman, *How Judaism Became an American Religion* (New York: Simon & Schuster, 2018).

30. H. Richard Niebuhr, *The Social Sources of Denominationalism* (New York: Holt, 1929).

31. Holifield, "Toward a History," 33.

32. On institutional isomorphism, see Paul DiMaggio and Walter W. Powell, "The Iron Cage Revisited: Institutional Isomorphism and Collective Rationality in Organizational Fields," *American Sociological Review* 48, no. 2 (April 1983): 147–60. On this process at work in the congregation as voluntary society, see R. Stephen Warner, "Work in Progress toward a New Paradigm for the Sociological Study of Religion in the United States," *American Journal of Sociology* 98, no. 5 (March 1993): 1044–93. On the Black church's expansion of the congregational form, see C. Eric Lincoln and Lawrence H. Mamiya, *The Black Church in the African American Experience* (Durham, NC: Duke University Press, 1990).

33. Donald M. Scott, *From Office to Profession: The New England Ministry, 1750–1850* (Philadelphia: University of Pennsylvania Press, 1978), xi.

34. Holifield, *God's Ambassadors*, 6.

35. Burton J. Bledstein, *The Culture of Professionalism: The Middle Class and the Development of Higher Education in America* (New York: Norton, 1976), 174.

36. Bledstein, *The Culture of Professionalism*, 84.

37. On this core dynamic of professionalism, I have learned especially from Samuel Weber, "The Limits of Professionalism," *Oxford Literary Review* 5, no. 1 (1982): 59–79.

38. GSS Survey, cited in Mark Chaves, *American Religion: Contemporary Trends*, 2nd ed. (Princeton: Princeton University Press, 2017).

39. Schaff, *America*, 74.

40. *The Memoirs of Charles G. Finney: The Complete and Restored Text,* ed. Garth M. Rosell and Richard A. G. Dupuis (Grand Rapids: Zondervan, 1989), chap. 7.

41. W. R. Harper, "Shall the Theological Curriculum Be Modified, and How?" *American Journal of Theology* 3, no. 1 (January 1899): 55.

42. Harper, "Shall the Theological Curriculum Be Modified, and How?" 59.

43. William Adams Brown, "The Seminary of Tomorrow," *Harvard Theological Review* 12, no. 2 (April 1919): 174.

44. John S. Brubacher and Willis Rudy, "Professional Education," in *The History of Higher Education,* ed. Harold S. Wechsler, Lester F. Goodchild, and Linda Eisenmann, 3rd ed., ASHE Reader Series (Boston: Pearson Learning Solution, 2008), 279–93.

45. William James, "The Proposed Shortening of the College Course," *Harvard Monthly* 11 (1891): 133. Quoted in Laurence R. Veysey, *The Emergence of the American University* (Chicago: University of Chicago Press, 1965), 61. On the larger movement toward specialization and utility, see also Chad Wellmon, "Whatever Happened to General Education?" *Hedgehog Review* 19, no. 1 (Spring 2017).

46. Bledstein, *The Culture of Professionalism,* 84–85.

47. James Fallows, "The Case against Credentialism," *Atlantic,* December 1985, https://tinyurl.com/2r2ata9r.

48. On the significance of inputs for evaluating professionals, see Fallows, "The Case against Credentialism."

49. Bledstein, *The Culture of Professionalism,* 125.

50. Edward Farley's landmark book *Theologia: The Fragmentation and Unity of Theological Education* (Philadelphia: Fortress, 1983) is sometimes read as a straightforward historical account that ascribes great influence to Schleiermacher in the formation of dominant models of theological education in the United States. I don't find evidence for that kind of direct influence. And I think that version of the story gives too much credit to the power of theological arguments to drive history. The better reading—both of the history of theological education in the United States and of Farley's book—lets Farley's account provide a theological genealogy that illumines the logic at work within present institutional forms.

51. Thomas Albert Howard, *Protestant Theology and the Making*

of the Modern German University (Oxford: Oxford University Press, 2006), 212ff.

52. See Friedrich Schleiermacher, *Brief Outline of Theology as a Field of Study*, trans. Terrence N. Tice, 3rd ed. (Louisville: Westminster John Knox, 2011; previous editions 1811 and 1830). See also Friedrich Schleiermacher, "Occasional Thoughts on German Universities in the German Sense," in *The Rise of the Research University: A Sourcebook*, ed. Louis Menand, Paul Reitter, and Chad Wellmon (Chicago: University of Chicago Press, 2020), 45–66. For a reading that attends to the subtleties of Schleiermacher for the sake of teaching today, see Mark D. Jordan, *Transforming Fire: Imagining Christian Teaching*, Theological Education between the Times (Grand Rapids: Eerdmans, 2021).

53. Brown, "The Seminary of Tomorrow," 178.

54. Robert L. Kelly, *Theological Education in America: A Study of One Hundred Sixty-One Theological Schools in the United States and Canada* (New York: George H. Doran Co., 1924); Mark A. May, ed., *The Education of American Ministers* (New York: Institute of Social and Religious Research, 1934).

55. Abraham Flexner, "Medical Education in the United States and Canada: A Report to the Carnegie Foundation for the Advancement of Teaching" (New York: Carnegie Foundation, 1910).

56. On the history of the ATS, see Leon Pacala, *The Role of ATS in Theological Education* (Atlanta: Scholars Press, 1998). For a more pointed history, see Daniel O. Aleshire, *Beyond Profession: The Next Future of Theological Education*, Theological Education between the Times (Grand Rapids: Eerdmans, 2021), especially chap. 2.

57. Willie James Jennings, *After Whiteness: An Education in Belonging*, Theological Education between the Times (Grand Rapids: Eerdmans, 2020), 101.

58. Elizabeth Hlavinka, "Racial Bias in Flexner Report Permeates Medical Education Today," MedPage Today, June 18, 2020, https://tinyurl.com/mtf757yp.

59. Pacala takes the story through the 1980s. See Pacala, *The Role of ATS*, 7–8. On Logos Evangelical Seminary, see Chloe T. Sun, *Attempt Great Things for God: Theological Education in Diaspora*, Theological Education between the Times (Grand Rapids: Eerdmans, 2020).

Chapter 2

1. Jeffrey M. Jones, "U.S. Church Membership Falls below Majority for First Time," Gallup, March 29, 2021, https://tinyurl.com/b8zrmt7j; Gregory A. Smith, "About Three-in-Ten U.S. Adults Are Now Religiously Unaffiliated," Pew Research Center, December 14, 2021, https://tinyurl.com/ewju2n6z.

2. For a recent instance of this perennial narrative—and a good recapitulation of some important precedents—see Timothy Keller, "The Decline and Renewal of the American Church: Part 1—the Decline of the Mainline," Life in the Gospel, Fall 2021, https://tinyurl.com/yhupnst8.

3. R. Albert Mohler Jr., "From Mainline to Sideline—the Death of Protestant America," Albert Mohler, August 26, 2008, https://tinyurl.com/2p84whch; Holly Meyer, "Southern Baptist Convention Membership Drops for 14th Year in a Row," Nashville Tennessean, May 28, 2021, https://tinyurl.com/2p9jehv4; Rick Seltzer, "Cuts at Liberty Hit Divinity," Inside Higher Ed, June 17, 2019, https://tinyurl.com/bd6zcxnm; Daniel Silliman, "Gordon-Conwell to Sell Main Campus, Move to Boston," Christianity Today, May 17, 2022, https://tinyurl.com/2pcxa3at.

4. David Voas and Mark Chaves, "Is the United States a Counterexample to the Secularization Thesis?" American Journal of Sociology 121, no. 5 (March 2016): 1517–56.

5. "In U.S., Decline of Christianity Continues at Rapid Pace," Pew Research Center, October 17, 2019, https://tinyurl.com/2cv49w8x.

6. David Brooks, "The Dissenters Trying to Save Evangelicalism from Itself," New York Times, February 4, 2022, https://tinyurl.com/cn3f3v3v; Ryan P. Burge, "So, Why Is Evangelicalism Not Declining? Because Non-Attenders Are Taking on the Label," Religion in Public, December 10, 2020, https://tinyurl.com/5n8fzszn.

7. Amelia Thomson-DeVeaux and Daniel Cox, "The Christian Right Is Helping Drive Liberals Away from Religion," FiveThirtyEight, September 18, 2019, https://tinyurl.com/2jx64m8p.

8. Emma Green, "Politics as the New Religion for Progressive Democrats," Atlantic, October 18, 2018, https://tinyurl.com/bt4fkrps.

9. See Melissa Florer-Bixler, "Capitalism Is Killing the Small Church," Faith & Leadership, April 30, 2019, https://tinyurl.com/2cbj2x6e.

10. Michelle Boorstein and Gary Gately, "More Than 300 Accused Priests Listed in Pennsylvania Report on Catholic Church Sex Abuse," *Washington Post*, August 14, 2018, https://tinyurl.com/3bhkxdyc; Derek Thompson, "Three Decades Ago, America Lost Its Religion. Why?" *Atlantic*, September 26, 2019, https://tinyurl.com/2p94n3am; "Abuse of Faith: A Chronicle Investigation," *Houston Chronicle*, accessed July 6, 2022, https://tinyurl.com/3x3w8y5c.

11. Ryan Burge, "Is Religious Decline Inevitable in the United States?" *Black Christian News*, accessed July 6, 2022, https://tinyurl.com/bdfabvr8. For a more comprehensive survey—and a more precise sifting—of secularization theories, see Charles Taylor, *A Secular Age* (Cambridge, MA: Belknap Press of Harvard University Press, 2007), 1–25 and passim.

12. "Religious Landscape Study," Pew Research Center, 2014, https://tinyurl.com/5xh3ucej.

13. For an overview of many of these currents, see Tara Isabella Burton, *Strange Rites: New Religions for a Godless World* (New York: Public Affairs, 2020). For more particulars, see Kevin D. Williamson, "'Mindfulness': Corporate America's Strange New Gospel," *National Review*, January 1, 2018, https://tinyurl.com/bdem4tny; Ariel Levy, "Glennon Doyle's Honesty Gospel," *New Yorker*, February 8, 2021, https://tinyurl.com/4hs7muaa; Kathryn Lofton, *Oprah: The Gospel of an Icon* (Berkeley: University of California Press, 2011); Josh Barro, "SoulCycle: You Say 'Cult.' I Say 'Loyal Customer Base,'" *New York Times*, August 7, 2015, https://tinyurl.com/2p86tdr8; Jessica Roy, "How Millennials Replaced Religion with Astrology and Crystals," *Los Angeles Times*, July 10, 2019. And for a classic analysis of how "occult" sensibilities are not just harbored but actively generated by modernity, see Max Horkheimer and Theodor Adorno, *Dialectic of Enlightenment*, trans. Edmund Jephcott (Stanford, CA: Stanford University Press, 1947).

14. Nancy T. Ammerman, "Organized Religion in a Voluntaristic Society," *Sociology of Religion* 58, no. 3 (1997): 203–15.

15. Russell M. Jenung, Seanan S. Fong, and Helen Jin Kim, *Family Sacrifices: The Worldviews and Ethics of Chinese Americans* (New York: Oxford University Press, 2019).

16. See Wendy Cadge, *Paging God: Religion in the Halls of Medicine*

(Chicago: University of Chicago Press, 2012); Winnifred Fallers Sullivan, *Ministry of Presence: Chaplaincy, Spiritual Care, and the Law* (Chicago: University of Chicago Press, 2019). On increasing interest at one school, see Chris Meehan, "Interest in Chaplaincy Is Growing," Christian Reformed Church, March 2, 2016, https://tinyurl.com/yr45f74c.

17. Faith Hill, "They Tried to Start a Church without God. For a While, It Worked," *Atlantic*, July 21, 2019, https://tinyurl.com/2p9ajuza.

18. Ulrich Beck and Elisabeth Beck-Gernsheim, *Individualization: Institutionalized Individualism and Its Social and Political Consequences* (London: Sage, 2002), 63. I am grateful to Gerardo Marti for pointing me to this work.

19. Beck and Beck-Gernsheim, *Individualization*, 65.

20. Beck and Beck-Gernsheim, *Individualization*, 63.

21. Beck and Beck-Gernsheim, *Individualization*, 63.

22. Of Wilson's many works, see especially William Julius Wilson, *When Work Disappears: The World of the New Urban Poor* (New York: Knopf, 1996). On neoliberalism more broadly, see Daniel Rodgers, "The Uses and Abuses of 'Neoliberalism,'" *Dissent* 65, no. 1 (Winter 2018): 78–87; Keri Day, *Religious Resistance to Neoliberalism: Womanist and Black Feminist Perspectives* (New York: Palgrave Macmillan, 2015); Ulrich Beck, *Risk Society: Towards a New Modernity* (London: Sage, 1992).

23. See Beck and Beck-Gernsheim, *Individualization*, 63–65; Tayyab Mahmud, "Debt and Discipline," *American Quarterly* 64, no. 3 (September 2012): 469–94.

24. See Beck and Beck-Gernsheim, *Individualization*, 70, 85–119.

25. Wendy Brown, *In the Ruins of Neoliberalism: The Rise of Antidemocratic Politics in the West* (New York: Columbia University Press, 2019), Kindle location 336.

26. See Shoshana Zuboff, *The Age of Surveillance Capitalism: The Fight for a Human Future at the New Frontier of Power* (New York: Public Affairs, 2019).

27. On the general phenomenon, see Ryan Burge, "Jesus Came to Proclaim Good News to the Poor. But Now They're Leaving Church," *Christianity Today*, November 27, 2019, https://tinyurl.com/5bnpaafp. For demographics on lack of affiliation among different racial and ethnic groups, see "Religious Landscape Study." For a closer study of the white

working class, see W. Bradford Wilcox et al., "No Money, No Honey, No Church: The Deinstitutionalization of Religious Life among the White Working Class," *Res Social Work* 23 (2012): 227–50. And on deaths of despair, see Anne Case and Angus Deaton, *Deaths of Despair and the Future of Capitalism* (Princeton: Princeton University Press, 2020).

28. Jennifer M. Silva, *Coming Up Short: Working-Class Adulthood in an Age of Uncertainty* (New York: Oxford University Press, 2013), 10 and passim.

29. See José Casanova, *Public Religions in the Modern World* (Chicago: University of Chicago Press, 1994). The "deprivatization" Casanova describes is happening via the category of identity.

30. Vincent W. Lloyd, "Introduction: Managing Race, Managing Religion," in *Race and Secularism in America*, ed. Jonathan S. Kahn and Vincent W. Lloyd (New York: Columbia University Press, 2016), 12.

31. Lloyd, "Introduction," 7.

32. Charles Taylor, "The Future of Religious Past," in *Religion: Beyond a Concept*, ed. Hent De Vries (New York: Fordham University Press, 2008), 202.

33. See Taylor, "Future of Religious Past," 178–79; Courtney Bender, *The New Metaphysicals: Spirituality and the American Religious Imagination* (Chicago: University of Chicago Press, 2010); W. E. B. Du Bois, *The Souls of Black Folk* (1903; reprint, New York: Vintage Books, 1990), 138.

34. Penny Long Marler and C. Kirk Hadaway, "'Being Religious' or 'Being Spiritual' in America: A Zero-Sum Proposal?" *Journal for the Scientific Study of Religion* 41, no. 2 (2002): 289–300; Yonat Shimron, "New Poll Finds Even Religious Americans Feel the Good Vibrations," Religion News Service, August 29, 2018, https://tinyurl.com/2p92hu6h; Hans Urs von Balthasar, afterword to *Meditations on the Tarot: A Journey into Christian Hermeticism*, trans. Robert Powell (1980; reprint, New York: Tarcher/Putnam, 2002).

35. Martin Marty, "Getting Organized," *Christian Century* 113 (1996): 439. Quoted in Marler and Hadaway, "'Being Religious' or 'Being Spiritual,'" 297.

36. Donald MacKinnon makes a parallel argument about the self-emptying of the standing order in England in Donald MacKinnon,

"Kenosis and Establishment," in *The Stripping of the Altars: The Gore Memorial Lecture Delivered on 5 November 1968 in Westminster Abbey, and Other Papers and Essays on Related Topics* (London: Collins, 1969), 13–40. And while David Hollinger does not speak of kenosis, he argues for a related view of Protestant liberalism in David A. Hollinger, *After Cloven Tongues of Fire: Protestant Liberalism in Modern American History* (Princeton: Princeton University Press, 2015).

Chapter 3

1. C. Kirk Hadaway and Penny Long Marler, "What Pastors Get Paid, and When It's Not Enough," *Christian Century*, June 6, 2019, 22–25.

2. I borrow this language from Jean LeClercq's great book on a mode of theological education that arose in a previous time between the times, *The Love of Learning and the Desire for God: A Study of Monastic Culture* (New York: Fordham University Press, 1982).

3. Jeff Brumley, "In BNG Webinar, Ryan Burge Details the Double Threat to Denominational Churches in America," *Baptist News Global*, April 27, 2021, https://tinyurl.com/wupv2s6s.

4. See James Hudnut-Beumler, introduction to *The Future of Mainline Protestantism in America*, ed. James Hudnut-Beumler and Mark Silk (New York: Columbia University Press, 2018), 1–15.

5. On the role of whiteness in the project of national reunification, see David W. Blight, *Race and Reunion: The Civil War in American Memory* (Cambridge, MA: Harvard University Press, 2002).

6. Robert Wuthnow, *The Restructuring of American Religion: Society and Faith since World War II* (Princeton: Princeton University Press, 1988), chap. 6.

7. Charles Taylor, "The Future of Religious Past," in *Religion: Beyond a Concept*, ed. Hent De Vries (New York: Fordham University Press, 2008), 202.

8. Mark Chaves, *American Religion: Contemporary Trends*, 2nd ed. (Princeton: Princeton University Press, 2017), fig. 5.1, p. 58; Yonat Shimron, "Study: Attendance Hemorrhaging at Small and Midsize US Congregations," Religion News Service, October 14, 2021, https://tinyurl.com/22yk6bn9.

9. "The Giving Environment: Understanding Pre-Pandemic Trends in Charitable Giving," Lilly Family School of Philanthropy, July 2021, https://tinyurl.com/472jbnms.

10. Yonat Shimron, "Study: More Churches Closing Than Opening," Religion News Service, May 26, 2021, https://tinyurl.com/mv6wb4jy.

11. Shimron, "Study: Attendance Hemorrhaging at Small and Mid-size US Congregations."

12. Chaves, *American Religion*, fig. 5.7, p. 72.

13. "Living by the Gospel," Board of Pensions of the Presbyterian Church (USA), updated April 1, 2021, https://tinyurl.com/2yrcbrj4.

14. Jeff Brumley, "In BNG Webinar, Ryan Burge Details the Double Threat to Denominational Churches in America," *Baptist New Global*, April 27, 2021, https://tinyurl.com/yvva9sny.

15. Bob Smietana, "Why the Minichurch Is the Latest Trend in American Religion," Religion News Service, November 16, 2021, https://tinyurl.com/bpsay25m.

16. Ted A. Smith Sr., conversation with the author, March 13, 2021. Used with permission.

17. Jean Hopfensperger, "Fewer People Are Entering the Seminary as Need Declines, Church Budgets Shrink," *Minneapolis Star-Tribune*, August 19, 2018, https://tinyurl.com/34m2ufh8; Adam DeHoek and Kenneth Inskeep, "The Supply of and Demand for Clergy in the ELCA," Office of the Presiding Bishop, Evangelical Lutheran Church in America, March 2016; Hadaway and Marler, "What Pastors Get Paid, and When It's Not Enough"; Barbara Wheeler, "Ready to Lead? The Problems with Lay Pastors," *Christian Century*, July 13, 2010, https://tinyurl.com/yaff72zv.

A focus on seminary placement rates can obscure this larger dynamic. PC(USA) seminaries, for instance, continue to enjoy relatively high rates of placements of graduates in ministry. Seminary graduates can still get jobs. But these placements are happening within an overall ecology that is rapidly contracting. In the 2010s, the PC(USA) lost about one thousand congregations. Even in this challenging environment, most of the 3,100 new ordinands could still find placements because more than 4,700 ministers retired. Higher numbers of retirees, lower numbers of new ministers, and a shrinking number of congregations have existed in a kind of equilibrium that has kept placement rates high. It is not clear that this equilibrium will be sustainable. Data from "Living by the Gospel"; Leslie Scanlon, "Full-Time Called Pastor as an Endangered Species," *Presbyterian Outlook*, March 18, 2013, https://tinyurl.com/2p9asbsz; and email from Lee Hinson-Hasty, February 21, 2019.

18. "May 2020 National Occupational Employment and Wage Estimates," US Bureau of Labor Statistics, https://tinyurl.com/36bb67et; Hadaway and Marler, "What Pastors Get Paid," 23; Jo Ann Deasy, "Black Student Perspectives," in *Bivocational and Beyond: Educating for Thriving Multivocational Ministry*, ed. Darryl W. Stephens (n.p.: Books@Atla Open Press, 2022); David Briggs, "Pay Gap for Women Clergy Is Decreasing," *Christian Century* 134, no. 18 (August 30, 2017): 12.

19. "May 2020 National Occupational Employment and Wage Estimates."

20. See Ted A. Smith, "Discerning Authorities," in *Questions Preachers Ask: Essays in Honor of Thomas G. Long*, ed. Scott Black Johnston, Ted A. Smith, and Leonora Tubbs Tisdale (Louisville: Westminster John Knox, 2016), 55–72. On the older roots of these practices in nineteenth-century revivals, see Ted A. Smith, *The New Measures: A Theological History of Democratic Practice* (Cambridge: Cambridge University Press, 2007), chap. 5.

21. On the role of finance capital in reshaping medicine, see Gabriel Winant, *The Next Shift: The Fall of Industry and the Rise of Health Care in Rust Belt America* (Cambridge, MA: Harvard University Press, 2021). On shifts in medical practices, see Carol K. Kane, "Updated Data on Physician Practice Arrangements: For the First Time, Fewer Physicians Are Owners Than Employees," American Medical Association Policy Research Perspectives, May 2019, https://tinyurl.com/cntd8yte; Bita Kash and Debra Tan, "Physician Group Practice Trends: A Comprehensive Review," *Journal of Hospital and Medical Management*, March 21, 2016, https://tinyurl.com/mry5eubx.

22. Yuval Levin, *A Time to Build: From Family and Community to Congress and the Campus, How Recommitting to Our Institutions Can Revive the American Dream* (New York: Basic Books, 2020), chap. 2.

23. "The Rise and Fall of Mars Hill," *Christianity Today* podcast, https://tinyurl.com/4duc2da6.

24. Chaves, *American Religion*, fig. 6.1, p. 76.

25. Asbury Theological Seminary, profile at ATS, accessed July 7, 2022, https://tinyurl.com/2s3eh8nn.

26. Justo González, *The History of Theological Education* (Nashville: Abingdon, 2015), 136.

27. David F. Labaree, *A Perfect Mess: The Unlikely Ascendancy of American Higher Education* (Chicago: University of Chicago Press, 2017), 93.

28. See Sacvan Bercovitch, *The American Jeremiad* (Madison: University of Wisconsin Press, 1978).

29. Karl Marx, "The Eighteenth Brumaire of Louis Bonaparte," in *The Marx-Engels Reader*, ed. Robert C. Tucker, 2nd ed. (New York: Norton, 1978).

30. On the connections between voluntary associations and the sacred mission of the nation, Taylor writes: "The point I want to make about British and later American patriotism, based as it was at first on the sense of fulfilling God's design, is that national identity was based on a self-ascribed pre-eminence in realizing a certain civilizational superiority. The superiority may have ultimately been understood as that of 'Christendom' over infidel religions, but within Christendom, Britain/ America stood at the cutting edge. This sense of superiority, originally religious in essence, can and does undergo a 'secularization' as the sense of civilizational superiority becomes detached from Providence and attributed to race, or Enlightenment, or even some combination of the two. But the point of identifying this sense of order is that it provides another niche, as it were, in which God can be present in our lives, or in our social imaginary—the author not just of design that defines our political identity but also of the design that defines civilizational order." Taylor, "Future of the Religious Past," 198. See also Charles Taylor, *A Secular Age* (Cambridge, MA: Belknap Press of Harvard University Press, 2007), 423–73. On Beecher's connection of the seminary to the saving role of white Protestant America, see his *Plea for the West* and my discussion of it in the parable at the beginning of this book.

The End

1. Thomas Merton, *Conjectures of a Guilty Bystander* (1965; reprint, New York: Image, 2014), 113.

2. James C. Collins and Jerry I. Porras, "Building Your Company's Vision," *Harvard Business Review*, September–October 1996, 73.

3. Unless otherwise indicated, all Scripture quotations in this book are from the New Revised Standard Version.

4. Walter Brueggemann, *To Build, to Plant: A Commentary on Jeremiah 26–52*, International Theological Commentary (Grand Rapids: Eerdmans, 1991), 71–72.

5. See Antonio Eduardo Alonso, *Commodified Communion: Eucharist, Consumer Culture, and the Practice of Everyday Life* (New York: Fordham University Press, 2021).

6. In defining determinate negation in this way, I am drawing especially on Max Horkheimer and Theodor W. Adorno, *Dialektik der Aufklärung: Philosophische Fragmente*, in Theodor W. Adorno, *Gesammelte Schriften*, 20 vols. (Frankfurt am Main: Suhrkamp, 1977), 3:40ff.; ET: *Dialectic of Enlightenment* (1947; reprint, New York: Continuum, 2000), 23ff. I am further developing ideas that are present in Ted A. Smith, "The Mark of Cain: Sovereign Negation and the Politics of God," *Modern Theology* 36, no. 1 (January 2020): 56–73.

7. Vincent Lloyd, *Religion of the Field Negro* (New York: Fordham University Press, 2018), 236.

8. Tina Campt, "Black Visuality and the Practice of Refusal," *Women & Performance*, February 25, 2019, https://tinyurl.com/y3w23by2. I am grateful to Joi Orr for pointing me to this essay.

Chapter 4

1. De'Amon Harges, "A Brief History of Broadway United Methodist Church (Indianapolis): Roving Listener," YouTube, September 3, 2019, https://tinyurl.com/36ry4huj. For Mather's reflections on Broadway, see Michael Mather, *Having Nothing, Possessing Everything: Finding Abundant Communities in Unexpected Places* (Grand Rapids: Eerdmans, 2018).

2. De'Amon Harges and Michael Mather, "Virtual Seminar on Asset Based Community Development," The Collegeville Institute, January 6, 2021.

3. Edward Farley, *Theologia: The Fragmentation and Unity of Theological Education* (Philadelphia: Fortress, 1983).

4. Theodor W. Adorno, *Problems of Moral Philosophy*, trans. Rodney Livingstone (Stanford, CA: Stanford University Press, 2001), 17.

5. Barbara Ehrenreich and John Ehrenreich, "The Professional-Managerial Class," *Radical America* 11, no. 2 (March–April 1977): 7–31. For a more recent reconsideration of the argument, see Barbara Ehren-

reich and John Ehrenreich, "Death of a Yuppie Dream: The Rise and Fall of the Professional-Managerial Class" (New York: Rosa Luxemburg Stiftung, 2013).

6. Barbara Ehrenreich, in Alex Press, "On the Origins of the Professional-Managerial Class: An Interview with Barbara Ehrenreich," *Dissent*, October 22, 2019, https://tinyurl.com/4uvttspe.

7. On the efforts of white professionals to reform Black communities, see Jamil W. Drake, *To Know the Soul of a People: Religion, Race, and the Making of Southern Folk* (Oxford: Oxford University Press, 2022).

8. See Evelyn Brooks Higginbotham, *Righteous Discontent: The Women's Movement in the Black Baptist Church, 1880–1920* (Cambridge, MA: Harvard University Press, 1994).

9. Ehrenreich and Ehrenreich, "The Professional-Managerial Class."

10. B. Ehrenreich, in Press, "On the Origins of the Professional-Managerial Class."

11. Stefano Harney and Fred Moten, *The Undercommons: Fugitive Planning and Black Study* (Wivenhoe, UK: Minor Compositions, 2013), 34.

12. For a brilliant description of "nothing music," see Ashon T. Crawley, *Blackpentecostal Breath: The Aesthetics of Possibility* (New York: Fordham University Press, 2017), 258ff.

13. Samuel Miller, *Letters on Clerical Manners and Habits: Addressed to A Student in the Theological School in the Theological Seminary at Princeton, N.J.*, rev. ed. (Philadelphia: Presbyterian Board of Publication, 1852), 10.

14. Carter Godwin Woodson, *The Mis-Education of the Negro* (New York: Associated Publishers, 1933), 4–5.

15. Woodson, *The Mis-Education of the Negro*, 66.

16. Keri Day, *Notes of a Native Daughter: Testifying in Theological Education*, Theological Education between the Times (Grand Rapids: Eerdmans, 2021); Willie James Jennings, *After Whiteness: An Education in Belonging*, Theological Education between the Times (Grand Rapids: Eerdmans, 2020).

17. Ignacio Ellacuría, "Is a Different Kind of University Possible?" trans. Philip Berryman, in *Towards a Society That Serves Its People: The Intellectual Contribution of El Salvador's Murdered Jesuits*, ed. John Hassett and Hugh Lacey (Washington, DC: Georgetown University Press, 1991), 188.

18. Ellacuría, "Is a Different Kind of University Possible?" 198.

19. Ignacio Ellacuría, "The Poor Majority," trans. Philip Berryman, in Hassett and Lacey, *Towards a Society That Serves Its People*, 174.

20. Throughout this section I have learned especially from Jennings, *After Whiteness*. And here, in talk of a "crowd," I borrow directly from his imagery. See chap. 5 and passim.

21. "Economic Challenges Facing Future Ministers," Association of Theological Schools, "GSQ Total School Profile," table 7, GSQ Question 13a, 2019–2020. The data appears on slides that can be found here: https://tinyurl.com/2p87dn2v.

22. "Economic Challenges Facing Future Ministers," table 7, GSQ Question 13b. See also Heather Grennan Gary, "Qualified for Admission, but in Debt," *In Trust*, 2018, https://tinyurl.com/mucadf8r.

23. "Economic Challenges Facing Future Ministers," table 7, GSQ Question 13b.

24. Maurizio Lazzarato, *Governing by Debt*, trans. Joshua David Jordan (Cambridge, MA: Semiotext(e), 2013), 66.

25. Lazzarato, *Governing by Debt*, 67.

26. Tayyab Mahmud, "Debt and Discipline: Neoliberal Political Economy and the Working Classes," *Kentucky Law Journal* 101, no. 1 (2012–2013): 5.

27. Sharon L. Miller, Kim Maphis Early, and Anthony T. Ruger, "A Call to Action: How Theological Schools Can Help Students Manage Educational Debt," *Auburn Studies*, 2014, 6–7.

28. Sharon L. Miller, Kim Maphis Early, and Anthony Ruger, "Taming the Tempest: A Team Approach to Reducing and Managing Student Debt," *Auburn Studies*, 2014, 15.

29. Mahmud, "Debt and Discipline," 42.

30. Lazzarato, *Governing by Debt*, 65–66.

31. "By the End of 2021, the Federal Government Had $28.43 Trillion in Federal Debt," DataLab, accessed July 8, 2022, https://tinyurl.com/3hah5rn2.

32. Here I have learned especially from the discussion of national debt in Maurizio Lazzarato, *The Making of the Indebted Man: An Essay on the Neoliberal Condition* (Cambridge, MA: Semiotext(e), 2012), 32.

33. Kathryn Tanner, *Christianity and the New Spirit of Capitalism* (New Haven: Yale University Press, 2019), 29.

34. See Johnna Montgomerie, "Webcast—Financial Melancholia:

Mental Health and Indebtedness," Political Economy Research Centre, July 15, 2015, https://tinyurl.com/mu3tfjst.

35. Miller, Early, and Ruger, "Taming the Tempest."

36. Edwin Chr. van Driel, "Rethinking Seminary," Pittsburgh Theological Seminary, March 27, 2015, https://tinyurl.com/5n6rsb8e.

37. Herbert Marcuse, *One-Dimensional Man: Studies in the Ideology of Advanced Industrial Society*, 2nd ed. (Boston: Beacon, 1964), chap. 3. I was pointed back to Marcuse by the analysis in Wendy Brown, *In the Ruins of Neoliberalism: The Rise of Antidemocratic Politics in the West* (New York: Columbia University Press, 2019), chap. 5.

38. I develop this argument more fully in Ted A. Smith, "The Politics of Christian Theological Education," *Religious Studies News*, April 28, 2017, https://tinyurl.com/ycpymev4.

Chapter 5

1. Sara Williams introduced me to the language of affordances as it has developed through the anthropology of ethics. See Sara Ann Williams, "Moral Apprentices at the Margins: Come and See Tours and the Making of the Ethical Self" (PhD diss., Emory University, 2021). For additional reading, see especially Webb Keane, *Ethical Life: Its Natural and Social Histories* (Princeton: Princeton University Press, 2016).

Christian Scharen introduced me to the ways a related conversation has developed around the significance of practice for knowledge. See Christian Scharen, "Learning Ministry over Time: Embodying Practical Wisdom," in *For Life Abundant: Practical Theology, Theological Education, and Christian Ministry*, ed. Dorothy C. Bass and Craig R. Dykstra (Grand Rapids: Eerdmans, 2008), 284ff. As background to this line of conversation, see especially Hubert L. Dreyfus, "Overcoming the Myth of the Mental: How Philosophers Can Profit from the Phenomenology of Everyday Expertise," in *Skillful Coping: Essays on the Phenomenology of Everyday Perception and Action*, ed. Mark A. Wrathall (New York: Oxford University Press, 2014), 104–26.

2. Maurice Merleau-Ponty, *Phenomenology of Perception*, trans. Colin Smith (London: Routledge, 1958), 130.

3. See Dreyfus, "Overcoming the Myth of the Mental."

4. Theodor Adorno, *Minima Moralia: Reflections from Damaged Life*, trans. E. F. N. Jephcott (New York: Verso, 1951), 247.

5. Lori J. Carrell, *Preaching That Matters: Reflective Practices for Transforming Sermons* (Lanham, MD: Rowman & Littlefield, 2013), 131.

6. Herminia Ibarra, "The Authenticity Paradox," *Harvard Business Review*, January-February 2015, https://tinyurl.com/2p8h57x9. For more on the authority of authenticity, see Ted A. Smith, "Discerning Authorities," in *Questions Preachers Ask: Essays in Honor of Thomas G. Long*, ed. Scott Black Johnston, Ted A. Smith, and Leonora Tubbs Tisdale (Louisville: Westminster John Knox, 2016), 55–72.

7. See, for instance, Jodi Dean, "Donald Trump Is the Most Honest Candidate in American Politics Today," *In These Times*, August 12, 2015, https://tinyurl.com/2nyjubp5; Doyle McManus, "Campaign 2016's Quixotic Quest for 'Authenticity,'" *Chicago Tribune*, November 2, 2015, https://tinyurl.com/bdeeapa2; Rachel Stern, "Trump's Authenticity Is What's Making Him Popular, UB Political Scientist Says," University of Buffalo, August 4, 2015, https://tinyurl.com/4s8ru5fh.

8. Asma Khalid, "'Authenticity,' 'Culturally Relevant': Why Bernie Sanders Is Resonating with Latinos," NPR, December 22, 2019, https://tinyurl.com/2mdpren8; "Georgia State Rep. Stacey Abrams Calls for Authenticity, Courage and Action in 16th Annual Barbara Jordan Forum Keynote Address," Lyndon B. Johnson School of Public Affairs, University of Texas, February 22, 2012, https://tinyurl.com/59n3m4b3.

9. Lionel Trilling, *Sincerity and Authenticity*, Charles Eliot Norton Lectures, Book 2004 (Cambridge, MA: Harvard University Press, 1972); Charles Taylor, *The Ethics of Authenticity* (Cambridge, MA: Harvard University Press, 1992); Ted A. Smith, *The New Measures: A Theological History of Democratic Practice* (Cambridge: Cambridge University Press, 2007), chap. 5.

10. Howard Thurman, "The Sound of the Genuine" (baccalaureate address, Spelman College, May 4, 1980), ed. Jo Moore Stewart, *Spelman Messenger* 96, no. 4 (Summer 1980): 14–15. Audio accessible here: https://tinyurl.com/2b87jmbv.

11. Robert N. Bellah et al., *Habits of the Heart: Individualism and Commitment in American Life* (New York: Harper & Row, 1985), 221.

12. Robert N. Bellah, "Discerning Old and New Imperatives in Theological Education," *Theological Education*, Autumn 1982, 7–29.

13. On *Rettendekritik*, see Ted A. Smith, "Redeeming Critique: Resignations to the Cultural Turn in Christian Theology and Ethics," *Journal*

of the Society of Christian Ethics 24, no. 2 (Fall 2004): 89–113. In trying to mortify and redeem authenticity, I have also learned from Taylor, *The Ethics of Authenticity*, passim, and Ulrich Beck and Elisabeth Beck-Gernsheim, *Individualization: Institutionalized Individualism and Its Social and Political Consequences* (London: Sage, 2001), 78ff.

14. Adorno, *Minima Moralia*, 153–54. For a more complete version of the argument, see Adorno, *The Jargon of Authenticity* (London: Routledge, 1964).

15. bell hooks, *Yearning: Race, Gender, and Cultural Politics* (Boston: South End, 1990), 15.

16. Victor Anderson, *Beyond Ontological Blackness: An Essay on African American Religious and Cultural Criticism* (New York: Continuum, 1995).

17. Patrick B. Reyes, *Nobody Cries When We Die: God, Community, and Surviving to Adulthood* (St. Louis: Chalice, 2016), 7.

18. Judith Butler, *Giving an Account of Oneself* (New York: Fordham University Press, 2005), 8.

19. Butler, *Giving an Account*, 40.

20. Butler, *Giving an Account*, 8.

21. Rowan Williams, "Making Moral Decisions," in *The Cambridge Companion to Christian Ethics*, ed. Robin Gill (Cambridge: Cambridge University Press, 2012), 4, 5.

22. Justo González, *The History of Theological Education* (Nashville: Abingdon, 2015), 119.

23. See Paul Reitter and Chad Wellmon, *Permanent Crisis: The Humanities in a Disenchanted Age* (Chicago: University of Chicago Press, 2021), 145.

24. Tyler Roberts, "From Secular Criticism to Critical Fidelity," *Political Theology* 18, no. 8 (2017): 704.

25. William H. Frey, "The US Will Become 'Minority White' in 2045, Census Projects," Brookings Institute, March 14, 2018, https://tinyurl.com/2p9c9uae; Juan Martínez, "It's Already 2040 at a Seminary Near You," Center for Religion and Civic Culture, April 2, 2014, https://tinyurl.com/3kpku6z2.

26. See Jodi Melamed, *Represent and Destroy: Rationalizing Violence in the New Racial Capitalism* (Minneapolis: University of Minnesota Press, 2011). For a history of center-left politicians' fusion of neoliberalism and the multiculturalism of progressive social movements, see Nancy Fra-

ser, "From Progressive Neoliberalism to Trump—and Beyond," *American Affairs* 1, no. 4 (Winter 2017): 46–64.

27. Fernando Cascante, Zoom conversation with the author, 2021.

28. Lovett H. Weems Jr., foreword to *Bivocational and Beyond: Educating for Thriving Multivocational Ministry*, ed. Darryl W. Stephens (n.p.: Books@Atla Open Press, 2022), 4.

29. Lindsay Armstrong, conversation with the author, 2021.

30. See Barbara G. Wheeler, "Ready to Lead? The Problems with Lay Pastors," *Christian Century*, July 13, 2010, 28–33.

31. See Winnifred Fallers Sullivan, *Ministry of Presence: Chaplaincy, Spiritual Care, and the Law* (Chicago: University of Chicago Press, 2019); Wendy Cadge, *Paging God: Religion in the Halls of Medicine* (Chicago: University of Chicago Press, 2013).

32. Gabriel Winant, "Professional-Managerial Chasm," *n+1*, October 10, 2019, https://tinyurl.com/26k8e9x2.

33. See Alex Press, "On the Origins of the Professional-Managerial Class: An Interview with Barbara Ehrenreich," *Dissent*, October 22, 2019, https://tinyurl.com/4uvttspe.

34. Alicia Garza, *The Purpose of Power: How We Come Together When We Fall Apart* (New York: One World, 2020), Kindle location 2193.

35. Garza, *The Purpose of Power*, locations 1993, 2007. See also "A Herstory of the #BlackLivesMatter Movement by Alicia Garza," *The Feminist Wire*, October 7, 2014, https://tinyurl.com/tzdc2ss3.

36. Garza, *The Purpose of Power*, location 814.

37. Garza, *The Purpose of Power*, location 2352.

38. Garza, *The Purpose of Power*, location 168.

39. González, *History of Theological Education*, 127.

40. Stefano Harney and Fred Moten, *The Undercommons: Fugitive Planning and Black Study* (Wivenhoe, UK: Minor Compositions, 2013), 26.

41. Aristotle, *Metaphysics*, in Aristotle in 23 volumes, vols. 17 and 18, trans. Hugh Tredennick (Cambridge, MA: Harvard University Press 1933), 9.6, 1048b18–34.

42. Aryeh Kosman, *The Activity of Being: An Essay on Aristotle's Ontology* (Cambridge, MA: Harvard University Press, 2013), 67.